KU-077-376

Contents

Acknowledgements — vii

Introduction — ix

Chapter One
Science and the state: a twentieth-century love affair — 1

Chapter Two
How science policy grew: national experiences — 17

Chapter Three
Life of a twentieth-century European researcher — 77

Chapter Four
Public perspectives of the scentific world — 97

Chapter Five
Science: cornerstone of culture or foundation of wealth? — 115

Chapter Six
Science goes international — 131

Chapter Seven
Pointers towards a new social contract for European science — 165

References and bibliographies — 177

Notes — 191

Name index — 194

Organization index — 195

Subject index — 199

The European Scientific Community

by Ros Herman

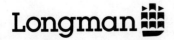

Longman Group Limited
Longman House, Burnt Mill, Harlow, Essex CM20 2JE, UK

First published 1986

British Library Cataloguing in Publication Data

Herman, Ros
    The European scientific community.
    1. Science—Europe
    I. Title
    509'.4   Q127.E8

    ISBN 0–582–90202–9

Typeset by The Word Factory, Rossendale, Lancashire
Printed in Great Britain by Robert Hartnoll (1985) Ltd.

Acknowledgements

This ambitious enterprise owes much to the dozens of people who have kindly taken the trouble to talk or write to me about science in their countries or organizations. I cannot name them all – many of their names appear in the notes and references.

A few people were so instrumental in setting me on the right tracks that I must single them out. The first was Dr Christoph Schneider, now working at the Science Council (Wissenschaftsrat) in Bonn, who translated some rather vague ideas into a thorough week-long programme of interviews in three cities of West Germany back in 1983. I was later able to use this programme as a pattern for people who helped me set up later visits to Spain, Italy, the Netherlands, Sweden and Denmark. The British Council science officer in Spain, Dr Robin Sowden (now in Turkey), was most conscientious in taking up the challenge; Dr Alessandro Vaciago, director of the Italian Institute of Culture in London, mobilized many of his contacts at home on my behalf. Niko van Schouwenburg, then at the Science Policy Information Department at the Netherlands Ministry of Education and Science, set up my visit to his country with the help of the national research council Nederlandse Organisatie voor Zuiver–Wetenschappelijk Onderzoek (ZWO). Dan Andrée, science attache at the Swedish embassy in London, and Anna Buremalm, of Sweden House in Stockholm, looked after me in Sweden, while Professor Flemming Woldbye, director of the Danish Research Administration, did the honours in Denmark. Alison Young of the Organization for Economic Cooperation and Development kindly helped me update the figures.

I have been grateful throughout for help in setting up additional interviews and contacts to Natasha Weyer-Brown, then of the European Science Foundation, now at the Royal Irish Academy in Dublin. These enabled me to gather much useful information and comment about countries I did not have the opportunity to visit. My initial interest in the European Science Foundation and indeed in science policy in general I owe to the generous friendship of Sir Geoffrey Allen during his time as chairman of the Science and Engineering Research Council. And for access to the necessary resources I am indebted to Michael Kenward, editor of *New Scientist*.

Gathering information is only the first part of writing a book: I have learnt that the mechanics of specifying how it is to be presented and actually carrying out the associated tasks are equally important. Dr Philip Gummett of the Department of Science and Technology Policy at the University of Manchester played an indispensable part in this from initial synopsis to completed work, while Mark Todd of Longmans had the courage to back the idea in the first place and has given helpful advice and comment throughout. Professor John Ziman of the Department of Economic and Social Studies at Imperial College, London directed me to important sources of background material and was good enough to make constructive and encouraging comments on the manuscript. I am also grateful for the hospitality and help afforded by Sally Grover of the Royal Society library.

Jane Moore, a freelance researcher who often works for *New Scientist*, provided me with extremely efficient help and support at crucial stages. She administered the questionnaire which we sent out in a (not altogether successful) attempt to gather consistent information about different countries, with references, and with compiling statistics. Neil Hyslop, another New Scientist freelance, used some of the numbers to make the story live visually. June Hull and Mandy Caplin, secretaries at *New Scientist*, kept cool and cheerful under the barrage of handwritten manuscript which they typed accurately and at remarkable speed in their evenings and weekends.

My family have had much to put up with. I am particularly grateful for the encouragement and forebearance of my husband Samson Abramsky and the constant support of my parents David and Ilse Herman. But it was the calming influence of my son, Joshua John Abramsky, over whom my writing hand had to be extended further and further as the book progressed, that really enabled me to complete the job. I only hope he can be persuaded not to tear up the proofs!

Ros Herman
London

June 1985

Introduction

For three hundred years, from 1550 to 1850, all the scientific developments of any importance took place in Europe. Although many important developments still take place here, few would dispute that the centre of gravity for most of the exciting disciplines is the US, with many expecting Japan to emerge as another serious force to be reckoned with. But with such a tradition, European science is not going to lie down and die, if for no other reason than the bodies politic cannot afford to let it do so. A sophisticated scientific community is, after all, one of the few assets that distinguishes some of Europe's more beleaguered economies from the more advanced of the world's developing 'Third World' countries.

Scientific research in Europe now is still a healthy, and occasionally glittering, enterprise. In this book I want to take a closer look at how the scientific community works in each of the 18 member countries of the European Science Foundation, and to give a more informal view of the 'feel' of the reality behind the neat, well-ordered organization charts. For reasons that combine practical considerations and personal preference, I will mainly confine my attention to research in the natural sciences (including engineering) whose primary aim is to increase our knowledge of the world, rather than directly solve a particular problem. The dividing line between such 'pure' or 'basic' research, and its more 'applied' counterpart, is not always a clear one. Many research programmes are fairly basic in character but concentrate on areas where the results are likely to be useful. This has long been true in the world of biology and medicine: now the demands of space technologies, microelectronics and the energy business are pushing the physical sciences in the same direction. Often these pressures result in a change in the character and aim of the work – hence the increasing popularity of the phrase 'strategic science'.

I will, therefore, not draw any sharp distinctions, but will try to concentrate on that type of research which is most speculative, least predictable – and least justifiable in terms of short-term results.

I make this choice not only out of perversity but also because such research is often the most demanding intellectually and provides the greatest challenge to those capable of pursuing it. It attracts able, imaginative students, trains them in painstaking and thorough craftsmanship, and inspires them to acts of creativity at least as breathtaking as those of their better-known peers in the world of the arts. Such work may in itself be esoteric, but it lays the foundation for the technologies of the future and the routine preventions and cures that have changed the face of the world for all its citizens.

For better or worse, most basic research is now funded by the state, particularly in Europe. Much of it takes place in the universities and other places of higher education, though many European countries have a substantial network of government funded research laboratories. A combination of factors makes basic research particularly vulnerable to changes. Firstly of course, governments assume that, in peacetime at least, they can alter the supply of funds to research without too much fear of immediate repercussions. Secondly, the universities are centres for both teaching and research, and an emphasis on the former can obscure growing deficiencies in the latter. Thirdly, decent work takes years to come to fruition and it is devilishly difficult to assess the quality and potential of any particular laboratory or group, or to detect a new burst of life or imminent stagnation. For all these reasons basic research is extremely vulnerable to economic, political and social changes.

It is this combination of creativity, importance and vulnerability that makes basic research such an interesting field of endeavour to examine, and I hope the reader will spare me a little time to try to share my enthusiasm.

CHAPTER ONE

Science and the state: a twentieth-century love affair

In the darkest days of the Second World War a civilian who had made her home in Europe summed up the cultural history of science like this: 'and science which meant progress in the nineteenth century in the twentieth century means simply useful things . . . and the discoveries of science are only used for war and destruction.'

This glib epithet of Gertrude Stein's is naive and simplistic; nevertheless it points to some profound changes in the shape of the scientific community and the motivation of scientists in Europe that have occurred in the twentieth century.

Western culture grew from roots in Greece and Rome, in Baghdad and Toledo. After the fallow period of the Middle Ages the curiosity of the Europeans produced a glittering culture of arts, music, commerce, and also a hunger for explanation of the why and how of the physical world. A common language allowed easy communication between the educated inhabitants of an enormous geographical area; and conquest, business and good husbandry led to release from physical toil and the possibility of a long education for an increasing number of people.

This is the culture that produced the renaissance, the scientific re-volution, the enlightenment, and the industrial revolution. For a millenium the traditions of Rome, overlaid with those of Christianity, linked the inhabitants of Europe in a common enterprise, with well-defined spiritual and later materialistic aspirations. The factions of Catholicism gave way to new religious groupings, and finally to nationalism as the creed of the committed European.

The scientific enterprise – the urge to understand, describe, and eventually predict the workings of the physical world – commanded the interest of a growing group of individuals throughout modern times. And it appealed to thinkers throughout the geographical area we are consider-ing: the history of science takes the student on a tour of each of its countries in turn. It also linked people of diverse nationalities as perhaps no other common activity, its practitioners usually considering themselves above such petty divisions as religion and, after the replacement of Latin by the various vernaculars, language. They often felt closer to their colleagues and correspondents who lived hundreds or thousands of miles away but were fascinated by similar ideas, than to their countrymen bent on pursuing more mundane and more locally focused pursuits.

But as this enterprise became linked with man's efforts to control the physical world with a view to making his life longer and pleasanter, and for some richer, the efforts of the cloistered natural philosopher acquired a larger and larger audience. It became fashionable to take an interest in the achievements of science. Partly this was a genuinely intellectual interest, appropriate for the leisure-time edification of the growing middle class. Partly it was a serious matter, for the exploitation of science's practical results was coming to play an increasingly important part in the life of the advanced nations of Europe.

In the nineteenth century the education of scientists started to become a matter for state intervention. Both industry and governments began to take a hand in harnessing the scientific enterprise for its own ends. At the same time science emerged as a potent shaper of society in its own right. Scientific concepts such as evolution had loosened the hold of religion over the minds of many millions, and developments in physics and astronomy threatened to encourage even more people to challenge the natural order as laid down in the various forms of Christianity. To be modern and sophisticated was often to reject faith in favour of some form of 'scientific' or 'rational' approach to life. And also to believe that it was only a matter of time before science cured the world's problems. It was a time for liberals and idealists – and enormous hope in what science could do for mankind.

The Prussian state was the first national government to tackle this task head on, investing enormous sums of money in modern forms of education including technical and vocational training at secondary level. It also initiated a revitalization of the universities through new funds for up to date research facilities and extra posts to give lecturers time for research. The investment paid off very quickly and in handsome measure, as the well-trained cadre of German chemical engineers snatched the initiative for the manufacture of synthetic dyes from Britain. Justus Liebig, whose brilliant career spanned the mid-century, is a prime example of the alliance of excellent science with filling a practical need. He developed the science of organic chemistry with the problems of agriculture in mind. And his deliberate efforts that his science should be harnessed to increase food production for a growing population are now held up as a model of how research can be both intellectually rewarding and useful.

The Prussian government soon recognized the need for a more applied form of education at the tertiary level, and opened the first technical university in 1825 at Karlsruhe to provide a focus for high-level training and research geared to the needs of industry. The idea was soon copied in other European countries: Italy, Sweden, Denmark and, rather later the Netherlands, Spain and Portugal. In these countries the local universities had even fallen far behind current developments, and the technical high schools became (and often remain) more prestigious institutions than their more traditional counterparts.

Alarm bells soon started ringing in the two nations with well-established scientific traditions – Britain and France. At the beginning of the nineteenth century British industry was way ahead of the rest of Europe. This supremacy had all been achieved by private enterprise and private education – there was as yet no tradition of government intervention in either research or innovation. Liberal thinkers such as the mathematician William Whewell and the philospher economist John Stuart Mill saw no place for the sciences in university education, and Oxford and Cambridge neglected to include them in the curriculum. Even the first two colleges in London University, opened in the 1820s, failed at first to provide any serious courses in applied sciences. In the middle of the nineteenth century Britain's main centre for science was still the Royal Institution. But two new London colleges, outside the universities, soon began to make an impact: the Royal College of Chemistry opened in 1845 to bring some of the excellence of German organic chemistry into English intellectual life, and in 1851, the year of the Great Exhibition, the Government School of Mines and Science Applied to the Arts began work. Government had also begun to support centres of scientific expertise for more mundane purposes: the Laboratory of the Government Chemist was founded in 1843 to perform analyses for the Inland Revenue on imported perishable goods. And 1850 was the first year of an annual grant of £1000 to the Royal Society to sponsor research projects by individuals.

Helpful as they were, these developments failed to provide enough trained experts to supply the growing demand from British industry for scientific expertise. Increasingly, companies in a wide range of industries brought over chemists from Germany and Switzerland to help. Others taught themselves or attended lectures at the Royal Institution. A serious lacuna in the higher education available in Britain became increasingly obvious as the century progressed.

Not surprisingly, it was industrialists who finally took the initiative in founding the civic universities that were to fill this gap effectively and quickly. At the end of the century there were a dozen of these institutions, of which by far the most notable grouping was the Victoria Federation which included the university colleges at Manchester, Liverpool and Leeds. The ancient universities also began to adapt themselves to changing times, and gradually drew sciences, both pure and applied, into their syllabuses, with spectacular results, particularly in the case of Cambridge. Thanks to the initiative of Lyon Playfair, the minister at the new Department of Science and Art, set up in 1853, the Royal College of Science was set up in London in 1872 by the amalgamation of two existing colleges. In 1890 Playfair initiated scholarships for science from money earned through the 1851 Great Exhibition. By 1900 the quality of scientific and technical education at least equalled that of Germany, though in terms of sheer quantity of graduates Britain was still well behind.

The new German empire (proclaimed in 1871) was still setting the pace in other directions, though once again Britain was quick to follow. Following the German Patent Act of 1870, the German companies such as BASF, Bayer and Krupp set up enormous research laboratories – and so did several American organizations, such as the General Electric Company. In this sphere Britain was beginning to catch up: among the earliest were Nobel's at Ardeer in 1871, United Alkali in 1891, Burroughs Wellcome in 1894, the Cambridge Scientific Instrument company in 1895, Ilford in 1898 and British Westinghouse just after, in 1899. The Prussian government was not resting on its laurels either. In 1876 it set up the Kaiserliches Gesundheitsamt or Federal Health Office and in 1887 the Physikalische Technische Reichsanstalt, which became a supreme authority in the field of weights and measures and served as a model for the National Physical Laboratory opened in 1899. It also provided some stimulus towards the foundation of the Imperial College of Science and Technology in 1907.

Two years later the British government started a Development Fund to sponsor the scientific development of forestry, agriculture and fisheries, and medicine took its turn in 1911 when the National Insurance Act was accompanied by the establishment of a new fund for medical research. The British government, however, did not have time to match the ambitious German scheme initiated in 1911 to set up a network of national research institutes under the title of the Kaiser Wilhelm Gesellschaft before the outbreak of the First World War in August 1914.

If British technical education had caught up with German, its industry had not, at least not in those areas crucial to twentieth-century warfare, or those crucial to the self-sufficiency of a state with severely restricted opportunities for trade. Gummett (1980) points out:

> the First World War brought wider recognition of the importance of science and technology, and a tightening of the bonds between science and government. The claims which had been made about the poor state of British manufacturing industry received disturbing support in the first few months of the war with the realisation of how dependent the country was on German drugs, dyestuffs, optical equipment and other materials needed for the war effort.

French industry was even further behind. The eighteenth century had seen the foundation of some pioneering state schools, the École des Ponts et Chaussées 1775, the École des Mines (1783), the École Polytechnique (1794). It was the last of these that had the main task of training the scientific elite of France, but the development of its research laboratories stagnated early in the nineteenth century, and the quality of its teaching subsequently deteriorated. Nevertheless, its prestige continued to attract the best students, who were thus denied to the newer institutions such as the École Centrale, set up by industry in 1829 to train its own scientific personnel. By mid-century distinguished thinkers such as chemist Louis Pasteur and philologist and historian Ernest Renan had brought to public attention the problems of shortage of funds for research, the elitism of the Écoles, and the separation of the worlds of industry and research.

The third republic, established after the disastrous Franco-Prussian war in 1870–71, soon became conscious of the need to encourage a cadre of well-trained scientists and engineers. It set in motion the expansion of faculties of science and created new schools of applied science, also providing new facilities for research. But these efforts largely failed to produce a cadre of practically minded scientists. Theoretical science was traditionally separated from its practical counterpart, with theory being considered by far the more prestigious of the two. Pierre Papon, describing scientific education at the *grandes écoles* and universities, says

> globally, the education of scientists favoured the deductive approach (based on general laws) rather than the inductive approach starting from observations.

France was also ill-equipped economically to cope with innovation: its companies were not geared up to make larger capital investments at crucial moments. The shortage of both adequately skilled personnel and the requisite capital investment resulted in France missing out almost completely on the chemicals industry, in spite of the excellent reputation of its pure scientists.

France did not miss out quite so disastrously on the next generation of new industries. French entrepreneurs were quick to appreciate the potential for automobiles, electrometallurgical manufacturing methods, electrical equipment, and finally and most spectacularly, aviation. Nevertheless, Papon reports, French industry in general did not realize the importance of science as a source of innovation and improvement. Out of 34 large industrial companies, only six possessed research laboratories worthy of the name.

It took the shock of the First World War to spur the French government into making some effort to initiate scientific developments itself. In the month the war broke out, August 1914, it set up the Commission Superieure des Inventions (Higher Committee for Inventions). The following year it was attached to a Direction des Inventions Interessant la Defense Nationale (Directorate for inventions concerning national defence) which came under the Ministry of Public Instruction.

In spite of this development, French scientists made little impact on the conduct of the war. One exception is the amazing heroism shown by the double Nobellist Marie Curie, who organized a service that arranged for the wounds of French soldiers to be assessed using X-ray equipment brought to the battlefield. In general, however, the initiative remained firmly with the Germans and later the British.

The brilliant synthesis of education, research and application achieved in Germany is exemplified in the career of Fritz Haber the man who eventually turned his talents to devising poison gases. Haber was a self-taught physical chemist who joined the staff of the Karlsruhe Technische Hochschule in 1894. Between 1907 and 1909, already a professor at Karlsruhe, he devised a process for manufacturing ammonia. This process filled a vital gap, for it enabled nitrogen to be fixed into a chemical compound from which it could later be released, a vital step in making the fertilizers that would help farmers grow enough food for the world's expanding population. Ammonia was also a key ingredient in the manufacture of explosives. Nevertheless, a practicable production process for ammonia had eluded some of the world's best physical chemists; Haber, however, was persistent enough to solve the problem, finding the correct physical conditions and a suitable catalyst for the reaction.

In 1911 Haber accepted the post of director of the newly formed Kaiser Wilhelm Institut für Physikalische Chemie und Electrochemie at Dahlem near Berlin. On the outbreak of war the government called on Haber to contribute to the war effort. He responded enthusiastically, turning over the whole work of the Institute to war work, in particular the development of chemical weapons, whose use he supervised and observed in the field. He meanwhile kept a watching brief on the supply of nitrogen products for explosives. Europe's chief source of nitrates was Chile, and in 1915 Germany lost access to the South American shipping routes. Germany was quick to exploit its newly developed process for making ammonia, so providing itself with a secure supply of both explosives and food.

As Robert Reid points out in his book *Tongues of Conscience*, Britain would probably not have been able to do likewise had she lost the battle of the sea routes. Nevertheless, Britain did eventually marshall its scientists to good effect in the First World War. Distinguished scientists hastened to offer their services: James Dewar, then at the Royal Institution, W. H. Bragg and Ernest Rutherford who worked on ways of attacking submarines, and W. L. Bragg (then 25) who was sent to France and ended up leading the work on sound ranging equipment placed close behind the front line to locate enemy guns. Britain also exploited its own pre-war chemistry. Cordite, used as a shell propellant, included acetone as a vital ingredient: Manchester University lecturer Chaim Weizmann had discovered in 1911 that acetone could be made by the bacterial fermentation of cornstarch.

It was during the war years also that the British government began to lay down the framework for state science in Britain. In 1915 a group of eminent scientists were convened in an Advisory Council on Scientific and Industrial Research responsible to a small committee of the Privy Council, a group of senior politicians and other distinguished citizens whose Lord President is a Cabinet minister. The following year science acquired its own Department of State, the Department of Scientific and Industrial Research (DSIR). Until the war ended the DSIR concentrated on stimulating research of military value, but afterwards broadened its scope considerably. It operated its own laboratories, including the National Physical Laboratory, which it took over from the Royal Society in 1918; it ran a new network of industrial research associations; and it provided the research grants for postgraduate students and university staff. The DSIR was the prototype of the type of body we now know as the 'research council', though its scope was far wider than what people now generally understand by that term. The first body actually to bear that name was the Medical Research Council (MRC) set up in 1920. From the very beginning the MRC took a different approach: it concentrated its resources in a few central laboratories and a large number of research units attached to universities and hospitals.

After the war the general bitterness of the allied nations against the central powers was carried over into the scientific community and even penetrated the realms of what was then pure physics. Organizers of the third Solvay congress in 1921 chose not to invite participants from Germany and Austria-Hungary, and the same omission marred the fourth congress in 1924. By the time the arrangements for the fifth congress began, Germany had joined the League of Nations and normal relations were resumed, German scientists being fully represented when it took place in 1927.

On the other hand, the 'chemists' war' had brought home to the Western world the importance of state science, and the efforts to promote world peace included at a very early stage an initiative to promote international discussions and cooperation in science and technology. The initiative came from the Paris Academy, the National Academy of Sciences in Washington and the London Royal Society. This led to the formation of a body called the International Research Council, formed in 1919 with its base in Brussels. Its twelve members were Belgium, Canada, France, Italy, Japan, New Zealand, Poland, Portugal, Romania and Serbia, the UK and Russia. The exclusion of the Central Powers of Germany and Austria proved a serious weakness, but it could not be overcome even when late joiner Sweden proposed in 1922 that all nations be admitted. The International Research Council finally disbanded in

1931 when the International Council of Scientific Unions was formed to replace it.

The International Research Council did have a lasting influence, however, in several of its member countries, because each had to have a suitable governmental scientific organization to send delegates. Both Portugal and Italy set up national research councils in the 1920s, though neither country had any effective research coordination until the late 1930s. Belgium set up a national foundation for scientific research in 1928, though this was initially privately funded after an appeal by the king.

The German government set up a fund for scientific research in 1920, the Emergency Association of German Science, to improve the backward condition of science after the First World War. Nine years later it became the 'Research Society'. Its funds came mainly from the state with a small contribution from industry.

These four research councils were mainly concerned with basic science but other countries were more interested in channelling efforts into science that would be useful to the state. The Netherlands, for example, set up its Central Organization for Applied Scientific Research in 1928, which was more of a confederation of national laboratories than a research council. It was not until 1939, however, that France set up its Centre National de Recherche Scientifique (CNRS). In the same year the Fascist regime in Spain set up the Consejo Superior de Investigaciones Científicas (CSIC) which was supposed to coordinate the state's research efforts. In the event CSIC limited its activities to setting up its own laboratories and units, some of which are sited at universities.

In spite of all this apparent activity, government science made little impact on the scientific effort of the smaller European countries between the wars. These years were spectacular ones for the development of technology and the associated industries. Turbines and engines were already quite sophisticated, as was electricity generation on a small scale. Sophisticated methods of making basic materials such as iron and steel were widespread. Handling of glass and ceramics was also quite well understood, with sheet glass readily available. The principles of the telegraph were well established. The 1920s saw varied and imaginative application of these techniques for the citizens of an increasingly democratic Europe and, as manufactured products became cheaper thanks to new techniques of mass production, more and more could benefit. The age of the 'consumer society' had begun.

Products such as refrigerators, vacuum cleaners, cookers and washing machines began to appear in the home; soon to be joined by telephones, radios and (less commonly before the war) televisions. Means of transport such as the motor car and the aeroplane became common sights and the volume of shipping increased rapidly.

As far as Europe was concerned, Britain and Germany were still the major innovators and producers. But there was still a very significant level of give and take between all the Western European countries, and there was scarcely one that did not make one or two significant contributions in terms of inventions and/or manufacturing. Sweden was for its size perhaps the most spectacular, pioneering Aga cookers and Electrolux fridges. Italian industry was quick to take up the manufacture of new polymers such as polythene and propylene.

Engineers were also beginning to acquire some confidence in their materials – enough to attempt ambitious feats of civil engineering such as the 20-mile long Princess Juliana Canal (1935) in the Netherlands. Italians invented a new way of making foundations for bridges in 1938, and built a dry dock in Genoa in 1940. The nineteenth century had already seen the completion of some quite long tunnels, but even more spectacular were underground systems such as the Rove Tunnel connecting the Port of Marseilles with the Rhône – it took fifteen years to build and was completed in 1927. But pride of place must surely go to the Netherlands for the tremendous feat of organization and engineering involved in the reclamation of 20 000 hectares of land in the Zuider Zee between 1920 and 1932.

As radio, telegraph and telephone, air transport, ships and motor cars shrank the world, Europeans became more and more aware that they would, in future, be sharing the fruits of their technological sophistication with others, in particular the US and Japan. But for the moment, the leadership in basic science remained in European hands. Physicists all over Europe were intrigued by the curious new discipline of quantum mechanics. The centre of the intellectual maelstrom was Germany, which boasted the grand old master Max Planck at Berlin University, succeeded in the chair of theoretical physics there by Erwin Schrödinger in 1928. Werner Heisenberg, having studied at Göttingen was professor of physics at Leipzig from 1927–42. Wolfgang Pauli was born in Vienna, studied in Munich, worked in Göttingen, Copenhagen and Hamburg, but left Germany in the late 1920s to spend most of the rest of his life in Zürich. Max Born was professor of theoretical physics at Göttingen from 1921–33; he spent most of the rest of his life in Britain.

Other European countries made significant contributions. The manic but brilliant Russian Paul Ehrenfest found refuge at Leiden and inspired a generation of Dutch theoreticians. Neils Bohr returned to his native Copenhagen, after working with Ernest Rutherford in Manchester, to found a school of theoretical physics that was almost as much of an attraction to visiting cognoscenti as the German centres. Nobel prizewinners James Chadwick, John Cockcroft and Ernest Walton all emerged from the Rutherford stable. Enrico Fermi visited Born at Göttingen and Ehrenfest at Leiden before returning to Italy to found yet another school of theoreticians.

Britons contributed more on the experimental side. J. J. Thomson studied at Owens College to prepare himself for scholarship exams at Cambridge, where he spent the rest of his life. Rutherford, strictly speaking a New Zealander, did most of his work at Manchester and Cambridge. Francis William Aston studied at Mason College (later Birmingham University) before joining Thomson at Cavendish Laboratory in Cambridge. Theoretician Louis de Broglie and experimentalist Frédéric Joliot-Curie provided most of the French input.

Physics was not the only discipline where Germany reigned supreme: Germans did much of the groundwork on the science of polymers and the manufacture of synthetic fibres and rubbers, and invented the insecticide DDT in 1939. Britain and Germany shared the honours in the new race to find safe and effective drugs, and Germans and Americans pioneered the new science of genetics. More quietly, the Germans were looking at ways of circumventing the disarmament provisions of the 1920 Treaty of Versailles. They could, for example, get away with supporting the development of completely new technologies – such as rocket propulsion. While the mysteries of quantum stole the headlines of the 1930s, Walter Dornberger and Wernher von Braun were hard at work on rocket weapons at Peenemünde on the Baltic coast.

German nationalism had had much to do with the creation of an excellent environment in which science could flourish. But in the late 1920s and 1930s nationalism turned into an ugly fascism. Adolf Hitler's wish to purge the German nation of any taint of Jewish influence led him to a distinction between 'Jewish physics' (bad) and 'Aryan physics' (good). The notion of Aryan physics was articulated by two German physicists, Philip Lenard and Johannes Stark. Lenard and Stark were both patriotic Germans who for various reasons found it difficult to come to terms with quantum mechanics and relativity, and allowed themselves to be persuaded that there was something intrinsically un-German about the new ideas. According to Alan Beyerchen (1977),

> the Aryan physicists . . . believed in a mechanical, yet organic, non-materialistic universe in which discovery could only come through observation and experiment. Aryan physics violently denounced mechanistic materialism, which was universally regarded as the underpinning of Marxism. At the same time Aryan physics . . . was opposed to relativity and quantum mechanics. . . . The Aryan physics adherents ruled out objectivity and internationality in science. . . . The Aryan researcher maintained a dialogue with nature. He asked questions in the form of experiments and observed the answers in the results. . . . Instead of observation the Jew had a predilection for theory and abstraction . . . the Jew presented his theories in the form of complex mathematical calculations with regard for experimental data.

Whatever the theory, the practice was simple. In 1933 all Jewish faculty members at German universities were dismissed, and many of their colleagues left in protest at such action or simply in despair at the devastating effect the dismissals were having on research. Göttingen University was particularly badly affected. Alan Beyerchen has counted twenty Nobellists who left German institutions of higher learning between 1935 and 1945 under this pressure. Born went to Britain, Pauli to Switzerland and the Austrian Lise Meitner to Sweden, but Albert Einstein and many others went to the US. Chaim Weizmann, an ardent Zionist as well as a distinguished chemist gathered a few of the refugee scientists in the Daniel Sieff Institute (now the Weizmann Institute) at Rehovot in Palestine, which opened in 1934.

Germany was not the only country where Fascism caused intellectuals to seek more congenial abodes. The Italian fascists also demanded extremes of patriotic fervour from its citizens, but failed to provoke much opposition among academics at least until their German allies insisted on a tough antisemitic line in 1938. Enrico Fermi chose the University of Chicago as his refuge and many of his outstanding team followed him there. Others, such as chemist Marco Tullio Levi stayed in Europe. Niels Bohr and his son Aage eventually made a hasty and undignified escape to Britain from occupied Copenhagen via Sweden. After the war Bohr and his son, also a distinguished physicist, returned to Denmark. Jewish scientists were also dismissed from positions in Dutch universities, though the Netherlands afforded a rather curious place of refuge for Dutch and even a few German Jewish physicists – the Philips Research Laboratory at Eindhoven. As the war drew to a close, scientists there even organized an *ad hoc* university where eighty young people could begin to catch up with their disrupted studies.

Spain too lost many of her best scientists, either as exiles from the Franco regime or casualties in the civil war. Some 5000 intellectuals left Spain, amongst them an absolute minimum of 200 natural scientists including Blas Cabrera, father of the new physics in Spain, and Nobellist Severo Ochoa. Many of them went to South America, others to Britain and the US.

There were a few scientists who found Fascism an attractive philosophy, but in general the ideology was almost universally rejected. But many scientists were among the Western intellectuals who were very much influenced by Socialism and Communism.

As we have seen many European countries, large and small, recognized in the second half of the nineteenth century that the possession of a well-educated cadre of scientists and engineers was a vital pre-requisite to future economic success. To achieve this, advanced scientific education had to be made available to as many as possible who could benefit from it, whether they came from the middle and upper classes to whom higher education had traditionally been restricted, or whether their backgrounds were more humble. The same was true of many other

11

of the new occupations for which a high degree of training and skill were required.

It is hardly surprising then that many of the new generation of scientists who studied in the first few decades of the century made a link between their intellectual passions and their wish to build a better world. For some this merely meant the exploitation of science and technology to improve the material welfare of as many citizens as possible – a perfectly respectable socialist analysis. But for others the scientific outlook had to be extended into a radical shakeup of the accepted economics and political structures. For the radicals, this was the only way to ensure that everyone would get a fair share of the material benefits of science, and also of its liberating and secularist influence on the mind.

Some very distinguished scientists joined this camp, most notably the crystallographer J. D. Bernal. His book *The social function of science* (1939) examined the relations between the scientific enterprise and the state, and pointed out how they could be improved to increase the benefit to society (and, incidentally, better the conditions of scientists). Bernal, like many contemporary scientists, was attracted to Marxism partly because of its socialist ideals but also because it purported to be the only possible scientific analysis of social relations and political history. It also allowed for a far more important role for science and technology in society, with the state taking a more aggressive part in planning and using science than had hitherto been the case in Europe.

The Soviet Union's efforts to put these ideas into practice initially commanded much respect in Britain, with visitors to the USSR such as scientific journalist J. G. Crowther writing glowing reports about new research institutes and factories. But the initial enthusiasm was soon dampened by more disturbing news of show trials, mass imprisonments and the widespread suppression of human rights and freedom of thought. Apart from the harsh punishment of any hint of criticism for the regime, scientists in the West also had to stomach the outright perversion of science in the name of political dogma. The official endorsement of Trofim Lysenko's genetic theories in the face of cogent arguments against it by distinguished experts was an important factor in encouraging some scientists to go public with their misgivings about the new utilitarian view of science. Manchester chemist Michael Polanyi was one of these. In his view 'scientific thought' was 'nowhere oppressed so comprehensively as in the USSR'. In 1941 he helped to form the Society for Freedom of Science, which aimed to promote a liberal view of science as an alternative to the growing international movement of socialist scientists as embodied for example in the World Federation of Scientific Workers.

But soon these debates faded into the background. World War II approached. Once again scientists on both sides became heavily involved. The stories of such developments as radar, code-cracking computers, rockets, and the atom bomb are now becoming well-known as documents are declassified.

In Germany more scientists left for allied or neutral countries, while a select few were drawn into the war effort, especially work on rockets and the atom bomb. The latter project harnessed the efforts of some of the most distinguished German physicists, who had hitherto been concerned with the purest of academic topics – a very different enterprise from the mad rush to build a very powerful weapon. They eventually decided, for whatever reason, to advise the military that they were unlikely to be able to make it work in the short term, and the research programme was subsequently given a low priority. Not so in the United States, where the sheer scale of industrial plant and technological expertise available made the construction of such a weapon feasible if only the science could be understood. And European scientists, whether refugees or seconded from allied nations were only too ready to help.

After the war in Europe ended the allies had to decide what to do with German scientists taken as prisoners of war. Both the Soviet Union and the US arranged complex and swift military operations to capture as many of these as possible along with papers, plans and equipment. The US eventually assimilated 500 such scientists for its research effort, mainly in defence and industry. The Soviet Union took many of their captives back home for debriefing, but sent them back after three years, giving them the choice of residence in East or West Germany.

Once again war had acted as a stimulus to science. Britain's scientists emerged proud of their achievements and keen to exploit the fruits of their work for peaceful purposes, especially atomic energy and the wartime medical advances. Germany too could be proud of her achievements, if not the way they had been used, and some of her most distinguished scientists, including Werner Heisenberg and Otto Hahn, insisted on returning, even though the political splitting into East and West Germany severely weakened even the remnants of her scientific infrastructure. The most promising youngsters were sent abroad to study and come back to help rebuild. France too could be proud of Frédéric Joliot-Curie, who had kept his position at the Collège de France as a cover for active participation in the resistance. As neutral countries, Sweden and Switzerland had continued to develop their scientific resources, swelled also by refugees, and had made remarkable strides in new industries such as drugs.

But in spite of the speed of postwar economic recovery, thanks in great part to American help, the centre of gravity of science and technology was no longer firmly placed in Europe. The Americans themselves were perhaps the first to realize this: in 1945 senior scientist and government policy maker Vannevar Bush wrote:

We can no longer count on ravaged Europe as a source of fundamental knowledge. In the past we have devoted much of our best efforts to the application of such knowledge which has been discovered abroad. In the future we must pay increased attention to discovering this knowledge for ourselves, particularly since the scientific application of the future will be more than ever dependent on such knowledge.

Bush was writing in a document called *Science – the endless frontier* and subtitled 'A Report to the President on a program for postwar scientific research'. In it he surveyed the progress of science and called for much enhanced government support for many types of scientific and technical research and education. In his view 'without scientific progress no amount of achievement in other directions can insure our health, prosperity, and security as a nation in the modern world.' Bush's document laid the foundations for the US government to set aside enormous budgets for new scientific agencies set up over the next decade.

Bush's arguments for state support for science applied equally to European countries. Even if they could no longer claim intellectual pre-eminence, they still had to make their way in a world whose technological sophistication they had largely brought about. To have any chance of keeping up with world science and technology, laboratories in the educational and industrial spheres alike were forced to turn to government for support. Already military science was a matter for government and the exploitation of atomic energy also joined the list of priorities for state support in many countries. One by one – sometimes only after much prodding from international agencies – the postwar European states added a new task to the machinery of policy making – that of developing a policy for science.

We have seen how, at the turn of the twentieth century, the growing importance of science in the world made it impossible for scientists to achieve their ambition to be left alone to pursue their researches. This was true whether their objectives were purely intellectual, or whether, as had often been the case throughout the history of science, they intended their discoveries to be put to practical use. The state needed to harness science for war and for economic development on an ever growing scale, whatever the prevailing political system.

Particularly in the case of science for war and for defence, the state also required that scientists give up their normal avenues of recognition in the form of publication in the open literature of the scientific community. Commercial considerations too tended to confuse and frustrate the normal functioning of these means of communication.

The scale of atrocity of the First World War, largely made possible by the application of science, forced some reconsideration of nineteenth-century ideas, especially narrow nationalisms. Scientists and politicians concurred in a desire to work together. At first these efforts amounted to little, particularly as it took a long time for the rest of Europe to come to terms with working with their German and Austro-Hungarian colleagues.

The Second World War again inspired supreme achievements from scientists in whom strong national feelings had again been aroused. It also shook up the scientific community more thoroughly than had ever happened before. The European scientific community had to face new challenges, particularly from the United States and the Soviet Union. So did European industries. Defence and reconstruction became a continental rather than a national objective, with new divisions between east and west. As science and technology embedded themselves more firmly into the infrastructure of the state, the expense of some vital projects also hinted at the need for international collaboration. This would go hand in hand with a desire to bring the poorer and less sophisticated nations of Western Europe nearer to the level of their neighbours and allies.

CHAPTER TWO

How science policy grew: national experiences

Science had never been harnessed so completely and purposefully by the state as in Britain, Germany and the USA during the Second World War. The scientists of the West were never to forget the horrors of Hiroshima and Nagasaki. Nevertheless they would also remember the triumphs of radar, cryptography and Alexander Fleming's discovery of penicillin. In the larger countries, governments concentrated on the benefits and decided that the scientific and technological machine that had been set in motion would have to stay in place. (Germany had to wait till the Federal Republic was granted full sovereignty and membership of the North Atlantic Treaty Organization (NATO) in 1955.)

At first the main object was to strengthen and maintain the nation's defences, often through further development of atomic weaponry. As relations between the USSR and the West deteriorated, scientists who had leaked atom secrets to the Soviet Union hit headlines: Allan Nunn May of King's College, London, unmasked in 1946: Klaus Fuchs of Los Alamos and the UK Atomic Energy Authority's Harwell laboratory; and Bruno Pontecorvo, an Italian refugee who had worked with Fermi and his student Emilio Segrè and later at Harwell, both in 1950. J. Robert Oppenheimer was deprived of his security clearance in 1954 because of suspicions that he was a Communist sympathizer.

Soon the lure of the peaceful atom came to play an important part in the research and development efforts of European countries. By 1958 seventeen of our eighteen countries had some sort of atomic energy commission – Ireland was the only exception. Many of them also set up or reviewed national planning bodies with the job of promoting research useful to industry and sometimes agriculture as well.

By 1957 the space race was on. Jean Jacques Salomon describes the subsequent period as an 'age of pragmatism' in science policy:

> The cry of alarm raised by the first Sputnik led most industrialized countries to set up institutions concerned with science policy and to increase their scientific and technological budgets. It was a huge and hurried effort of financing but the effort was only concentrated on a small number of objectives; three-quarters of the public funds went towards military, nuclear and space research. Most European countries wished above all to make up for the time lost by the war and the immediate post-war period in matters of manpower, equipment and structures. And Europe – once the birthplace of the Scientific Revolution and the very heart of the international system – discovered at the same time that from now on it stood on the outskirts of that system and that no country in it was capable any longer of undertaking individually and on the same scale the r&d programmes undertaken by the superpowers. From that moment, the European countries, even those who were members of the 'Atomic Club' and who allocated the same proportion of their resources as the United States or the USSR to the three priority sectors of military, nuclear, and space research, were compelled to go through the process of cooperation in order to achieve their scientific or technical objectives in a more rapid or economic manner.

But this cooperation did not extend to topics of industrial and commercial interest. In fact Salomon asserts that serious discussion showing 'general awareness of the role played by scientific and technological research in international economic competition' did not begin until the mid-1960s. By this time a whole generation had grown up with heightened aspirations and, in many countries, a belief in democracy and reasonable improvements in economic prosperity for a large proportion of the population. Demand for education, firstly at school and later for higher studies, increased rapidly, and many of the new graduates were natural scientists.

Salomon describes the effect of the new interest in research related to industry:

> Research activities were undertaken by ten times more people than before World War II; all industrialized countries increased their scientific and technical investments. But the general picture of national research work cannot hide the gaps existing between work undertaken on the one hand by the United States and the USSR and on the other by the European countries which, far from joining forces in this matter, competed among themselves and often set themselves against one another. . . .

Europe's weak point in both the industrial and the academic field lay not only in the resources it allocated to research activities or even in the structures it displayed; it lay also in its aptitude for innovation, that is, in its aptitude for exploiting the results of research.

Several countries that were slow to set up national networks of scientific and technological research were chided and cajoled into action by the Organization for Economic Cooperation and Development (OECD) which during the 1960s and early 1970s reviewed the science policy of all its member states.

The trend towards harnessing science to serve socially useful rather than nationally expedient ends matured during the early 1970s. At this time science, especially in Europe, was coming under attack from two directions: firstly from those who pointed out the negative effects of science and technology such as pollution, and secondly from observers who pointed out that, especially in Europe, investment in scientific research, for whatever reason, was failing to keep industry competitive.

During the 1970s many countries tried to devise more sophisticated approaches to science policy, often defining priorities relating to both economic and social development. With varying degrees of success they opened new laboratories or institutes, provided extra funding, encouraged programmes of research in universities. Rarely, though, was any attempt made to link state-funded research efforts directly to those of industry. Research and development in industry increased: quite rapidly in some countries, particularly where it had fallen behind. Often the growth in industrial r&d was faster than in the public sector.

With the oil crisis of 1973, many countries ran into financial difficulties. A common response was to cut back on expansion in higher education. In general r&d was given higher priority and usually maintained or allowed to grow slightly faster than national economies. Even so, by the beginning of the 1980s, many structural problems were beginning to emerge, particularly for basic science, whose share of total r&d spending almost invariably declined during the 1970s. These will be discussed in more detail later; suffice it for the moment to list a few of them: a shortage of secure jobs for young researchers; a decline in the average support for each researcher (financial and in terms of technical support for example): heavier teaching and administrative loads for academics; greater pressure to seek outside funds, from industry for example, often resulting in work with short- rather than long-term emphasis; lowered morale because of financial uncertainties.

In the following brief reviews of national efforts in science and technology, I have attempted to sketch trends, and where possible motivations in patterns of funding in both government and industry. Some feeling for comparisons can be gained from the diagrams 2.1 and 2.2. As in the rest of the book, the emphasis is on basic or fundamental

Diagram 2.1 Patterns of employment and r & d personnel 1981/2. General economic data apply to 1982; r & d statistics refer to 1981 or nearest available year.

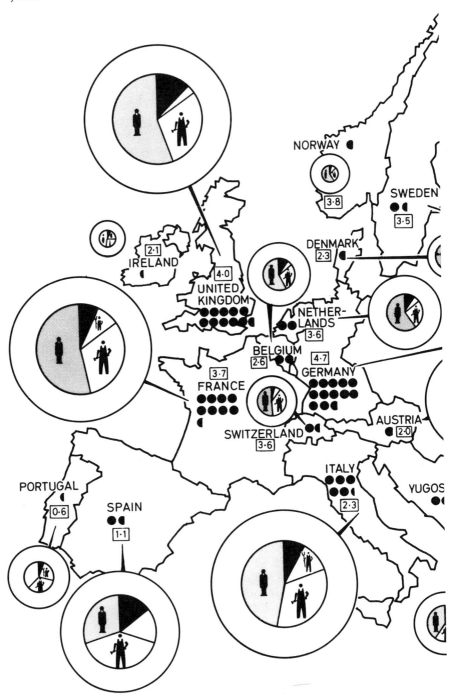

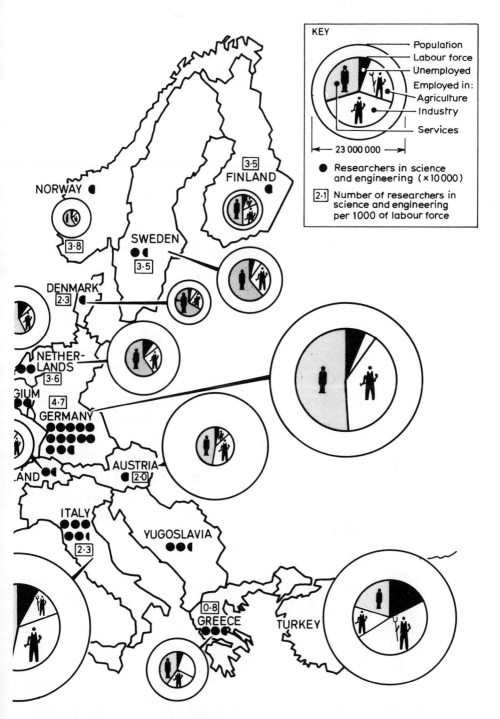

(*Source:* OECD Observer June 1984 *OECD science and technology indicators 1984* and subsequent updates OECD, Paris)

Diagram 2.2 Economic indicators and r & d spending 1981/2. General econom
data refer to 1981 or nearest available year.

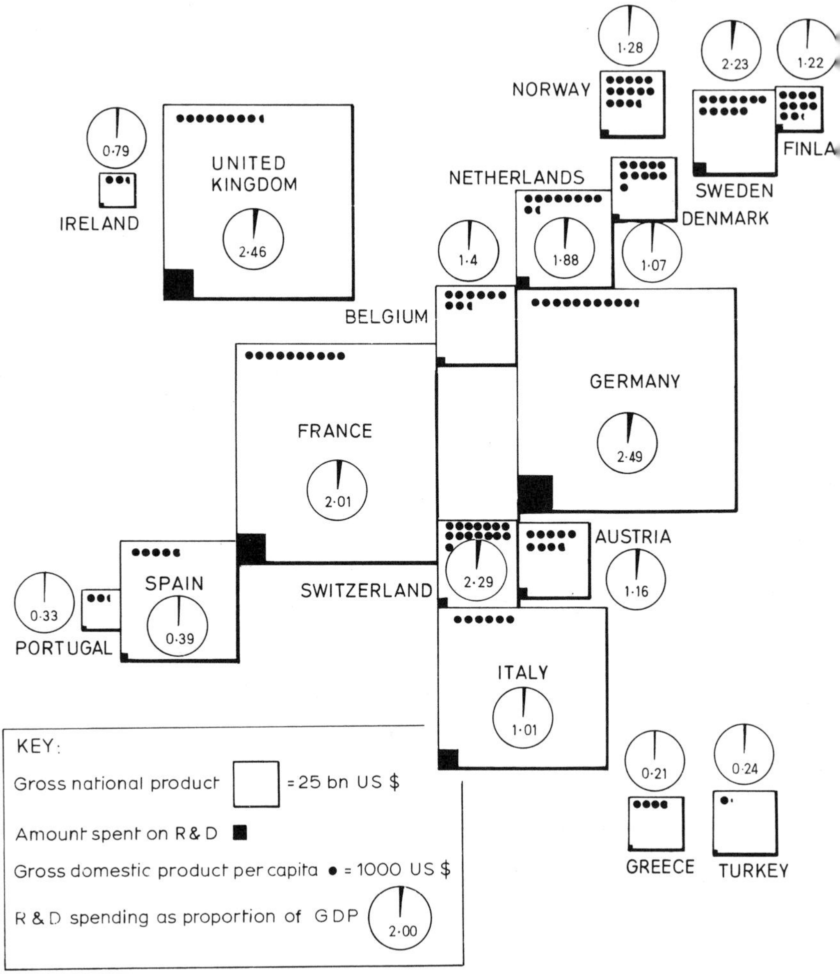

NORWAY 1·28

2·23   1·22

FINLA

0·79

UNITED
KINGDOM

NETHERLANDS

SWEDEN

IRELAND

2·46

DENMARK

1·4   1·88   1·07

BELGIUM

GERMANY

FRANCE

2·49

2·01

SPAIN

SWITZERLAND   2·29   AUSTRIA

0·33

1·16

PORTUGAL   0·39

ITALY

1·01

KEY:

Gross national product ☐ = 25 bn US $

Amount spent on R & D ■

Gross domestic product per capita ● = 1000 US $

0·21   0·24

GREECE   TURKEY

R & D spending as proportion of G D P (2·00)

(*Source:* OECD Observer June 1984 *OECD science and technology indicators*
1984 and subsequent updates.)

aspects of research, though I have tried to give some impression of how this relates to the rest of science and technology in the country concerned. Information of the kind I needed is often hard to come by and even more difficult to interpret. In the absence of previous attempts along these lines, I have done my best under the prevailing constraints. I hope others will one day improve on them.

Austria

Over the last fifteen years, Austria has brought about a quiet revolution in its approach to science and technology. A steadily buoyant economy has allowed Austria to increase the proportion of gross domestic product (GDP) spent on research, and political stability has allowed long-term plans for the gradual encouragement of chosen areas, both in the universities and at new research institutes created and funded by government. Austria makes predominantly low-tech products such as paper, textiles and relatively simple metal products with industrial machinery and road vehicles also playing an important role. These and other industries also sponsor their own research, contributing about half of total Austrian r&d funds.

The Second World War left the once noble and prestigious Austrian universities − Vienna, the oldest university in a German-speaking country, Graz, Salzburg and Innsbruck − in ruins. Six specialist schools of medicine, economics and technology, dating mainly from the nineteenth century, were in a similar state. Nevertheless, these institutions were the main sites of research in the postwar years and were eventually integrated into a coordinated system of higher education in 1955. The state had founded its own Institute for Experimentation and Research in the 1940s, though this eventually came to concern itself only with atomic energy.

Science policy proper began in Austria with the setting up of the Austrian Research Council in 1960, along with an umbrella body for scientific institutes called the Ludwig Boltzmann Society for the Development of Scientific Research in Austria. In 1967 the Lower Chamber of the Austrian government passed the Research Promotion Act which set up two separate funds under the Austrian Research Promotion Council. The Science Foundation funds any scientific research that promises to add to knowledge and is not yet of commercial use, while the Industrial Research Promotion Fund supports all types of research and development projects in industry, including prototypes and pilot plants.

In 1969 and 1970, the OECD planners came to investigate. Their report, published in 1971, criticized a number of features of the system. The Austrians responded by setting up a Ministry of Science and Research. The Ministry appointed a team of scientists, economists and government experts, which defined weaknesses more specifically. They specified absence of research awareness; insufficient information coordination and communication; too much traditionalism; unsatisfactory manpower policy; insufficient means, and no overall research concept.

The team then drew up a 'research conception' that oriented research according to social, economic, cultural and socio-political demands and set up mechanisms for coordination. Within this framework more than seventy project teams and advisory committees have developed strategies for research in different fields, ranging from the history of knowledge through development studies, through ecology to recycling and innovation. The Austrian view of research is a very broad one and it seems to be impossible to persuade their statisticians to provide breakdowns of spending either by subject area or by social objective, so this description will of necessity be in rather general terms.

The Federal Ministry of Science and Research has been busy applying the interim advice of the commissions over the last ten years, vastly helped in its planning efforts by its control of about 80 per cent of federal r&d funds. About two-thirds of the ministry's r&d money is spent in higher education. Unusually the Science and Research Ministry pays for maintenance and new premises as well as individual research projects.

Higher education is open and free to all Austrian citizens who have passed a secondary school leaving certificate (Matura): there is no *numerus clausus* in any subject except for foreigners. A University Organization Law passed in 1975 provides for democratic procedures in all forms of decision making within the university. It also aims to encourage training geared to employability and professionalism, and to meet student demand for subjects such as information technology.

Teaching in technical subjects has been stimulated by some of the new institutes, such as the technical-scientific faculty at Linz, but the proportion of students taking natural sciences and engineering remains lower than average for Europe. Graduates are beginning to experience some difficulty in finding work, though graduate unemployment is reported to be only one per cent.

Research activities have expanded steadily in higher education: just under half of all Austria's research man-hours are put in there. And just over half of university research is applied r&d, an unusually high proportion.

University salaries are 'fair'. Nevertheless academics, who must all do some research, do sometimes have trouble obtaining equipment and consumables and employing technical help. Mobility between universities, between universities and industry, and internationally is a matter for national concern. Austria is also having some problems finding academic jobs for young researchers and there is a federal programme for on-the-job training of young academics to help tide over waiting aspirants.

Under a 'scientists for industry' scheme established by the Ministry of Science and Research and the Federal Chamber of Industry, future young researchers will be able to take up temporary postings in industry with the option of returning to university or taking up an industrial post.

The Ministry of Science and Research also funds the Academy of Sciences, which doubles as a prestigious gathering of senior researchers (thirty-three full members in each of two categories, mathematics and natural sciences, and philosophy and history) and an umbrella organization for commissions and institutes of basic research. The Ludwig Boltzmann Society is another umbrella organization for research institutes. Its work has a more socially relevant flavour, including such topics as human and veterinary medicine, psychology and sociology. The ministry also provides the bulk of the funds for the Austrian Research Centre in Seibersdorf (industry also makes a contribution). Research across the entire spectrum from fundamental to applied takes place there, with an emphasis on large-scale projects and international cooperation.

By the early 1980s the strategists in the Ministry of Science and Research had made a wide ranging but thorough analysis of research in Austria – what was being done and what the guidelines for the future should be. The 1981 Research Organization Law embodied a sort of social contract for science. This restates the basic ground rules of research, including 'the multiplicity of scientific opinions and methods' and the provision of adequate financial resources for scientific and research purposes. In return, research should deliver 'a responsible contribution to the solution of social, economic, cultural and scientific problems, particularly with a view to securing and raising the overall quality of life and economic progress' and the research system should also aim to 'encourage the recruitment of a younger generation of scientists.' The decision makers of the Austrian Science Foundation were joined by representatives from industry, trade unions and student bodies.

The law also provides for two senior advisory bodies that will take over the job of formulating overall policy and advising government. The Science and Research Board will act as a council of elders while the Science and Research Conference will be a parliament where various relevant interest groups can be represented.

These bodies will be particularly valuable in the next serious task that faces the Austrian research machine. Its planners have realized that such a small country cannot afford to be pre-eminent in all areas of science. Now they have to decide which areas to pursue. The document 'Research Conception for the 80s' puts forward some proposals: energy and raw materials; ecology and environment, awareness and a basic effort in the new advanced technologies such as microelectronics and biotechnology; peace studies; sociology of work. It also stressed the importance of access to the latest information for the rest of the world, and of international collaboration, with all parts of the developed and developing world.

Belgium

Belgium is one of the most densely populated countries in Europe and is very short of indigenous raw materials. Its economy is mainly concentrated on services and industrial production. Important manufactures include machinery and transport equipment, chemicals, mineral fuels (including the enormous Petrofina company). The food industry is also significant. The balance of payments has been seriously hit by the recession. The government is desperately trying to cut public spending. Recent efforts in this direction have slightly reduced general funding, for example, for the universities, though total public spending on r&d has stood up well. Meanwhile industry has increased its r&d efforts.

In spite of a sometimes turbulent political scene, the Belgian government has developed a coherent r&d policy over the last two decades. But government spending on r&d as a percentage of GDP remains low by European standards.

The Belgian higher education system expanded rapidly in the 1960s, with no deliberate attempt to influence subject choice. This expansion was in line with a national belief that a better-educated populace would encourage technological progress. Student numbers grew especially in agriculture and medicine, with natural and applied sciences showing a less than average rate of expansion. Belgian universities have, for more than thirty years, been the most important sites of fundamental and basic research. There are no large national laboratories except for the nuclear research centre.

At the time Belgian politicians became aware that the country was scientifically lagging behind neighbours such as the Netherlands. Since the late 1960s funds for university research came either from the general university budget, or from the Fonds National de la Recherche Scientifique (FNRS) though its funds are now declining along with the general university budget. Today the FNRS is still an important national institution for the financing of university research, but there are a number of other sources of funds, each geared towards a specific type of postgraduate training or research.

In 1968 the government created the post of science policy minister and a science administration (the Science Policy Office). This was Belgium's first attempt to assess and control the national r&d effort. From that year on the science policy department has drawn up an annual science budget. This document has a wider scope than many other nations' documents of similar title: it includes the budget for higher education and for public services such as libraries. Research and development performed by all government ministries also figures in the document, though the running of such research is left mainly to the ministries.

Control over the size and detailed division of this budget gives the government a fairly sharp instrument for imposing national policy on the system.

In the 1970s two trends began to change the pattern of research in higher education. The first was that general university funding became far less generous, particularly after the energy crisis of 1973. The second was the increased emphasis placed by the government on research linked to the priorities of society, particularly the needs of small and medium sized firms and industries. The Science Policy Office introduced the concept of national research programmes. These are aimed at promoting r&d in specific fields important for the social and economic development of the country but where not enough research would be carried out without specific government encouragement.

Financial stringency has become much more severe in the 1980s; in 1983 universities were asked to make ten per cent cuts in academic staff by the end of the decade. Very little money is available from general university funds for research or equipment. A new scheme to grant universities special allowances for these purposes was under discussion in 1985.

Special provision for bailing out centres of excellence in research, whether basic or applied, which could not otherwise survive the general malaise, is available in the form of large rolling grants called *actions de recherche concertées*. These grants are managed by the Science Policy Office itself. The projects include a number of fashionable areas of research with potential industrial applications, including microelectronics, integrated optics, robotics, catalysis, new metal and polymer based materials, molecular and cellular biology and oceanology. The National Institute for the Stimulation of Research in Industry and Agriculture has a healthily growing budget out of which it provides aid in various forms to companies. Much of the research it sponsors is performed jointly with university groups.

The Institute also provides almost all the country's studentships for postgraduates working towards a doctorate. It claims not to exert any influence over the subject work of the PhD and that its object is to make available a supply of people with the right background of training and skills to make a contribution in industry. A separate scheme sponsors good graduates to acquire university and industrial training in useful skills and techniques. The purpose is to improve their employment prospects and their contribution to the renewing of industry through experience in research.

Since 1983 the institute has dealt separately with the Fleming and Walloon regions, with the allocation of funds being adjusted in 1984 to ensure each received its fair share. Under the new rules information about research must not pass across regional boundaries. In April 1985 the Flemish regional assembly decided to change the rules by which the institute dealt with local industry. Now proposals from companies based in Flemish areas will be scrutinized by the regional assembly's minister of economics, and subsidies will have to be repaid. The old system of non-repayable subsidies will continue in Brussels and the Walloon regions.

Belgium's universities are going through a tough time, and the situation is not helped by difficulties with the age structure of academics. In 1977 two-thirds of all tenured academics were over forty, and prospects are bad for aspiring assistants on limited contracts: 45 per cent of university researchers held such positions. As a result 'mobility' of researchers often turns into 'brain drain', but expatriates who work in France or the US do sometimes return. Subjects such as nuclear energy development and civil space research have research laboratories administered by government. Such institutions employed just under 800 researchers in 1977. On average the permanent staff were even older than academics, but again they are balanced by an almost equal number of temporary assistants. In the private non-profit sector, including industry's collective research centres which the state funds to the tune of 40 per cent, the average age is far younger: 64 per cent of staff were under forty-five in 1978.

The government seems to have succeeded in persuading industry of the importance of r&d, though enthusiasm seems to have declined a little since 1979. Nearly 60 per cent of the total spent on r&d in 1983 was put up by industry (compared with 70 per cent in 1979), and on average only 9 per cent of the r&d money spent in industry comes from the government. And industry has clearly taken the hint about taking on trained personnel from the universities: it now employs nearly 20 000 of the country's 32 000 researchers. Most of the money is spent in high-tech industries: one-third of the industrial r&d effort goes into chemicals, including drugs and 13 per cent into electronics, with metallurgy and metal manufacture taking another 11 per cent. And the message seems to have got through to more and smaller companies. In 1983 900 companies reported some r&d activity.

Denmark

In spite of Denmark's highly honourable scientific traditions it has not yet developed a solid base of science-based technological expertise. Its economy includes a large chunk devoted to agriculture. Manufacturing industry, which now accounts for two-thirds of its industry, is largely based on fairly simple and well-established technologies. The general population is not really geared up to thinking of their country as being competitive with more technologically sophisticated neighbours such as Germany. Nevertheless, among the policy makers and leaders of the engineering and science worlds, there is a growing will to keep Denmark up to date with the latest developments in computing and information technology. There is also a special local interest in biotechnology, where it is thought experience in brewing, agriculture and chemicals could give Denmark an edge in some areas. One major problem is Denmark's severe balance of payments problem which has persisted throughout the 1970s and has forced continuous restraint in public spending. Unemployment is also high.

Denmark now has five universities and one technical high school. Copenhagen University, founded in the fifteenth century, is still by far the largest of these, with Aarhus, founded in 1928, also training a substantial number of students. These universities do not teach engineering and have very little contact with industry: students at Copenhagen have even strongly resisted attempts to institute such contacts. The study of physics, chemistry and mathematics is in the decline, and jobs that fall vacant are not filled, which in the short term tends to increase the teaching load. The effect is, however, partially masked by an enormous demand for courses in computer science – for which qualified teachers are in very short supply. Not surprisingly most of the research in the natural science faculties is basic rather than applied, with the bulk of support coming from general university funds, though each group now has to negotiate individually with the Ministry of Education.

The three smaller, one might almost say regional, university type institutions account for only one fifth of the student population, but they have provided the opportunity for experiments in completely new types of education. Of particular interest to the technical world is the Aalborg University Centre, where students learn through project work conducted in small groups rather than taught courses. This approach has made it particularly easy to set up collaborations with local industry and may well lead to the establishment of a local research institute for the fishing industry alongside a graduate course in fishing economics and technology.

Technical education of a more traditional kind is provided at Denmark's single Technical University, which since 1829 has provided the country's main supply of graduate engineers and has housed the most academic end of research in practical subjects in the Danish system. Collaboration with industry is much more apparent here, and 10 per cent of r&d funds come from industry.

Nevertheless, the stagnating research budgets of the 1970s have had their effect here too. Throughout the higher education system much equipment is out of date, and there is also, as almost everywhere else in Europe, a shortage of jobs for young researchers.

Over the last few years the Danish Research Administration, which provides 12 per cent of r&d funds in higher education through a number of research councils, has begun to get the message through. It has persuaded the government to come up with a small fund for the renewal of instrumentation, and a number of special research posts.

Before the expansion of the universities in the 1960s and early 1970s, a majority of Denmark's researchers worked in the fairly large network of technical institutes. The most prestigious of these is the Risø National Laboratory, founded after the Second World War in the worldwide wave of emphasis for atomic energy and with the active help of Danish theoretical nuclear physicist Niels Bohr. In 1980 the Danish parliament resolved not to build nuclear power stations in the immediate future so Risø's nuclear work is of no practical interest. Nevertheless, the laboratory houses research of high quality into energy supply technology, environment and safety, materials, and biotechnology and radiation research. Risø's research reactor is a source of neutrons for experiments in the structure of materials, and this facility attracts researchers from all over Northern Europe.

Government also provides substantial subsidies to the fairly complex network of technological service institutes and information centres maintained by industry. Only a very small proportion of r&d executed directly by industry is paid for by the state. Some of the institutes have been of immense use to their industries, but the general trend has been away from r&d work, especially basic or long-term, in favour of testing, information gathering, and very short-term product development.

Recent heart-searchings over science policy in Denmark have concentrated on working out ways of stimulating a more dynamic and systematic approach to 'technical scientific research' and developing a 'national strategic research plan'. The discussion is twofold. Firstly there are the basic structural weaknesses of a system with a rather old-fashioned higher education system and underfunded facilities for research. These will have to be tackled to some extent before universities can offer any kind of contribution to industry. And in August 1984 the Danish government announced plans to revitalize basic research in the universities and attract back some of her most distinguished emigré academics. There will be well-funded five year fellowships for 25 'super-researchers' who will each earn a professor's salary plus a supplement. Each fellow will report annually to the relevant research council. The rate of recruitment of lower-level researchers will double, with 1100 vacancies being available over the next decade to help ease the age structure problem. Then there is the challange of finding out what industry needs and/or wants in the way of help.

While the government has not wholeheartedly committed itself to tackling all the problems, it has supported a number of quite imaginative schemes to improve the situation. For example, it started in 1977 a training scheme leading to a diploma in 'industrial research'. Equivalent to a PhD, this involves two years of research in industrial development departments and r&d institutions, and is funded 50:50 by the state and a sponsoring company. Another is a 'co-operative organization for higher education of Fyn' (Fyn or Funen is the Danish island whose main town is

Odense) which aims to ensure the establishment of educational and course offerings which are relevant to the needs of the area, and, through close cooperation with the local business community, to ensure that new graduates will not simply be graduated into unemployment. Graduates who are already on the dole can take advantage of a national scheme to fund projects that allow them to extend their skills. Projects in private enterprise are preferred.

In 1980 the Technology Council (part of the Ministry of Industry) made an important venture into setting priorities in research. It set up initiative groups in eleven specific disciplines to decide how best the council could stimulate activity in these areas.

Finland

For a country with a population half the size of Greater London's, Finland has a remarkably well-established and diversified system of higher education and research. Finland's economy has been very precarious since the early 70s, particularly as Finland has to import 69 per cent of its energy requirements. But in spite of stringent attempts to cut back on public spending, the government has continued to increase its outlay on r&d in line with a fairly consistent policy established in the 1960s.

Finland trades actively with both the Communist bloc and the EEC. Its major export is pulp and paper with manufacturing accounting for only 24 per cent of GDP. There is great faith in the possibility of developing high-technology industries if the correct r&d policies are pursued with government and industry working together.

In spite of its small and thinly spread population and its apparently isolated geographical position, Finland has maintained a continuous tradition of scholarship since the foundation of its major university in 1640. In the late nineteenth century many of its scholars, by then based in Helsinki, turned their attention to the natural sciences. A network of state research institutions was founded in the early years of the twentieth century – the first were in geotechnology and agriculture and forestry.

The Finnish university system began to expand in the late 1950s, with even faster growth in the early 60s and early 70s. The average length of study increased too, so the total university population increased faster than annual intakes, though both are now beginning to level off. Student numbers in the natural sciences, engineering and medicine have formed a growing share of the total, a trend encouraged by the foundation of three universities of technology and two faculties of technology (out of a total of seventeen universities or higher education institutions which carry out research). The government too has encouraged this trend. Every two years the Finnish Cabinet makes a recommendation about the number of new students to be admitted in the various fields of study and in-

31

stitutions, though the universities themselves have the final word on the matter. These cabinet decrees are made within the framework of a long-term Development Plan for Higher Education, which also lays down staff and space requirements in terms of the number of students in each of four different subject groups. Postgraduate students (8 per cent of graduates) are employed by the universities as assistants or researchers.

Government attempts to reform degree courses in order to make them more career-oriented and efficient were implemented in 1980. The changes have been severely criticized by academics, particularly in the pure sciences. Nevertheless, in the second half of the 1980s student intake will expand slowly, according to plans reported in February 1985. The Ministry of Education is optimistic that graduate unemployment will not rise appreciably. The Finns are considering a plan to specify the proportion of GDP that will go to university funds each year. The final draft of the plan, which includes guarantees of autonomy and for support for researchers, has been cautiously welcomed by academics.

Graduate unemployment is a serious reality in Finland today, though graduates stand a better than average chance of getting a job. PhDs looking for jobs in the research world are in a rather worse, though not yet desperate, situation as the student populations level off. Since then holders of university and institute posts intended to be short term have been allowed to stay permanently and this leaves fewer opportunities for future aspirants.

Research in higher education accounts for less than half of government funded r&d in Finland; though not surprisingly three-quarters of state-funded, basic research is carried out there. About a quarter of the research funding in universities comes via the Academy of Finland, an umbrella organization for Finland's six research councils. The academy's funds, like those of the universities, come from the Ministry of Education.

Other ministries such as Trade and Industry, Agriculture and Forestry, Social Affairs, Health and Defence run their own research institutes, which account for most of the rest of the state r&d support. Attempts at coordination of this began in the 1950s: in 1963 a Science Policy Council was formed to allocate the research appropriations in the state budget. This council is chaired by the Prime Minister with five members of the cabinet and seven other appointees. Its major achievements have been to lay down an outline for Finnish science policy in the 1970s (in a document published in 1973) and a new policy for the 1980s.

In the recession years of the 1970s, the focus of the policy's objectives was basically economic. In line with OECD recommendations, the proportion of GDP spent on research rose to just over 1 per cent. The priority areas of the programme were public health, living conditions of the population and the development of national production structures, environment, promotion of democracy and equality, working life and working conditions.

In the late 1970s particularly, industry began to put more effort into research on its own account, and its share of the country's spending on r & d now exceeds 50 per cent. Part of the extra funds are accounted for by 'risk loans' from various public or semi-public agencies including the Ministry of Trade and Industry. The number of businesses involved grew from 340 in 1975 to 500 in 1980, though most of it is still conducted by large companies. Among product groups the electrotechnical industry is the biggest spender with over 20 per cent; machinery is next with almost one fifth, then chemicals, with the paper industry, which used to head the list, in fourth place.

The Finns are proud of this progress (and the OECD, incidentally, has applauded it recently too). But in its development guidelines for the 1980s the Science Policy Council has noted some weaknesses. In particular it comments on the relatively slow rate of growth in basic research, with social sciences particularly deprived. It proposes a 40 per cent increase of funds from 1982 to 1986 for basic research, compared with a 50 per cent total increase.

Basic research's share of the state cake will thus continue to drop slightly over the period, from 39 per cent to 37 per cent, but more slowly than before (between 1970 and 1981 it dropped from 54 per cent to 41 per cent). Early indications are that funding for r&d in universities and in particular the Academy of Finland is indeed rising more quickly than before.

Although the Science Policy Council acknowledges that growth in r&d spending must slow down during the 1980s, its plan includes the objective that over 2 per cent of GDP should be spent on r&d by 1990.

Planners also have some ambitious schemes for the fastest-growing section of the state's r&d budget: technology, promotion of industry. They want to stimulate the growth of new technology industries such as microelectronics, telecommunications, data processing, biotechnology, materials science and process control and automation technologies.

In February 1985 the government reported that r&d allocations had grown from 0.89 per cent of GDP in 1971 to 1.32 per cent in 1983 and announced plans that the amount should grow by a further 10 per cent each year for the rest of the decade.

France

Socialist governments in Latin countries seem to have a special talent for trying to initiate change through enormously complex legislation fronted by grandiose statements of principle. Often these worthy actions have very little effect in the long run. One partial exception to this rule appears to be the French efforts to enshrine science and technology as the main element of strategy to revitalise French industry and stimulate the economy. The new socialist government of 1981 created a new Ministry for Research and Technology and declared its intention to raise the percentage of GDP spent on r&d from 1.8 per cent in 1981 to 2.5 per cent in 1985; and increasing the number of employees in the public research effort by 4.5 per cent a year. Under the leadership of Jean-Pierre Chevènement it identified six priority areas for research and launched a very broad national debate on the nature and purpose of research that would involve all interested parties: industry researchers themselves, and not least the trade unions which had played an important part in bringing the new government to power. France's severe economic problems are affecting the ability of both government and industry to meet all the objectives of the plan; nevertheless the new initiative has undoubtedly changed the philosophy and the practice of research in France.

Postwar France was quick off the mark with government interest in science; it drew eminent scientists such as Frédéric Joliot-Curie into the mainstream of national planning. In the great French tradition of government acting through prestigious state funded and controlled organizations, the institutes of the Centre National de la Recherche Scientifique (CNRS) took the central role in providing France with an adequate effort in all fields from theoretical physics to ancient history. France was also the first country in Europe to set up an Atomic Energy Commission which has since been another important sponsor of research, as have state industries such as energy and defence, including aerospace.

As far as research is concerned, the enormous French university system has never quite come to terms with the challenge of the CNRS. Since the very rapid expansion in student numbers of the 1960s, when many staff of varying degrees of research ability were taken on and given absolute security of tenure, the scientific output of university departments has been variable to say the least. More recently this disproportionate influx has left jobs blocked to new aspirants often of higher quality. The university law of 1968 enshrined the principle of freedom of access to universities for all holders of the baccalauréat and also encouraged institutions to take on as many students as possible by relating their income directly to student numbers. In general subsequent governments have done little to enforce any standards of teaching or research performance.

The 1968 law did have some positive effects. It laid down that among the multifarious committees responsible for the running of each university should be a (non-democratic) scientific council, which allocates research funds and approves research programmes. Within the limitations of their powers, these councils have worked reasonably well, though attempts to coordinate the universities' research activities nationally through a council for higher education and research have proved less successful.

There are, of course, exceptions to this generally gloomy picture.

Where strong research teams have evolved, the CNRS often injects funds for equipment, research posts and technical support to maintain and continue a centre of excellence. The new universities with special status such as the Technical University of Compiègne and the university institutes of technology can be more choosy about students and take pride in developing practical subjects and working closely with industry, a traditionally weak area of the French education and research system as a whole.

French universities have also failed to provide an adequate supply of well-trained researchers, the shortage being worse in engineering and applied skills in general. The highly politicized universities have been reluctant to tailor their students to meet the needs of employers. Also, they suffer because the intellectual cream of the nation is taken by the *grandes écoles*, elite training colleges that provide an excellent specialized education geared to mainly administrative careers in government or industry. Such organizations do virtually no research themselves neither are they a major source of research manpower.

The socialist regime is keen to introduce reforms here too. In general the philosophy of the Higher Education Guideline Bill (passed in July, 1983, but still under discussion in 1984) is to encourage the universities to provide graduates with a more professionally oriented training and to work far more closely with industry at the level of research. Universities should also provide more flexible forms of education, particularly vocational, for people of all ages, and in general share the knowledge and expertise they develop and preserve with a far wider community. Since then the government has announced that there should be more student places in key technological subjects such as electronics.

The government appears to be slightly ambivalent about the role the universities should play in the country's basic research effort. Objectives seem to be far better defined in the thrust towards industrial collaboration and the transfer of technology, and with the shortage of cash there are already signs that basic research will lose out. In the universities these problems may be exacerbated by new measures (in the Higher Education Guideline Bill) to increase the range and influence of democratic decision-making procedures. But a lobby of senior university researchers, most of them distinguished and well-known scientists in their own right, has forced the government to go back on some of these proposals, in particular one-man one-vote electoral colleges. How far the government can afford to go on denying the wishes of the university trade unions who provide the administration with loyal support remains to be seen.

The new super-ministry created in 1981 took over the CNRS and all the other 'organismes de recherches' that constitute the main thrust of the state-funded research effort. With increased funding these organizations have managed to find a few posts of various kinds for young researchers, though the average age of scientific personnel is still increasing: it now stands at just over 40. Closer relationships with university groups are being actively fostered, but the main thrust of the government's efforts are clearly the priority programmes or *programmes mobilisateurs*. In 1983 there were seven of these: six concerned specific areas of science: biotechnology; use and diversification of energy; electronics; science and technology for the developing countries; employment and conditions of work; industrial materials. The seventh concerned the cultural context of science: in particular the promotion of French as a scientific language and the diffusion of scientific information to non-scientists. The biotechnology programme was the first of these to get off the ground, with a plan drawn up by experts from the research institutes, industry and government. The programme has the ambitious objective of securing at least 10 per cent of the world market in the next decade, and will involve many types of activity from basic science to projects suggested by and performed in industry, as well as the development of a precise industrial strategy.

By 1984 it was fairly clear that some objectives of the grand plan would not be met, in particular levels of overall funding forecast for both science and government. Nevertheless, the plan has a combination of economic sense, structural hardheadedness and appeal to national pride that has definitely caught the imagination of those concerned directly and indirectly with research in France.

At the end of 1983 Chevènement lost his job at the (renamed) Ministry of Research and Industry to be replaced by Laurent Fabius. In July 1984 Fabius took over from Mitterand as prime minister when Mitterand took the president's job. Fabius brought back Chevènement to become education minister, while the research and industry job went to Hubert Curien, a well known space scientist.

During 1984 and the first half of 1985 Chevènement and Curien both kept up the pressure for increasing the quantity and quality of research, making research jobs more numerous and attractive, and promoting links between basic research and industry. The traditional two-stage PhD system in the universities has been replaced by a shorter three-year single step degree, and it has been suggested that the grands écoles should be able to award doctorates. Student numbers are increasing and there are new jobs, primarily for teachers, in the universities. Universities are being encouraged to develop their own special identities and to compete for students and research funding. All undergraduates will, in future, have to learn computer programming. The government is asking universities to produce more graduates in science and technology, particularly with a view to meeting local needs. And there will be a new elite first degree course with highly restricted entry. The idea is to bridge the gap that currently exists between universities and grands ecoles. There will be a new committee to 'evaluate' the work of the universities. It will be chaired by Laurent Schwarz, a distinguished mathematician who has openly criticized standards in the universities and reports directly to the president.

There will be changes too in the CNRS, which has done fairly well in recent years with an average of 5.5 per cent more funds (in real terms) each year between 1981 and 1985, and 3 per cent a year growth in jobs. The number and variety of types of post in CNRS has been reduced, simplifying the system. All CNRS employees are now civil servants, enjoying such benefits as tenure of jobs. This change is designed to improve mobility by making jobs more attractive, an important point as the uptake of opportunities for CNRS employees in industry has been disappointing. In the long term CNRS will concentrate its resources by continuing to develop links with universities. A new plan announced in April 1985 suggested that 40 per cent of CNRS funds might be spent in 20 selected research areas, most of which have fairly close links to practical objectives.

In May 1985 the socialist government proposed a new bill for research policy that would continue the upward trend in spending on r&d, which by that year had reached 2.25 per cent of GDP. By 1988 the figure should be 2.6 per cent, but government expected most of the remaining expansion to be paid for out of private funds. Nevertheless there will be 4500 new research jobs and it is proposed that all industrial employees will have the right to take one year's leave to conduct a project at a recognized research institution.

Germany

Germany is truly Europe's science policy 'wunderkind'. In absolute terms and by almost all relative standards it is Europe's biggest r&d spender. And it has achieved this pre-eminent position by substantial growth in investment in r&d from both government and industry since the early 1960s when in terms of GDP its r&d spending was much smaller, and far behind that of the UK for example. The level of spending has been maintained in recent years in spite of serious economic problems in the late 70s and early 80s.

In 1945 most of the prewar base of scientific research and education, already weakened by the policies of the Nazi regime, was in ruins. Those German scientists not lost in the fighting, the concentration camps, or in exile were rounded up by the occupying armies and interned or deported, often never to return. When the Federal Republic of Germany was formed in 1949, rebuilding the research system was a priority. As with many aspects of the new German government the emphasis then was on de-centralization, and for the next fifteen years regional government took the bulk of the responsibility for planning and executing research. Of course, many aspects of basic research, particularly that of the specialized research institutes belonging to the Max Planck Society, and the newly founded Fraunhofer Society for the Advancement of Applied Research, had to be nationally coordinated. Such coordination is now done by bodies such as the Standing Conference of Ministers of Education and Cultural Affairs, (for the Länder) and the Federal-Länder Commission for Educational Planning and Promotion of Research. Both are advised by the Science Council.

During the 1960s federal agencies began to take a stronger role in r&d planning. In 1955 a ban on German research into nuclear physics was lifted, leading to the formation of the Federal Ministry for Atomic Energy. In 1962 this became the Federal Ministry for Scientific Research. During the 1960s the percentage of GDP spent on r&d in Germany rose from under 1.5 per cent to nearly 1.8 per cent. This was also a time when the universities were expanding quickly to cope with the raised expectations of young people; and educational planning too was thought to need more central control. Hence, in 1969 the science ministry was transformed into the Federal Ministry of Education and Science.

The new ministry had to deal with all aspects of technological r&d, nuclear technology and data processing; space research and technology, and aeronautical research, as well as many aspects of education, including universities and vocational education. In 1972 the research functions (except for federal funding of university research) were handed over to the new Federal Ministry for Research and Technology which now provides a central focus for encouraging both applied and basic research to meet the needs of the state and increasingly those of industry. The Federal Ministry for Education and Science continued to be responsible for the general university legislation and the federal funding of university building, university research and assistance for young scientists. This situation remains approximately the same today, though it should be remembered that central government's control of universities and basic research and universities is still far from complete: the Länder provide much of the basic running costs of the universities and half of the funds of the Max Planck Society and the German Research Society (Deutsche Forschungsgemeinschaft, the DFG).

The Germans realized as early as 1919 that for a concentrated effort in a particular research discipline, especially where teamwork and specialized equipment is needed, special institutes can be extremely effective. Today they have built up a number of such networks with differing purposes. Apart from the institutes of the Max Planck Society there is a group of thirteen 'big science' establishments which carry out a wide spectrum of work from the very pure (such as high energy physics), to the much more down to earth applied work, sometimes within one institution. More at the applied end of the spectrum are the laboratories of the Fraunhofer Society (Germany's equivalent of industrial research associations, though some have more government-oriented objectives) and the Bund or Länder (federal or regional) research establishments.

Of the government's total spending on r&d a remarkably high proportion (about 40 per cent) goes on basic r&d. Of this, the lion's share goes to the universities, and the bulk of this tranche comes from the Länder, which bear almost all the general running expenses of higher education. German universities have always maintained the tradition of combining education and research, and of an academic's basic freedom to pursue the topics that interest him. Estimates suggest that one-third of general university funding is spent on research. In addition funds for special projects can be obtained from the German Research Society (DFG) from ministries and from a number of fairly rich private foundations. Academics can also collaborate with the staff of research institutes, particularly if they need to use specialist equipment, and participate in federal research programmes.

In the early 80s the emphasis on basic research has increased even further, especially as far as support from within the research and technology ministry is concerned.

Nevertheless, the extremely rapid expansion of student numbers that has continued from the 1960s to the present day has taken its toll on research, which has not grown at anything like the same rate. Heavier teaching loads; more administrative work due to increased bureaucracy and democratic procedures; union legislation that limits employment on short-term contracts; shortage of tenured posts for young researchers and lack of reward for good research performance have all been blamed for a general air of malaise about research in universities.

University education too has come under attack. Any student who has passed the Abitur examination, which marks the end of secondary education, can apply to the faculty and university of his choice: in general he will be admitted unless the course is oversubscribed in which case he will be offered a place at another institution. But there are stronger restrictions in some fields. This applies particularly to medicine, where new admissions procedures involve the hitherto unprecedented measure of using interviews to select candidates for a fixed number of places.

The influx of students has swelled the older universities beyond all recognition and facilities are sometimes less than adequate even for basic teaching. Only a quarter have been attached to the twenty-five newer universities created since the war. Already aged about twenty when they enter, students take an average of six years to take their first degree.

The growing spectre of graduate unemployment has, however, begun to sharpen the mind of many prospective students, who now make sharper choices, preferring the technical universities, the Fachhochschulen, (similar to the British polytechnics) or other forms of vocational training to studies at a university.

The government is beginning to propose some remedies for these problems: in particular more power in decision making and administration for senior staff and a new professional structure for academics that will provide jobs for good young people. It is also encouraging universities to diversify and to compete for outside research funding from industry, the foundations and the DFG. In recent years the DFG itself has tried to stimulate research by defining certain priority areas, in which universities can compete for extra support including senior staff posts. It also sponsors a small number of five-year fellowships to tide over exceptional young researchers until jobs become available (the Heisenberg programme).

Reforms in training – in particular shortening the length of courses – have met with more resistance. In Germany the shortage of jobs for graduates is seen as an argument against the measure, as it would have the effect of increasing the unemployment figures.

The basic research institutes have also been criticized, often with justice, for their failure to keep up with modern developments especially those related to industry's needs such as biotechnology and those that involve knowledge of and exchange between many disciplines.

In late 1984 the university population was continuing to grow. There were 1.3 million students for 760 000 places. Finance ministers of the 11 Länder wanted the universities to accommodate 200 000 to 300 000 more students without spending more money, which would be the implication of expanding the system to allow for 850 000 students as requested by the university rectors.

The federal government had a different perspective. In a draft amendment to the university law it proposed measures to improve the autonomy and effectiveness of German universities. Fewer decisions would be taken democratically, putting more power back in the hands of senior academic staff. Special courses would be offered to the most talented students, admissions being restricted to those who passed a special exam in addition to the Abitur. And restrictions that discouraged the sponsorship of research in universities by outside bodies such as industry would be removed. By July 1985 students, states and even the rectors' organization had lost enthusiasm for the government's new measures, suggesting that they represented a distraction from the real issues of overcrowding, poor financing, and the shortage of job opportunities for academics.

The academics are still concerned about the stagnation of the research community, and continue to call in vain for implementation of the Fiebinger plan to increase the number of senior academic posts by 200 per year. They backed an idea to allow short term contracts to be offered to aspiring academics who were continuing their research training or working on projects paid for by outside organizations. Such posts would be offered by universities and state run research organizations such as the Max Planck institutes. The idea has, however, been opposed by the trade unions which regard it as contrary to the constitution.

The image of university training is changing, however. More and more career-minded young people are choosing shorter and more vocational higher education options such as courses at polytechnics, and industry is increasingly keen to recruit people with the qualifications they award. Even so, many of their contemporaries seek personal development and fulfillment through university study, and appear not to be too disappointed when finding a job proves difficult. Attempts to widen the scope of the *numerus clausus*, for example to heavily over-subscribed subjects such as computer science, have been unsuccessful. Measures to control the numbers undergoing expensive medical training, where there is already a *numerus clausus*, continue to be controversial. In April 1985 the state culture ministers finally decided that 15 per cent of medical students would be selected by personal interview. And when in May 1985 it was announced that nearly half of first year medical students failed their preliminary exams, it was widely interpreted as a trick to cut student numbers.

Greece

Modern Greece has suffered one political upheaval after another, and its scientific and technical development has consequently been much retarded. Its expenditure on r&d is 0.2 per cent of GNP – the lowest in Europe. The bulk of this comes from government and is spent in government institutes. Industry plays only a small part in the research effort and usually has no financial or organizational link with the government's effort.

Since the defeat of the Colonels and the return of democracy in 1974 the government has acknowledged the importance of planning research and linking it to industrial development. In spite of severe economic problems the government has committed itself to spending 0.8 per cent of GDP on r&d by 1987 and in 1982 it created a Ministry of Research and Technology to develop a national plan within the framework of which the budgetary objective could be achieved. A previous attempt at a national plan, launched in 1977, ran into a number of serious difficulties: the planners found they had too little information about what industry was doing. Bureaucratic hassles also held up the cash they allocated to individual research projects – an idea rather new to the Greek system.

The sector best catered for in the Greek system is agriculture. Through the Ministry of Agriculture the government runs no fewer than eighty or so separate units dealing with specific crops or specialist topics. Together with a dozen or so larger agencies and institutes with more generalized remits, this network accounts for about 30 per cent of Greece's r&d spending.

Another 30 per cent or so goes to 'general promotion of knowledge' in a number of basic research institutes such as the six run by the National Hellenic Research Foundation. Greece's research council houses centres for Byzantine Studies, Graeco Roman antiquities and neo-Hellenic studies as well as the centres for biological research, organic chemistry and theoretical chemistry. The Academy of Athens also runs eleven research centres across a similarly wide spectrum of subjects to conduct investigations in the natural sciences. Two other state-sponsored institutes have established reputations for excellence in natural science: the Demokritos nuclear research centre, and the Institut Pasteur Hellenique, where biochemistry is the main theme.

Greek universities do not make a substantial contribution to research. Nor do they provide much in the way of post-graduate training. So most Greek researchers have learnt their trade abroad. At undergraduate level too many Greeks study abroad, particularly prospective doctors and engineers, who go to Italy. The mass exodus occurs partly because the seven Greek universities are crowded and oversubscribed.

In some fields an old-fashioned style of education predominates, with the professor as the dominant figure and involving a great deal of bookwork as opposed to experiment and original thought. The shortage of teachers (in the Aristotles University of Thessaloniki, where over a quarter of Greek students are educated, the staff/student ratio is 1:82) and the comparative rarity of research work may also play a part. The national technical university at Athens, which teaches only practical subjects including all forms of engineering and architecture, is better off with a staff/student ratio below 1:10.

In 1983 the parliament passed a law under which Greek universities would be organized in departments rather than by 'chairs' and would give students more say in the running of their institutions. There would also be more emphasis on continuous assessment rather than examinations, and on scientific method and the solution of problems rather than rote learning. A national academy to supervise the appointment of teachers and coordinate research was also planned.

It is not yet clear, however, how substantial a part the universities will play in the grand new plan for research now being elaborated by the Ministry of Research and Technology. In 1982 the new ministry set up a Research Centre of Crete associated with the University of Crete at Rethymnon. Its three institutions will deal with informatics and computer science research; molecular biology and biotechnology; and electronic structure of matter and lasers.

Greece is clearly keen to develop new technologies. The National Plan also includes quite a lot of catching up with the technologies that underlie Greece's new low-tech industries. Manufacturing has now just outstripped agriculture as a contributor to GDP, mineral resources are particularly important raw materials and so the plan will include 'special attention to metallurgical research as well as to industry-related minerals which may eventually become resources of paramount importance for the national economy'. A completely new venture will be to encourage innovation by establishing new funding mechanisms and sorting out the legal details of patents. In general the ministry hopes to 'direct research activities towards the needs of industry as well as towards the goal of dissemination and utilization of research results'.

Developing basic research does not figure highly in the new plan: perhaps this would require an effort that Greece just cannot afford; or perhaps the government thinks that Greek research has been too biased in that direction in the past.

Ireland

The Republic of Ireland is a small country where industry has only recently encroached on a largely agricultural economy, with tourism another important factor. In spite of a rapid growth in GDP during the 1960s Ireland now faces serious economic problems including high inflation and a large and growing level of unemployment, exacerbated by the increasing population.

The lack of an industrial tradition has, of course, weakened the development of a national research base and the level of spending on r&d in terms of GDP is one of the lowest in Europe. There is some excellent basic research done (mainly at the universities), but not surprisingly sciences associated with production such as engineering are weaker. In spite of recent encouragement for technical training Ireland still produces far fewer engineers per head of population than industrialized countries.

There is a positive side to Ireland's late industrialization, however. There is less inertia in the higher education system obstructing the introduction of research and training geared precisely to the new technologies such as electronics and biotechnology. As there are relatively few jobs in traditional industries, new developments such as automation are not seen as a threat to employment.

Much of the industrial growth of the 1960s was due to investment by overseas companies in manufacturing plant in Ireland, and the country's future prosperity will depend on maintaining and encouraging this trend. Technical support in the form both of r&d and trained personnel is seen as a key element in keeping this investment and attracting more. So far though, the parent companies rarely see Ireland as a place for their own major investments in r&d, though piecemeal collaborations, for example with university departments, are growing.

Ireland has some very honourable scientific traditions, associated in particular with Trinity College, Dublin, the Royal Irish Academy, and the Royal Dublin Society. With the formation of the Irish Free State in 1922, Eire finally gained control over its own affairs. A Commission of

Enquiry reviewed 'the Resources and Industries of Ireland', and as a result of its reports, many steps were taken towards the development of energy resources and agriculture, often with substantial technical knowhow built up along the way.

Science planning began in the late 1950s. At the same time Ireland's network of research institutes began to develop, beginning with the Agricultural Research Institute in 1958, which remains the largest of the government laboratories today. The second is now the Institute for Industrial Research and Standards. The bulk of government r&d money is spent on this network.

Meanwhile in 1967 the National Science Council took on responsibility for areas such as fundamental research, utilization of natural resources, technological change in the business enterprise sector, the social sciences and promotion of scientific and technical information. Most of its money went to support science of various types carried out in Ireland's university level institutions. Specific schemes provided for scientific research grants (starting from 1969) and a university/industry cooperation grant scheme that began in 1971. These schemes certainly fuelled the growth of expansion in university research, but often the message failed to get across to industry. Providing a network of industrial liaison officers went some way towards improving matters.

During the 1970s this style of science policy was superseded by another structure, the National Board for Science and Technology (NBST), which has a dual role as an advisory body for government on all aspects of science and technology and a disburser of grant money for both pure and applied types of research in higher education. Following recommendations by an OECD review, the BST, formed in 1977, took on the more grandiose task of formulating a national science policy 'which would draw together the various threads of scientific and technological activity into a composite and integrated whole, to secure the optimum contribution towards medium and long-term economic development. Its advice in this area is now delivered in the form of commentary to an annual science budget, which it formulates after discussion with all the other government agencies that spend money on education and maintaining technical services and running r&d.

The 1981 and 1982 science budgets review the past performance of the economy and the economic impact of science and technology. In 1981, the review concluded that

> Science and technology in Ireland, as reflected in r&d, has remained . . . at the lowest level within the EEC. [This is not quite true today: Greece is relatively worse.] This applies both nationally and in particular to industry. . . . Technology transfer of the kind currently being promoted while it has compensated for job losses in traditional sectors, has not led to any dramatic growth in manufacturing

employment. A stronger indigenous sector using technology to exploit raw material advantages is required. Indigenous r&d will be a key element in this.

As far as the world of the Irish research worker is concerned the NBST addresses itself to three major issues. The first is how to plan for an adequate but not excessive supply of skilled manpower. In the early 1980s the NBST predicted a shortage of graduate engineers that would last until 1990, but as recession has bitten deeper the talk is rather of trying to come to terms with graduate unemployment. Together with the Institute for Industrial Research and Standards the NBST runs a programme to find suitable posts for a year at a time for unemployed holders of science ad engineering degrees. Nevertheless, the long-term need for engineers particularly in electronics has led to the establishment of new centres for training and research (see below).

At the same time the serious economic crisis has led to a cutback in resources and calls for 'more efficiency' in the education system. As in other sectors of the civil service, only one in three academic jobs that fall vacant may be filled. Spending on other physical resources such as equipment has also been cut back.

NBST has voiced serious concern about such stringencies and recommended a proper capital investment programme which concentrates on expanding facilities at the National Institutes of Higher Education (NIHE) at Dublin and Limerick (founded in the 1970s to meet the growing need for technological education at degree and other levels) and a new engineering school at University College Dublin. The last of these fell victim to government spending cuts in October 1983.

But other institutes already established are beginning to work together with industry. NIHE at Limerick, for example, has set up the Plassey Technological Park. A number of companies and government agencies have rented space near the campus, and cooperate with the NIHE in both training and research. Since 1981 the site has also contained the National Microelectronics Application Centre. Other national institutes include the National Microelectronics Research Centre at University College Cork and the National Software Centre at the Industrial Development Authority's Enterprise Centre in Dublin.

The Plassey Park is also playing an important part in pursuing another of the NBST's aims: increasing Irish industry's investment in r&d, and encouraging foreign firms to conduct more of their r&d in Ireland. The business enterprise sector provided about 40 per cent of total Irish r&d expenditure. Of this almost half was spent by foreign companies.

The NBST is also concerned about a lack of innovativeness in Irish industry, as indicated for example by the low level of patenting. It is donating an increasing share of its resources to work relevant to industry. There is a Higher Education-Industry Cooperative r&d Scheme, now run jointly between the NBST and the Industrial Development Authority. NBST has also embarked on a 'strategic research programme' for projects involving 'pre-competitive research or the development of a particular technology relevant to a group of companies or industrial sector or the further understanding or development of a national resources' in the areas of biotechnology, engineering and materials science and technology and information technologies. The strategic research programmes will no doubt include much basic science, but the emphasis is definitely on applicability.

There is, in addition, one NBST programme specifically concerned with promoting excellence in scientific research, attracting and keeping top researchers, and keeping Ireland at the forefront of at least a few areas of science. Scientists also have access to funding from international bodies and are keen participants in multilateral collaborations: particularly important for a small and poor but often scientifically sophisticated country.

The financial problems of Irish universities were highlighted by a memorandum that Ireland's Higher Education Authority sent to the Education Minister in August 1984. It noted that many proposed new courses could not be started because of shortages of staff (due to recruitment restrictions) and cash. Many of the courses are in modern and vocational subjects such as biotechnology, information technology, telecommunications, agribusiness and marketing.

In October 1984 the government's new economic plan for the years 1985 to 1987 predicted a growth in student numbers by 4 per cent a year. Funds will now grow by nearly 5 per cent over the three-year period. Later in the year a British expert on universities suggested that Northern Ireland (part of Britain) might help relieve the threatened overcrowding of Irish universities as demand from Eire's rapidly growing population of young people expands.

Italy

Italy is a country where the best and the worst appears to be able to coexist quite happily, and any attempts to preserve the former and root out the latter encounter almost insuperable bureaucratic obstacles. This is as true of the world of science and technology as of many other aspects of Italian life: Nevertheless, the last few years have shown consistent attempts to focus national efforts in various areas and to improve the resources and incentives for research, particularly in the universities. The proportion of GDP spent on r&d has also been growing, rising above 1 per cent for the first time in 1981 and reaching 1.3 per cent in 1983.

Since the end of the Second World War the state has been closely involved with many sectors of the Italian economy, well beyond those sectors normally associated with government control. Thanks to dynamic and innovatory management Italy achieved an unprecedented economic boom in the 1960s. The 1960s also saw heightened aspirations: many more young people aspired to a university education, and their elders in the political world set about the business of long-term investment in science and technology.

The government's main agent for change in basic research was, and still is, the Consiglio Nazionale delle Ricerche (CNR). Set up in 1923, but not seriously in business till the late 30s, the CNR now spends just under a fifth of the state's r&d budget. Funded directly by the Treasury, the CNR answers only to the Prime Minister and to Comitato Interministeriale per la Programmazione Economice (CIPE), the interministerial committee for economic planning. Italy's Minister for Research has limited influence because parliament has never got around to giving him a portfolio or a secretariat. CNR's wide remit includes national planning of scientific activities and administering international collaborations. It also funds its own institutes and research centres and groups, and provides *ad hoc* support for university research.

Italian academics are proud of their right, embodied in the constitution, to freedom of teaching and research. Especially since the bitter experience of the prewar fascist regime, they have been reluctant to accept intervention of any kind (except funding of course) from the state. There was also a traditional reluctance in the universities, apart from the two high-calibre polytechnic universities at Milan and Turin, to tackle applied topics. Thus it was that the CNR pioneered applications-oriented research programmes. The first batch of these started in 1964. They were to develop areas of very practical national interest such as water supplies, energy and building. The CNR encouraged research in these areas through all its traditional mechanisms including work in its own institutes and that commissioned from universities. A new batch of projects began in 1976 and since then several more have been added. The 1976 group was wound up in 1981 with another new set starting in 1982. By 1983 the proportion of CNR resources spent on these projects had grown to one half, a signal of the increasingly applied emphasis within the CNR as a whole.

That is not to say that CNR has lost interest in basic research: many of its institutes and sponsored centres in universities continue to pursue essentially basic objectives. CNR also organizes regular meetings of scientists in particular disciplinary groups to discuss progress on a national basis. But since 1980 the responsibility for funding basic research in universities has rested with the Ministry of Public Instruction and not with the CNR.

This new approach grew out of widespread dissatisfaction with the arrangements for research in Italy's universities. Entry to any university course is now a matter of right for every school-leaver with a secondary-school leaving certificate, and over a million students now crowd the existing institutes. Increases in available funds have rarely matched the needs of the extremely rapid increase in student numbers since the 1960s, and extra teaching loads have fallen on the faculty, who have also had to cope with the decreasing overall size of the research budget. In 1983 the CNR spent four times as much per researcher employed as the university research budget provided for. Democratic procedures take up yet more of an academic's time, and Italian academics are particularly sore at an enhancement in the power of the university administrators that came into effect in the early 1970s.

A British Council report (*Italy, a science profile*, 1983) described university research in Italy as follows:

Although a great deal of research is done in university institutions, the sector is large and heterogeneous. At its best it is represented by institutes which are well staffed, equipped and administered, in which teaching and research are well integrated and the research out-put is internationally recognized. At the other end of the spectrum are institutes poorly organized and equipped, where little or no research of note is carried on, or where individuals attempt to carry out research but are hampered by lack of the necessary administrative financial and technical back-up necessary. The system of scientific and administrative direction of university institutes varies, as does the degree of coordination between institutes to prevent duplication of effort and to try and group complementary equipment. There have been instances of successful collegiate direction of the research being carried out by institutes working in complementary subjects. Equally there are instances of total lack of cooperation and collaboration when ostensibly it would have appeared to be worth attempting.

Serious young researchers have found extreme difficulty in making a career for a number of reasons. Chief of these are the chaotic procedures for appointing research staff, both permanent and temporary, and the subsequent permanent employment of almost everyone in the system, regardless of quality, every time new legislation was passed. The last time this happened was in 1980, when the last university reform law was passed. The situation was further complicated by the lack of a doctoral training scheme throughout the 1970s. To be fair, though, much of the new law was designed to streamline the arrangements for university research by reducing the types of faculty posts available to three: professor, associate professor and university researcher. It also made provision for a graduate training programme leading to a research doctorate. Responsibility for providing the funds for all these posts and grants, as well as equipment and consumables, and for new projects in basic research, now rests with the Ministry of Public Instruction. Early indications suggest that the supply of funds will not always match up to forecasts and promises in terms of either amount or speed.

One promising sign, though, is that the state of university research continues to figure prominently in the authoritative report that the president of the CNR makes annually on the state of scientific and technological research in Italy. This document ranges over all types of research from basic, through directed and applied to development work, and it records progress in Italy's valiant efforts over recent years to devise national plans for research relevant to different sectors of the economy. Work in all four categories is encouraged and is to be carried out by the most appropriate organization whether university, research institute or company. National plans for energy and space are already well established; new schemes for microelectronics, chemistry, biomedical technology and iron and steel were approved in 1983.

Like the two smaller para-governmental organisms that carry out research, the energy and nuclear energy agencies, the CNR has worked hard to conform to government policies such as development of education and research in the economically beleaguered southern regions. Nevertheless, it is not immune from criticisms: among the most serious are complaints about appointments made for political reasons rather than scientific reasons, and about the difficulty of dealing with bureaucracy.

Complaints, mainly over low pay, from the researchers who work in the CNR, surfaced in early 1985 as one of the major issues to be resolved by the organization's new president. The researchers pointed out that their pay and career prospects compare badly with those of academics even though the CNR staff publish more scientific papers on average and work longer hours.

CNR seems likely to move some way towards settling these grievances but only at the price of weeding out small and unproductive institutes. Under a new plan announced in May, institutes will apply for extra funds by filling in a detailed application form. Other elements of the plan include restrictions on leave to spend long periods abroad, and concentration of research into centres of excellence with access to a full range of facilities such as libraries. Strategic research priorities will continue to play an important part in CNR's future, as will projects that encourage links with industry. Indeed, it has been suggested that CNR staff supplement their incomes by contracts and consultancy work for companies.

Netherlands

The Netherlands is a small country which has for centuries maintained a sophisticated awareness of the ebb and flow of world economics. Its intellectual world enjoyed close contacts with Germany at the end of the last century. Nevertheless it did not begin to develop its industrial potential till after the humiliations it suffered at German hands during the Second World War.

Once decided on the need for industrialization progress came quickly, thanks particularly to large companies such as Shell and Philips. The Netherlands' scientific expertise was quickly applied to the new aspirations, mainly via a national network of laboratories that do research underlying a wide range of state and industrial objectives (Organisatie voor Toegepast Natuurwetenschappelijk Onderzoek – TNO). The universities meanwhile expanded rapidly. Research standards dropped on average, but the research objective continued to command a vast chunk of state funds. Relations with industry have until recently been fairly weak, even worse in the universities than in TNO.

Efforts to establish a national plan for science and technology reached a fairly serious level by the mid 1970s, when the Netherlands appointed its first minister for science policy. Since then the occupant of this post has been the focal point of a wide variety of advisory and planning committees both inside and outside government. Since 1981 the title has been taken over by the minister of education and science, which has also absorbed the science policy secretariat. The people in this group attempt to keep track of spending on science throughout the government machine, leading to the annual task of formulating a science budget to be presented to parliament.

Back in the 1970s the first Science Policy Minister, a Mr F. H. Trip, saw the reform of TNO as the first priority as far as fundamental research on applied topics was concerned. In time his comments were heeded. In the 1970s the Minister for Science Policy gained control of TNO and since then it has been remoulded into a centrally directed and far more professional outfit. More recently, saving money has been another constraint, and TNO will have to make substantial cuts in staff including possibly compulsory redundancies. Another part of the plan is to increase the proportion of income from contract work, especially from industry. TNO incidentally includes the Netherlands' small effort in defence research.

Pressure for change in the universities has been more recent, but once begun has taken effect quickly. One clear direction, particularly by the more right-wing governments of the early 1980s, is to relate university research more closely to national needs, particularly those of industry. Just to make sure that this takes effect, the science policy secretariat now has an offshoot based in the Ministry of Economic Affairs. It is from here, for example, that the initiative has come for developing a national plan for biotechnology. The detailed legwork for this has been done by a consultancy called the Central Institute for Industrial Development (CIVI) who worked with a committee of industrialists and academics. The result is a carefully thought through proposal which gives a realistic assessment of which areas of biotechnology are likely to flourish best, given the resources and scientific, industrial and agricultural experience already available in the Netherlands. It also differentiates carefully between fundamental, strategic and product-oriented work, assigning separate streams of funding and assessment to each. The execution of the plan should draw university and industry closer together without making too much intrusion on the distinct approaches of different types of institution.

Another strong engine for change in the universities is the Foundation for Technical Sciences (STW). The STW is an outgrowth from the Nederlandse Organisatie voor Zuiverwetenschapelijk Onderzoek (ZWO) which at the moment is not allowed by its constitution to fund applied work. STW's board chooses projects that involve basic research techniques but are likely to find some useful application usually, but not necessarily, in industry, biomedicine or agriculture. STW has made good use of the opportunity to adapt the traditional review system operated by ZWO. ZWO is essentially a research council: it is an extra source of funds for university research as well as providing centralized facilities in nuclear physics and astronomy for example. The STW has also instituted a more flexible system whereby its own secretariat choose the referees (industrial, academics and also TNO scientists where appropriate). In the 1980s STW looks set to be the fastest growing science policy agency in the Netherlands.

The university system as a whole has received a number of shake-ups recently. The Ministry of Education and Science for example is trying to exercise some control over the large chunk of university funds allocated to research. It has stipulated that 60 per cent of this (the proportion may change somewhat) will be 'conditional funding' – that is, allocated by a set of procedures operated nationally, mainly at the moment by ZWO. The government's view is that funding for the really good projects will receive extra protection, being guaranteed for five years once approved under the new system. There is quite a lot of unease, particularly because the judgements seem to be made by the same organizations as those which provide the 'second stream' of funds. Nevertheless, even the objectors admit that money was wasted under the earlier system.

More recently the conditional funding debate has been pushed into the background by an average eight per cent cut in overall university funding. The details of where the axe would fall were arrived at after a long national assessment of resources for teaching and research in each discipline and although academics are obviously not particularly keen on cuts, there are no severe complaints about the procedures adopted. The cuts exercise was performed bearing in mind the development of a closer relationship between the country's needs for trained people and the education offered by the universities. Academics too are becoming increasingly conscious of the large numbers of unemployed graduates, a symptom of the severe effects recession has had on the economy and unemployed generally.

The education and science ministry has already gone some way towards tackling this problem by introducing a streamlined under-graduate degree that should take four years to complete instead of the more usual six years. Only a limited number of graduates will be allowed to pursue postgraduate studies and most of these will be vocationally oriented.

In the longer term the minister also plans to change the structure of university staff, providing more temporary posts at junior level and fewer permanent professorships. While this should help to provide more jobs for young researchers, a topic of serious concern at the moment, it is viewed by some scientists as yet another attempt by the government to get science on the cheap.

The presence of substantial research efforts on behalf of multinational companies, especially Philips, has had an important influence on re-search in the Netherlands in the natural sciences. Contacts between academics and senior company researchers have kept up standards in the universities. But the companies have also acted as a drain on the country's stock of good researchers, often offering better terms and condi-tions than the universities could provide. Even Philips' research efforts have been hit by the recession, though in late 1984 the company an-nounced that research would now begin to expand again. A Philips employee turned down a professorship at a university because it would have meant a pay cut. He commented that university cuts in personnel and equipment had reached a level where serious research was threatened and where competent staff could no longer be attracted.

Norway

Norway's tiny population of just over four million has been remarkably well-endowed with one of the most important commodities of the twentieth century: energy. First hydroelectric power, and more recently petroleum, have accelerated industrial development and economic performance. The Norwegians have been careful to ensure that oil com-panies who are licensed to drill in its waters carry out r&d work and train local employees. This has contributed to the rapid growth in indus-trial sponsorship of r&d and has also provided a focus for new avenues of government-sponsored research, for example in investigating the likely sociological consequences of the new 'petroleum economy'. On the other hand it is generally accepted that basic research has suffered during the 1970s as a result of the government's increasing emphasis on short-term and applied work to meet the needs of industry, and efforts to restore balance have been proposed for the early 1980s. One rather unusual feature of Norway's public research effort is that a substantial part of it (9 per cent in 1983) is funded by the state-run football pools.

After the war Norway was quick off the mark in setting up a network of institutes to perform research to meet the needs of state and industry. The Norges Teknisk-Naturvitenskapelige Forskningsråd (NTNF) was set up in 1946. In the 1950s and 1960s the government set up more institutes, this time directed more towards social rather than industrial policy, embracing issues such as environment, transport, urban planning and working conditions. Some of these were established within the NTNF framework.

Today the NTNF is the largest of Norway's research organizations, taking just over one-fifth of the government's total spending on r&d. The bulk of this comes from the Ministry of Industry with contributions from most of the other ministries with an interest in research. Until a substantial reorganization now under way (see below) NTNF has administered fourteen institutes and four more affiliated bodies. Some of these have operated more like independent ministerial research establishments than those belonging to a research council. Commissions to carry out specific research projects account for about a third of the NTNF's outgoings.

Research in universities and colleges, half of which is basic research, accounts for about one-third of government r&d expenditure. Most of the money for this comes directly in university budgets – the research councils are another important source.

Norway has four universities. The oldest and largest is the University of Oslo, established in 1811, which teaches all the traditional disciplines. Just under 20 000 students are enrolled there, just under a quarter of those at institutions of higher education in the country (which include regional colleges as well as universities). The second largest university is that of Trondheim, created in 1969 by a federation of three existing bodies: the Norwegian Institute of Technology, set up in 1910, the State College for Teachers, founded in 1922, and the museum and library of the Royal Norwegian Society of Science and Letters, an institution that dates back to 1760. Trondheim is also the home of the Foundation for Scientific and Industrial Research (SINTEF), which since its creation in 1950 has been linked with the Institute of Technology. SINTEF has a number of research laboratories that supplement the institutes of the technical university. It has a staff of just under a thousand, and is still growing.

The main research council concerned with basic research is the Norwegian Research Council for Science and the Humanities or Norges Almenvitenskapelige Forskningsråd (NAVF), which was established in 1948. Its existence stems largely from a national debate on what to do with the proceeds of the state football pool. A professor at the University of Oslo suggested dividing the proceeds between 'physical and spiritual athletics' and proposed that in the case of the latter a council of ten members should allocate the money to research projects. An agricultural research council was founded the same year in much the same way. Both were given considerable independence from central government.

At the end of the 1960s politicians took a great deal of interest in reforming the research council structure. The basic problem was the difficulty of relating the councils' activities to the objectives of government as divided into ministries. The debate eventually sidetracked into a discussion about whether there should be a separate ministry for research, and no structural changes were made.

During the 70s the ministries developed needs for research, if only to help them plan future policy, and they satisfied such needs by sponsoring research projects themselves, with money allocated by central government specifically for that purpose. The projects were organized and funded *ad hoc*, and without interministerial coordination.

Two new research councils were set up in the 1970s: a fisheries research council (1972) and a research council for societal planning within the NAVF (1976).

In 1982 the Central Committee for Norwegian Research, the most important forum for these debates, reported that the organization of research needed adjustments rather than a total shakeup. But a year later a review of Norwegian science policy conducted under the auspices of the OECD deplored the lack of useful action to meet the challenges of the 1980s.

It praised the work of SINTEF in collaborating on r&d with companies of all sizes, but the main government research laboratories, the NTNF network, came in for much criticism, in particular the difficulties posed for medium-sized and small companies in planning and executing research that would give rise to innovation and improved productivity. In general the report recommended much more flexibility in relations between government institutions and industry.

The universities and colleges also need to change, according to the OECD assessors. Both they and the research councils who fund research activities there should coordinate their activities and make long-term plans in line with well-defined priorities. As research councils are generally better at this, it is suggested that these be preferred as channels for resources. The report also advocates concentrating research efforts, for example by amalgamating small research institutes with university departments and by discouraging very small departments.

The report also proposes that existing machinery for science policy making in government is used efficiently and in association with a secretariat that has an overall grasp of research performed by all the ministries.

The government has already taken up some of these suggestions. Substantial changes in the organization of NTNF were begun in 1984. The council will cease to control and administer individual institutes: its function will be to look at research strategies, to distribute funds to the institutes, and to evaluate the research performed. Meanwhile each institute will be independent, with its own board of directors.

The 1985 allocation of funds for higher education, research and development records a small increase (3.5 to 4 per cent) in the total funds available for research and identifies two major new objectives: to fund research which can stimulate technological development and economic growth, and to promote basic research and the long-term strengthening of research expertise.

New priority areas under the first heading are information technology, aquaculture, materials research, and offshore technology. Actions to strengthen basic research will include increasing funds for the NAVF, making more money available for scientific equipment, and funding a programme of basic research in petroleum.

Funds for universities and colleges will grow very slightly in real terms. Priority for spending must go to areas determined by the Ministry for Cultural and Scientific Affairs – namely technological and economic/administrative education.

Norway's strong economy continues to allow expansion. In government plans announced in May 1985 student numbers are scheduled to grow from 90 000 that year to 100 000 in 1995. Research funding will benefit too. It has already risen from 1.2 per cent of GDP in 1980 to 1.5 per cent in 1985. Five main areas for growth have been specified. Three are technological: information technology, biotechnology, and petroleum and gas. The fourth concerns management – the government wants to use new tech to improve public planning and administration. The fifth is culture.

Portugal

Portugal is a smallish country where technical and economic development is rather behind that of the rest of Europe. The policies of the fascist regime that dominated Portugal from the 1930s until 1974 were largely based on the idea that Portugal would be able to rely on cheap raw materials for manufacturing from its overseas colonies, mainly in Africa, and at home the economy remained largely agricultural until the 1960s and 70s when control over the colonies declined.

Portugal became a republic in 1910 and in spite of political instability the government found time to set up two new universities in Lisbon and Oporto, to join the ancient university of Coimbra. The new universities were set up to train people for government and also for the slowly growing manufacturing industries. In 1930 a number of professional schools were joined into a federation with the title of the Technical University of Lisbon. The number of students did not expand nearly as rapidly as in other European countries until the mid 1970s. Nevertheless, such expansion as there was, was not matched by significant rises in either financial or staff resources. As a result teachers experienced very heavy teaching loads. In Portugal the universities have always been seen largely as teaching institutions.

The main thrust of government research in Portugal, small as the overall effort is, remains in the network of national laboratories, from the National Agronomical Station, created in 1936, through the Board for Overseas Scientific Research (1945) and the National Civil Engineering Laboratory (1946) to an agency for nuclear energy in the 1950s and a truly national institute for industrial research in 1957. For the promotion of research linked with higher education a Board of National Education was created in 1929. This took the place of the Directive Board of Studies a kind of research council planned in 1923–4 that never got off the ground. The Board started the Instituto de Alta Cultura in 1936.

In the 1960s the OECD initiated a project under which senior Porguguese researchers assessed their country's arrangements for r&d, and as a result of its report several changes took place. In 1967 the government set up a National Board for Scientific and Technological Research (Junta Nacional de Investigação Cientifica e Tecnologica) and in the early 1970s began to plan for changes in and new roles for university education. The revolution of 1974 overtook the implementation of this plan. As a Council of Europe study puts it: 'after a reformist period more condensed in time and vigour than in most other West European countries, a number of guidelines were decided upon in 1976 and 1977 concerning the future expansion of the whole higher education system.' One part of the plan was for a number of polytechnics, though these have been slow to get off the ground.

Since 1973 six more state universities and two university institutes have been founded. All have science courses, but only three teach en-gineering. According to Professor F. R. Dias Agudo, a professor at the University of Lisbon, there have been many changes in the variety of courses and administration of universities but 'we cannot say that the standard is different'. The new universities necessitated 'great increase of posts with a too rapid promotion of young staff'. Universities can give contracts to non-academics (from industry and elsewhere) to teach temporary courses.

In spite of the expansion of the system the Portuguese government found it necessary in 1976 to impose a limit on the number of entrants to each course. The object of this exercise was to avoid overcrowded courses, increase quality in teaching, and force some students to attend polytechnic rather than university courses. In recent years the *numerus clausus* has been fixed annually, and, rigidly enforced. The Council of Europe report says that, 'The number of places at the old universities is gradually decreasing until there is re-established the delicate balance, lost after 1974, between the capacity of the institutes and the number of students enrolled.'

The year 1976 also saw the splitting of Portugal's Instituto de Alta Cultura into an institute for Portuguese culture and language and the National Institute for Scientific Research (Instituto Nacional de Investigação Cientifica). INIC provides a small amount of funding for research in universities, including grants for postgraduate students, but academics regard this arrangement as rather unsatisfactory as it cannot guarantee adequate support for a wide-ranging research effort. They would like to see INIC as complementary to university research support rather than as a substitute.

In 1982 civil science outside the universities was drawn under the National Council for Scientific and Technological Research (Conselho Nacional para a Investigação Cientifica e Tecnologica) which had been created two years earlier. It took over JNICT as its secretariat.

Dias Agudo, who has also been president of INIC, lists the main features of the Portuguese scientific system as follows: very limited financial resources by European standards; scarcity of human resources; and underemployment of high-quality staff because of a shortage of technical and auxiliary personnel, especially in the higher education sector.

He also complains of the weak links betweeen 'the scientific and technological system and the productivity activities', an aspect which is being improved, he says, with improved links between universities, state institutes and industry. The 'high degree of scientific and technological dependence' has also been a drawback with 'a lot of money for royalties, many PhDs got abroad'.

But perhaps the most serious problem is the 'non-existence of an overall scientific and technological policy'. This perhaps is partly due to another serious flaw in the system: 'ambiguity in the definitions of the bodies coordinating and promoting research, with useless duplications'.

Early in 1985 Portugal's new secretary of state for higher education announced extra money for research including £50 000 for academic research projects and basic research in universities. The problem of the 14 polytechnics and teacher training colleges planned since the mid 1970s but not yet opened is still on the agenda.

Spain

Spain is the third largest and sixth most populous country in Europe. But, largely due to the fascist regime that ruled it with a rod of iron between the mid 1930s and 1976, it has remained far behind the rest of Europe in terms of both economic and technological development. Since fascism was replaced by democracy in 1976, Spain has tried to respond to external and internal pleas to increase and focus its efforts in scientific training and research. The socialist government elected in 1982 seems at last to be taking up the challenge with an impressive degree of seriousness. Perhaps surprisingly for a country with such a weak economy, private funding, mainly from industry, more than matches the government's contributions to research.

The twentieth century opened with a number of promising developments in Spain: King Alfonso XIII created in 1907 the Committee for Research and Scientific Investigation, which supervised the construction of state-funded laboratories. Regional scientific societies and cultural centres also began to appear at this time, and the standard of research at the country's universities also began to improve. The Higher Technical Schools provided a separate network of education and research facilities for engineers of a fairly high standard.

This slow but steady progress was rudely interrupted by the bloody civil war of 1935–39. Many intellectuals and scholars, including hundreds of natural scientists, engineers and doctors, were either killed in the fighting or fled to other parts of Europe or the Americas. The refugees included Blas Cabrera who has been called 'the father of the new physics in Spain' and Severo Ochoa, who went on to share the Nobel prize for physiology or medicine in 1959.

The Franco regime paid little attention to developing the research capacity and scientific expertise of the universities. University appointments were often made on political grounds rather than academic merit so that the professioriate would provide a prestigious and authoritative body of support for the government. In keeping with this plan the syllabuses were strictly controlled by the Ministry of Education and each university had to arrange each detail of its financial affairs with the Ministry.

In spite of the restrictions on intellectual freedom and contacts with institutions, enrolment in the universities expanded just as rapidly in the 60s and 70s in Spain as in the rest of Europe, thanks to relatively easy access. But only a small proportion of students (one of the lowest in Europe) ever succeeded in graduating.

Academics who want to put a lot of effort into research have had to struggle with the education ministry for resources and support in the form of technicians has been additionally hampered by bureaucratic rules. These constraints have made other sources of funding such as banks and foundations, and even a fund provided by the USA as part-payment for the right to site military bases in Spain an important and attractive alternative.

Active researchers have also been discouraged by a promotion system that involves competition by an ancient Spanish institution called *oposiciones*, a combination of written examination and public oral grilling by a selection committee. Because the number of tenured academics is too low to deal with the enormous numbers of students, a large population of teaching and research assistants of one kind or another has grown up to meet *ad hoc* needs. These people have no clearly defined rights or responsibilities.

The state is far more committed to research at its own laboratories. Of the ministerial laboratories, the Junta de Energía Nuclear (JEN) probably comes closest to basic research – in the 1950s it provided good opportunities for theoretical and practical physicists to travel abroad and come back to work in an exciting and relatively well-equipped team. It was largely pressure from JEN that resulted in Spain joining the European Organisation for Nuclear Research (CERN) in 1961. Franco had other motives, hoping this involvement might be a first step to acceptability in grander collaborations such as the EEC. This hope disappointed, the expense soon became too much of a burden and Spain pulled out in 1969.

But the state's major effort in basic research takes place under the auspices of the Consejo Superior de Investigaciones Científicas (CSIC). Set up by the new fascist government in 1939, CSIC was supposed to coordinate such research activities as already existed as well as stimulate new ones. It spanned a large network of basic research institutes in natural sciences and humanities, whose work ranges from the very pure to the fairly applied. There has been little control or review of the work of the CSIC laboratories and by the early 1980s CSIC's leadership undertook a radical shakeup.

CSIC never quite rose to the coordinating role and neither have several interministerial committees that have been assigned this task in the intervening years. But promising signs of action are coming from the Advisory Committee for Scientific and Technical Research (Commission Asesora de Investigación Científica y Técnica (CAICYT) set up in 1958. In 1981 CAICYT defined a series of priority programmes that embody Spain's first attempt at a national science and technology policy. One priority is to direct a substantial amount of money towards private research institutes, industrial research organizations and industry itself. Specific priority areas are aquaculture, agroenergy, microelectronics, urban transportation, high energy physics and biotechnology. It is intended that a National Committee for Scientific and Technical Research will link CAICYT with government and draw up a more global long-term plan for research involving the whole of the government sector.

The new Socialist government that took office in 1982 has also worked hard to introduce reforms in the university system. New legislation passed late in 1983 grants far more autonomy to each university: these can now set their own syllabuses and design new courses. They are also free to negotiate research contracts with industry, an option that was not impossible before but certainly not encouraged under Franco. The new law abolishes the *oposiciones*, although public examination of candidates will continue. It also streamlines the number of types of teaching post to four, hoping that this will reduce the current chaos. There will also be a closer eye kept on staff who do various types of work outside their university duties.

Another aspect of government policy that will affect both universities and the research institutes is the government's commitment to decentralize as many activities as possible, giving far more power to the new autonomous regions. It seems likely that funds for the universities will come via the regional governments, giving them some say in a university's priorities in research and training. The government also plans to fund the national (CSIC) institutes on a regional basis – a change that may prove problematic if national priorities conflict with local ones. The regions may well press for a fairer distribution of such institutes, which are currently concentrated around Madrid and Barcelona. A potential problem is the extremely pronounced regional variations in industrialization and local interest in and appreciation of science and technology.

Implementing the university reform law has not been easy. Allowing universities to appoint their own staff has been a popular change. Social councils have been set up to link universities to local affairs, though not without murmurs about drawing politics into university life. But sorting out academic jobs has been more difficult. The government suggested that the occupants of non-tenured posts, 80 per cent of the teaching staff, take exams to determine their competence. After these took place in the summer of 1984 there were many accusations of unfair discrimination. Eventually the secretary of state for the universities, a distinguished geologist with excellent Socialist credentials, was forced to resign over the issue in July 1985.

The new Council of Universities remains in place as a forum for discussion about these and other problems. Chaired by the education minister, it will act as a channel for the government to influence the future shape of the university system without exercising quite as much centralized control as in the past.

Reform of the state's research effort is at an earlier and so far less controversial stage. In April 1985 the Spanish government approved legislation which would simplify and streamline the various state organizations and provide a mechanism for defining research priorities. There will be a national plan for r&d – the first will give priority to microelectronics, biotechnology, transportation technology and high energy physics. It also includes measures that would double the number of Spanish researchers. Meanwhile the CSIC and the Junta de Energía Nuclear will be combined into a single body called the Centre for Energy, Environment and Technological Research.

Sweden

Thanks to its early involvement with industrial development and continuing steady progress, Sweden has managed to defy all the rules that predict slow economic and technological growth for small countries. Another apparent paradox is Sweden's exploitation of the unashamedly capitalistic industries, such as consumer goods and drugs, to fund an enormous state sector and a society committed to humanitarian and egalitarian goals. The government (almost continually dominated by socialists except for a short spell in the late 1970s) has been consistently generous with r&d funds and the large high-tech industries have funded impressive research efforts. Rapid growth in both sectors took Sweden to a leading position in the European r&d league in the early 1980s, with 2.5 per cent of GDP going on r&d.

During the 1980s Sweden has not been immune from the effects of the recession, and some of the ideals of the welfare state, such as full employment and a completely free health service, have fallen victim to government spending cuts. But the government still sees r&d as a priority and hopes to maintain its support.

An important feature of the Swedish government system is that ministries rarely tackle the day-to-day administration of the state's complex nationwide activities. Instead these are run by boards or agencies, which have their own permanent secretariat and hierarchy, but of course are answerable to their parent ministries as well as parliament, and have to gear their actions to state policies.

This arrangement works quite neatly in the case of the two largest agencies with an interest in research. The state's largest research outfit is the National Board for Technical Development (STU) which administers 12 per cent of the government's r&d budget. It works mainly with the Ministry of Industry, but runs laboratories and funds research and development in almost all the subjects of interest to government and/or industry, such as energy, medical technology, general industrial processes as well as general acquisition and dissemination of technical information generated overseas. Two-thirds of STU's budget goes on grants. Universities and cooperative research institutes for the various industrial sectors each take about a quarter of this. Another 10 per cent goes to projects at government research institutes, and the remainder is in the form of grants and loans to individual enterprises. STU's activities can also be broken down into five technology areas which account for just over a third of the budget as well as support for a number of 'action areas' when STU aims to provide a stimulus for research with well-defined goals in view. STU also provides a wide range of support services such as advice on technology procurement for local authorities and patenting for small firms.

STU's general objectives are 'to promote development of products and systems satisfying the needs of society, to increase the competitiveness of Swedish industry in world and domestic markets; and to increase technical knowledge in general in Sweden'.

The other large agency with an interest in research is the Universitets – och högskoleämbetet (UHÄ) or National Board of Universities and Colleges. This is the agency that deals on the one hand with the higher education policies as set by Parliament and the Ministry of Education and on the other with each of the nine universities and all the numerous colleges. It was up to the UHÄ to effect the reforms of the higher education system decided upon in 1977 which committed the government to providing a full range of higher education in each of Sweden's six geographical regions. The 1977 reforms also initiated a new division of subjects into five sectors, which relate to the types of professions that graduates who have followed a particular line of study would be eligible for. It also expects to play a growing part in making decisions about selective changes in patterns of funding to different departments in accordance with national needs: examples include closing departments of dentistry and choosing sites for centres for teaching and research in new subjects such as microelectronics. As the university system is under threat of a 2 per cent cut in overall funding each year for five years the UHÄ can exert quite strong pressures on institutions to go along with its recommendations, even though technically the universities are supposed to enjoy a large degree of autonomy.

The universities certainly have to cope with some structural problems. In spite of the parliament's control over student numbers many faculties are overcrowded, and students in general do not receive a lot of guidance about the progress of their studies. Many drop out along the way to a degree and a lot of those that survive hang around for many years trying to complete a doctorate, often on a part-time basis. The situation is better than average in the sciences, where appointments for postgraduates often include some teaching or demonstrating work or technical duties, sometimes connected with externally funded research projects.

For lecturers in tenured posts teaching has to take first place, and the heavy burden of work for academics in their most intellectually productive years is perhaps the greatest discouragement to research in Swedish universities. Full professors do little to help; it is not part of their job to do undergraduate teaching. A lucky few manage to persuade research councils such as the STU to pay half or all their salaries as part of research grants; this is usually only possible in subjects that are fashionable from the point of view of technical potential.

Extra funds for research are available from the research councils that come under the Ministry of Education, as well as the STU. The biggest research Councils are the Statens Naturvetenskapliga Forskningsråd (NFR), the Natural Science Research Council, and the Council for Social Sciences and Humanities. The first of these assesses proposals from academics by a peer review system administered by its five committees. In recent years it has taken a more active role through its committee for 'mission oriented research', which provides money for research in important but unfashionable subjects such as analytical chemistry. It is also rather proud of the reviews of Swedish research in various disciplines that commissions from teams of foreign academics.

Recently the scientific community has achieved a somewhat louder voice in the corridors of power. The Swedish Cabinet Office, where government policy is formulated by a team of card-carrying civil servants, now has a science team headed by the deputy prime minister. Most of the day-to-day work is done by a junior minister who convenes monthly meetings of an advisory committee of top-notch academics.

It is largely through this committee that an important message penetrated in the early 1980s: that the pursuit of societal goals had unbalanced the Swedish research effort; it had become so concentrated to meet the needs of industry and state that much basic, long-term, strategic work was being neglected. The academics have also identified a gap in the spectrum of research between the rather applicable work sponsored by the research councils and the more long-term work sponsored by STU.

These ideas have made a large contribution to the drafting of the 1984 Research Bill, which summarizes the government's science policy in general, and in particular lists future allocations according to the ministry providing the cash. One measure is to set up a technological research council within STU where applications will be judged by peer review rather than be assessed in terms of immediate relevance to a particular project.

Reforms in the career structure of the Swedish higher education system were proposed by the government at the end of 1984. Under the new legislation many different kinds of post available in universities would be abolished. Only three would remain: professors, lecturers (who possess a doctorate), and others with a first degree. Teachers with a doctorate in science (or equivalent) in science would be allowed to do research – this measure is primarily designed to promote links with industry.

Graduate unemployment is growing, largely because of the shortage of jobs in the public sector, which at one time employed 60 per cent of graduates. But at the same time the country remains desperately short of technically skilled personnel, ranging from technicians to university graduates, mainly in computer science and electronics. Industry rates such skills so highly that it pays qualified researchers three to four times what they earn in a university – with the result that the most talented scientists are lost to the higher education system. The government has proposed that researchers in industry do spells of research and teaching at universities.

Switzerland

Switzerland is a small country at the heart of Europe which has managed to remain efficient and prosperous throughout its 350 years of existence, thanks to a combination of political neutrality, respect for personal freedom and enterprise, and unashamed burgeois values. For many purposes, including education and voting rights, local rules are laid down by the twenty-three cantons, with populations ranging from 34 000 to just over a million. The federal government has limited powers and often has difficulty in forming coherent policies. In spite of some small setbacks to the economy in the early 1980s, Switzerland has weathered the recession well and has kept unemployment low.

The proportion of GDP spent on r&d in Switzerland is one of the largest in Europe, running neck and neck with Sweden. In fact the state's contribution is comparatively quite low: the outstanding overall performance is largely due to the r&d effort mounted by industry. Over half of this takes place within four companies: Sandoz, La Roche, Ciba Geigy and Brown Boveri. Industry invests a small proportion of this in university research: but contacts between industry and the universities are strong and exert a far wider influence than the small financial investment would imply. For example scientists from industry often come to lecture for several hours a week. These contacts have also helped to maintain standards of both teaching and research in spite of the rapid expansion in student numbers over the last two decades. Industry's influence has also helped the country to avoid an undue emphasis on university education as opposed to other useful and effective forms of technical and vocational training.

Of the federal r&d effort, about a quarter takes place in government institutes. A significant part of this is related to defence and agriculture. There are also institutes related to normal state interests such as energy and health. Very little basic research is done in these institutes. Scientists who work in these organizations are well paid and secure, and they can draw on relatively generous funds for equipment and technical support. The same in general applies to researchers in industry, and universities.

Apart from a small amount of support for r&d carried out in industry, the rest goes on r&d in higher education where most of Switzerland's fundamental research is carried out. Switzerland has seven cantonal universities and two federal schools of technology (where the vast majority of engineers are trained, along with a fair number of natural scientists).

Swiss universities continue to attract a high proportion of foreign students. Although student numbers continue to rise, expansion of academic staff has stopped, as budgets level. Shortage of money has also led to decline in money for equipment and technical support.

There is a noticeable shortage of academic jobs for young people – the usual response is to prolong postgraduate study. Bureaucracy and democratic procedures take up to a third of an academic's working hours.

Nevertheless, Swiss academics maintain that the quality of research has not deteriorated and they point to the fact that the number of research projects submitted to the National Science Foundation, is still increasing. Some of the universities have advanced research institutes which have managed to distance themselves from the worst of the effects.

The National Science Foundation, founded by the federal government, is the oldest and best established agency on the Swiss r&d scene. Its funds go mainly to sponsor individual research projects, but it also supports publication and funds a few research professorships. The Foundation also provides advice to government about devising and funding national science policies. In this it works together with the Swiss University Conference, which coordinates the work of the universities on a federal basis and handles applications for federal funds. The Swiss Science Council advises the federal government on science policy, especially as far as the allocation of funds for research and the support of universities is concerned. Its members represent political, social and business groups as well as those bodies more traditionally involved with science. It has a secretariat inside the Division of Science and Research of the Department of the Interior.

In the early 1970s the federal government tried to increase its control over the universities and the research system in order to improve coordination and to establish a national framework for research. Since 1974 the government has had the power to instruct the National Science Foundation to set up a programme in a priority area, and there are now 'national research programmes' in energy, health, and urban and rural planning. Materials science, and electronic and biomedical technology are now also sponsored in this way. The National Science Foundation devotes 12 per cent of its funds to these programmes. Formal legislation on science policy was passed by the Swiss parliament in 1974, but rejected by the electorate. In 1984, however, a science policy bill passed into law.

The federal government has also set up a fund to help medium and small businesses develop knowledge and skills through a fund administered by the Department of the Economy. Money from the fund is granted if industry will put up half the cost of research projects.

These measures have succeeded in promoting more mutual interest between industry and academic researchers.

Consider for example the Swiss Centre for Electronics and Microtechnology (CSEM) at Neuchâtel. With money from the federal parliament it also enjoys the support of local groups including trades unions and the local chamber of commerce. The main aim of the institute is to promote education and training at the university while helping industry develop new technology. It keeps track of relevant advances worldwide and informs local companies of them. It provides a wide range of technical support for medium and small companies that cannot afford r&d efforts of their own. The enterprise has paid off by attracting electronics companies, many based on investment from other European countries and the USA, to open up in the region.

Academics are not particularly concerned about a threat to basic research, though they want to see current funding maintained. They are beginning to recover from the shock of a 10 per cent cut in the real value of the National Science Foundations budget in the 1980s, which prompted internal evaluations and some selective cutbacks. From now on they hope the budget will at least remain level in real terms until 1987.

Turkey

By population Turkey is a large country compared to most mentioned here, but its ambiguous relationships with Europe, its rather poor state of economic development, its unstable and repressive politics and its low investment in r&d all combine to reduce its influence. Geographically most of Turkey is in Asia Minor rather than Europe; to the east it shares borders with Syria, Iraq, Iran and the USSR, and 99 per cent of its population is nominally Muslim. Since the dissolution of the Ottoman Empire, after the First World War, Turkey has committed itself to the Western alliance and Western values. The state was secularized in 1928. Its position makes it an extremely important strategic asset to NATO, of which it has been a member since 1952. Although it is not a member of the EEC it has received EEC funds for economic development including r&d, as well as substantial economic support from the US in return for the right to run military bases on its territory.

More than half of Turkey's resident working population still works in agriculture, but substantial efforts have been and continue to be made to establish modern industries based on locally available raw materials such as cotton and chemicals. Much of this development has been directly under state control: food, agricultural supply, nitrogen, chemicals as well as energy industries have been arranged in State Economic Enterprises since 1929. Turkey's total r&d effort is thus virtually synonymous with government expenditure. The consequences of rapid development have included severe inflation and high unemployment. These have contributed to political unrest, which has several times resulted in military coups and civil violence. The latest, in 1980, led to the establishment of a National Security Council which still exerts much influence over Turkey's internal affairs, though technically democracy has been restored and the country has a government and a parliament.

Since the war the government has invested seriously in the education system and expansion has continued recently in spite of the country's economic problems. In 1965 just over 90 000 students were receiving higher education, 60 per cent at universities. The corresponding figure for 1981 is 240 000. In 1979 funding for university research amounted to 0.057 of GDP, about a quarter of the national research effort. University intake jumped again, increasing by a dramatic 70 per cent in 1982 and the expansion has resulted in heavier teaching loads for academics. As a result the time available for research has noticeably declined.

University life has changed much since 1981, when the military regime established a Higher Education Council. To cope with demand the HEC has established many new universities over the last few years, by 1983 there was a total of twenty-seven. Legislation passed in 1981 substantially reduced job security for academics. Since then there have been sporadic attempts to impose tidiness and discipline on students including dicta against jeans, beards, make up and high-heeled shoes.

More seriously many academics – over seventy at Ankara University alone – have been summarily sacked for reasons that are at best unclear. Most of these are social scientists or economists, suggesting that political motives play a large part in the sackings, but natural scientists and mathematicians have also been affected. The HEC seems set to maintain its strong control over the system, especially with a new ruling giving its president the power to reappoint university employees to different institutions. But there were signs in 1984 that sheer expediency would temper some of its harshness, and in particular to stem the mass exodus of academics who prefer voluntary exile and more comfortable jobs overseas to braving the arbitrariness and insecurity of the Turkish system.

By October 1984 Turkey's universities faced a serious shortage of teachers, due partly to the sackings and consequent protest resignations. One calculation put the number of staff lost at 2500 between March and September 1984. Student numbers continue to grow, but the government is taking tougher measures to regulate their studies, in particular by levying fees, which were introduced for the first time in November 1984. Extra fees will be charged for the substantial number of students who fail end of year examinations. A few months later the HEC decided to expel 5000 students who failed mid-year resits following failure in one of their courses last year.

Early in 1985 a national newspaper published a detailed report of plans by the HEC to keep files on the activities of all university teachers and students.

Private universities appear to be one way of avoiding the iron grip of the HEC – according to the 1982 constitution non-profit making foundations may set up institutes of higher education. The first of these, called Bilkent, was set up early in 1985 on behalf of eleven private companies to teach mainly technical subjects. Planners hope that 5000 students will be studying there by the end of the decade.

In 1963 the government set up the Scientific and Technical Research Council of Turkey (TÜBITAK) to 'develop, promote, organize and coordinate basic and applied research in the positive [apparently the natural] sciences'. The council provides scholarships and funding for postgraduates, advises research institutes, university and governments on policy as well as funding university research and its own institutes. The science council that runs TÜBITAK supervises the work of seven research groups: six in different disciplines, and one concerned with the training of scientists. Initially TÜBITAK's own institutes and interim activities veered mainly towards the applied sciences. Its Building Research Institute, established at Ankara in 1969, was followed by the Marmara Research Institute at Gebze in 1972, whose purpose is 'to identify and solve problems of industry pertaining to the utilization of technology and the advancement of industrial processes'. TÜBITAK also runs an 'industrial relations unit' to identify 'problems encountered by industrial organizations during the application of technology and endeavours to find solutions to these problems through TÜBITAK agencies or outside sources'.

In recent years Turkey has become conscious of its weakness in basic research: in 1977 the socio-economic objective 'advancement of knowledge' accounted for only 16 per cent of government r&d expenditure rising to a still comparatively puny proportion of 25 per cent in 1979. In 1982 TÜBITAK started work on its own Basic Sciences Research Institute which when complete will have departments of mathematics, physics, chemistry, biology and earth sciences. The same year saw the foundation of the Ballistics Research Institute in Ankara.

TÜBITAK and the Turkish Atomic Energy Authority are attached to the Prime Minister's office. The ministries of industry, energy and natural resources, and agriculture run their own research establishments and institutes – the latter with the help of a scientific council to advise on research projects.

November 1983 saw the publication of a national science policy document that proposed a rise in the ratio of r&d spending to GNP from its present level of 0.24 per cent to 1 per cent by 1993. The next five years should see a net increase of 15 per cent. Future planning will be the job of a recently formed Higher Council of Science and Technology headed by the Prime Minister, with ministers and heads of research organizations, with the power to coordinate all government research establishments and promote concerted actions in accordance with the science policy adopted.

United Kingdom

By the outbreak of the Second World War in 1939 the efforts of British governments to institutionalize science were already substantial – probably at least rivalling the effectiveness of the German system – and the quality and relative scale of her scientific research were probably second to none. The research council system was already in place (see Chapter 1) except for the Nature Conservancy Council founded in 1949, and efforts to mobilize science to help fight the war came fairly promptly and often to great effect: the development of radar, the early research on the atom bomb and the sophisticated efforts of the code-breakers are outstanding examples – all of course paid for by the government.

The influence of government procurement for the war effort penetrated far beyond the research community into many parts of the chemicals and the embryonic electronics industries (as well, of course, as textiles and steel). Companies rapidly became accustomed to mass production of the most sophisticated equipment available – with the help of effective government subsidy. After the war this pattern proved impossible to break, and two characteristics still distinguish the UK from many countries in Europe: defence takes a comparatively large share of the r&d budget: and government as well as paying for a substantial civil science effort, continues to subsidize much industrial r & d. It pays for well over half the total national r&d effort, while industry performs well over half.

The Department of Scientific and Industrial Research (DSIR) continued to supervise and fund a wide range of civil science ranging from basic research in the universities (including postgraduate training) to a network of industrial research associations and laboratories related to national needs such as transport, building and fire fighting. Medicine and agriculture retained their own separate research councils. Spending on the research councils as well as on direct support for research in the universities grew enormously in the two postwar decades.

After the war new agencies began to command considerable r&d funds and attract a substantial number of trained scientists and engineers. The most significant of these were Ministry of Defence, the Ministry of Aviation and the United Kingdom Atomic Energy Authority.

Throughout the civil science system, but particularly in the research councils, scientists were largely left alone to plan and execute their own research. The rapidly expanding universities were also very much left to their own devices to cope with the extra demands for both teaching and research. By the early 1960s the *laissez faire* approach was no longer adequate: the Labour government had to come to terms with a worsening economy, rapidly increasing costs of scientific equipment, and a shortage of scientific manpower. The response was to formulate a policy that would provide economic renewal through 'the white heat of technological revolution'. A vital part of the plan would be to direct the country's scientific and technological efforts in appropriate directions.

In 1964 machinery was set in motion to split the DSIR. Responsibility for the more basic research activities went to a new body, the Science

Research Council, (SRC), which soon began, in a small way, to foster areas it considered to be of interest to industry as well as meeting demands for basic research funding. Along with the Medical Research Council and a new Natural Environment Research Council, the SRC moved into a new Department of Education and Science. The new Ministry of Technology (Min Tech) took over the more applied aspects of DSIR's work, including the industrial research associations and several other national laboratories such as the National Physical Laboratory and the National Engineering Laboratory. Min Tech also took over the Atomic Energy Authority and later the Ministry of Aviation. In 1969 its brief was extended to cover the textiles, chemical and other manufacturing industries. Committees within each ministry advised ministers on the distribution of budgets. Recommended mechanisms for cross-coordination were never introduced, and in the 1970s science policy within government was dominated by the Rothschild principle (p 123–4).

Thinking about higher education in the 1960s was dominated by the Robbins report published in 1963. The government immediately endorsed the report's recommendation that higher education courses should be available for all those qualified by ability and attainment to pursue them and who wished to do so. As Robbins recommended, the University Grants Committee – government's interface with the universities – was reorganized, but few attempts were made to influence directly the way universities handled their internal affairs.

Towards the end of the 1960s science planners began to notice a 'swing from science' in sixth form and universities. One report suggested a broadening of the sixth form curriculum and a revision of university entrance requirements. Another studied the employment of qualified scientists, engineers and technologists: it concluded that too many such people went into fundamental research in universities and government and proposed measures to encourage more people to go into teaching and industry.

In the event, the numbers of qualified students outstripped the forecasts and gradually successive governments fell away from their commitment to provide higher education for all those able enough to benefit. It was also gradually becoming obvious that, particularly in an economy in recession, it was not going to be a simple task to find jobs that matched the aspirations of graduates. Nevertheless, in 1972 the government endorsed even more ambitious plans for expansion in higher education.

Throughout the period of rapid expansion the universities, old and new, made sure that their support for research grew roughly proportionately with their student numbers: indeed roughly one-third of total university budgets were supposed to go on the support of research. Even so, projects became more expensive, particularly in the natural sciences, academics became increasingly reliant on the research councils for additional funds.

This 'dual support' system worked well while budgets on both sides grew, but after 1973 problems began to arise. Funding for universities ceased to keep pace with student numbers, so resources began, almost imperceptibly at first, to drift away from the support of research. In the research councils the building and maintaining of central laboratories and facilities of one kind or another began to take larger and larger chunks of the now more slowly growing resources.

The overall effect of this squeeze on basic research was not fully assessed until the end of the 1970s, when a review committee began to look at it. The committee had just completed a draft of its report when in 1982, the Conservative government announced a drastic reduction in overall funding for universities, with a total effect estimated at a 15 per cent cut over three years. A new version of the report redrafted to take the new cuts into account finally appeared in 1982. Although dogged by a lack of suitable national statistics it concluded that the effects on research had been serious and looked likely to worsen considerably. It called for increased funding for research and it recommended that universities should take steps to safeguard research from unequal depredation, but it advocated that the 'dual support system' should be left alone. It also noted a severe shortage of tenured jobs for young people with good research track records. This has been alleviated to some extent by a 'new blood' scheme in which 1000 new lectureships will be funded centrally for five years.

In spite of the general government policy of cutting public spending the research councils have not received swinging cuts, although their spending power and flexibility of action was certainly eroded in the early 1980s. By 1984 all of them were working towards strategies that would bring at least some of their work closer to industrial applications and at the same time safeguard important innovative work. Although under constant pressure from the government to help produce economically useful results, pleas for extra funds for priority areas and new initiatives have not met with a sympathetic response. But the government has backed a three-year programme for r&d in information technology to be funded and executed jointly with industry and academics. The programme is known by the name of its chief planner, John Alvey.

The universities too are under pressure to produce more graduates with skills required by industry, in information technology and science and technology generally. The universities, accustomed to a great deal of autonomy, are not keen about a rapid shift to meet current 'fashions' but are being forced to respond to these pressures to a considerable extent.

In late 1984 and early 1985 the consequences of level funding for the research councils began to become clear. The Natural Environment Research Council (NERC) and the Agricultural and Food Research Council (AFRC) suffered worst. Both do much of their research in their own institutes rather than at the universities – also both have built their programmes around extra funds that government departments pay them for doing specific jobs. Lately such funds have been severely cut back. Both NERC and AFRC have drawn up detailed corporate plans that describe in detail those parts of the research councils' programme that would be retained and those that could no longer be supported. The (AFRC) announced the impending closure of several laboratories and the loss of hundreds of posts for researchers.

The other natural science research councils, the Science and Engineering Research Council (SERC) and the Medical Research Council (MRC) were levied to pay for restructuring costs of AFRC and NERC, which put even more pressure on their own strained resources. The Advisory Board for the Research Councils, in its advice to the secretary of state for education and science, continued to point out the difficulty of keeping up Britain's tradition of world class science under these circumstances. It noted particularly that new opportunities to open up areas of research in strategic subjects such as biotechnology and microelectronics were being lost.

It also reported its intention to consider seriously pulling out of a number of areas of basic research, such as astronomy or particle physics, in order to release funds, and it launched a review of Britain's future in particle physics to be conducted by scientists from other disciplines. The review group reported in June 1985, recommending that Britain had benefited greatly from membership of the European Organization for Nuclear Research (CERN) and should remain a member. But that it should also press strongly for cuts in the cost of its subscription and pull out if it could not be cut by 25 per cent by 1991.

At the end of 1984 the government announced a small increase in the Science Budget, for new initiatives. But the scientists are still complaining that level funding is not enough because the cost of doing science rises each year by more than the official inflation figure. The reason is that to keep up with the competition researchers need ever more complex and therefore expensive equipment.

The situation in the universities is even bleaker. In mid 1985 student numbers were no longer falling, but big cuts are planned for the 1990s when the population of the appropriate age group will have diminished substantially. A special initiative to train more students in the subjects where skills are short – such as electronic engineering and other forms of design and manufacturing technology – has brought a small amount of extra funds to selected institutions. But the block grant to universities is still due to fall by 2 per cent a year till 1990.

The UGC published a strategy document in September 1984 in which it expressed its determination to allocate research funds more selectively. To help it do this it has set up a number of committees and sent out a questionnaire to universities asking them to rank their research efforts and define research policies and priorities. Eight research groups have already benefited from a UGC hand-out of £4 million of extra government cash for equipment needed to keep them in the forefront of their subjects. But it seems clear that at the other end of the scale some departments will lose research funding and may have to close down completely.

Things may go even further. A government green paper (draft legislation) on higher education published in May 1985 stressed the need for economies and selectivity in universities, in both teaching and research, the emphasis being clearly placed on subjects with vocational and industrial relevance. Greeted by most academics as a philistine's charter, it clearly signalled the possibility of closing one or more of Britain's 44 universities.

Yugoslavia

Yugoslavia is still one of the poorest countries in Europe as measured by gross domestic product per capita, but it spends about one per cent of GDP on r&d and has a sophisticated and unusual approach to science planning and funding. An intensive postwar programme of industrialization has posed a severe challenge to the country's rapidly growing population of researchers. Science is now organized mainly at local and federal level, and, in theory at least, initiated on a communist version of the customer-contractor principle.

There is no science budget as such, but, according to a review by Yugoslav academics published in 1980, economic organizations (what other countries would call industries) and others formulate their research requirements and arrange for the appropriate research institute to do the work. The initiators may be acting alone or as part of a group of organizations committed to a fairly broad programme of research. Science can also be planned and funded by self-management communities of interest for scientific work. Each province or republic has an assembly charged with this task, and these are bound in a national grouping called the Association of Republican and Provincial Self Management Communities of Interest for Scientific Activities.

In practice the science policy for each region is implemented and coordinated by a committee or secretariat whose precise sphere of influence differs from region to region. Slovenia, for example, which has the largest number of scientific researchers per head of the population, has a Republican Committee for Research and Development, while the regions at the lower end of the research league lump science in with education and culture. Research may also be commissioned by committees representing subregions or even individual communes. Self-management communities for public health, education, culture, etc, may also commission research.

This setup is not seen as being one where research is 'bought' and 'sold': the phrase used to describe it is 'the free exchange of labour', which implies that the researchers have quite a lot of say in how they meet the requirements of the sponsoring organization. Indeed, the freedom of research is guaranteed under the Yugoslav constitution.

The bulk of Yugoslovia's research is concentrated in independent institutes, which may stand alone or be closely associated with a university department (whose job is primarily to teach rather than produce research). Independent institutes derive about a third of their income on average from 'economic organizations'; just under a third through self-generated income from economic and secondary activities, with a further fifth from self-management communities of interest. R&d units within economic (and other) organizations account for another substantial chunk of research: here the parent organizations provide the bulk of the funding. Science units within the academies of science take only a small proportion of total funds: they used to be funded from central administrations but are now largely dependent on the self-management communities of interest for science.

The Yugoslav academics describe three phases of development of r&d since the Second World War.

From 1945 up to the beginning of the sixties, science policy was primarily aimed at creating the basic constitutional, material and personnel requirements for its own development . . . science had a kind of enlightening function: the basic objectives of science were of a scientific cognitive and scientific educational nature . . . From the beginning of the sixties up to the mid-seventies . . . the process was under way of the abolition of 'state' science . . . from fundamental (predominantly motivated by academic cognitive and pedagogical interests) research projects began to turn towards research and development . . . throughout this period, the scientific potential was primarily used (by the economy) as a kind of special selector in the transfer (import) of foreign applied knowledge and technology . . . and only partly as an authentic 'producer' of applied sciences . . . since the mid seventies . . . Yugoslav society has taken a new approach to the development of science . . . according to the principle of current social policy, science should be . . . functionally linked to the flows of social development, sharing both the risks and benefits of the application of its results.

Numbers of researchers approximately doubled between 1965 and 1977, with medical sciences and engineering achieving the largest growth rate, and natural sciences the smallest. This trend reflects the heavy emphasis, implicit in the recent policies described above, towards applied and away from fundamental work. The trend is also reflected in a decline in the proportion of completed research projects that are fundamental in character. Nevertheless, there is an explicit intention to maintain the level of support for fundamental work in future.

An increasing proportion of researchers hold higher degrees – but the average age of researchers is rising. This is seen as a problem that needs to be tackled.

In 1981 the Yugoslav parliament adopted a 'general development plan of scientific activities for the period 1981/4'. This document embodied the state's acknowledgement of the importance of r&d for economic growth, and its intention that spending on r&d and the number of researchers should grow faster than the Yugoslav economy as a whole. The aim is that by 1985 1.5 per cent of GDP should be spent on r&d compared with 0.9 per cent in 1979.

So much for the theory. The reality is not quite so rosy. Partly due to Yugoslavia's economic crisis spending on science fell from 1.07 per cent of the national income in 1978 to 0.91 per cent in 1983. And even the limited resources available are often wasted. The problem, according to some scientists is that the government undervalues science and scientists and the contribution they could make to the country's future. One of the major problems is that each of Yugoslavia's nine provinces runs its research activities autonomously – there is little coordination and the result is much duplication. Even within provinces research institutes and universities often fail to coordinate their work. Research institutes are however encouraged to be commercially minded and now levy realistic charges when they do work for other government agencies or for commercial organizations. Yugoslav academics, more usually in humanities and social sciences, are still being tried and receive prison sentences for criticising the Yugoslav social and political system.

CHAPTER THREE

Life of a twentieth-century European researcher

The diversity of the scientific worlds in Europe, as outlined in the last chapter, should be a source of pleasure, pride and hope to every European. Nevertheless, the careful reader will have noticed that many common themes underlie the events and trends I have described. In the next two chapters I want to bring some of these out. I have tried to choose the ones I think will be most important for the development of science in Europe to the end of the century and beyond.

Whatever the important issues are, they relate always to real individuals, whether researchers or ordinary taxpayers. I intend to keep this obvious fact constantly in my mind and I hope that this will protect me from launching into highly theoretical discussions of individual factors that cannot really be tackled in isolation from one another. That is why I have chosen to structure this chapter around the various stages in the life of a researcher and to bring forward at each point the pressures that seem relevant at that stage.

In Chapter Four, I have tried to look at the research world from a different perspective. I have followed an imaginary path through the perceptions of a reasonably intelligent lay person who takes an interest in science and its ramifications. In each case, of course, the protagonist may be male or female: I have usually taken the old-fashioned view that the male embraces the female.

Education and intellectual creativity

There are few small children who do not express curiosity about how and why the world works. Fewer still lack the desire to learn how to control

Table 3.1 Provision of Education for young West Europeans (1981 or latest available figures)

Country	1st level		2nd level			3rd level				National expenditure on education as % of GNP
	Per cent Enrolment	Age range	Per cent Enrolment (trend)	Age Range	Student/ staff ratio	Enrolment per 1000 inhabitants (trend)	Per cent foreign students	Student/ staff ratio	Per cent science & technology students (trend)	
Austria	100	6–9	73 →	10–17	11	1.8 ↑	9	na	36 ↔	6.0
Belgium	100	6–11	90	12–17	18	2.0 ↑a	7 a	na	51 ↔a	6.1
Denmark	100	6–11	100 a	12–17	8 b	2.1	3 a	na	38 ↑a	7.0 a
Finland	100	7–12	100	13–18	13	2.5 →a	(0.5) a	na	50 ↔a	5.9
France	100	6–10	86 ↑	11–17	20 a	2.0 ↑a	11 a	na	37 ↓	5.0 a
Germany	na	6–9	na	10–18	14 a	2.0 ↑	5 a	7	47 ↑a	4.7 c
Greece	100 c	6–11	81 c	12–17	na	1.3 ↓c	7 c	15 c	49 ↓c	2.2 c
Ireland	100 a	6–11	93 ↑a	12–16	14 a	1.6 ↑a	5 a	9 b	44 ↑a	7.0 a
Italy	100	6–10	73 ↔	11–18	10 c	2.0 ↑a	2 a	23 b	50 ↑a	5.1 c
Netherlands	100	6–11	95 ↑	12–17	na	2.6 ↑	1	na	33 ↓	8.4 a
Norway	100	7–12	97 a ↑	13–18	na	1.9 ↑	1 c	10 c	37 ↑a	9.0 a
Portugal	100	6–11	53 b	12–16	16 b	0.9 ↑c	1 c	9 c	41 ↑c	4.5 a
Spain	100	6–10	88 ↑	11–17	na	1.8 ↑a	1 a	16 a	40 ↓a	2.6 c
Sweden	100	7–12	85 ↔	13–18	9.4 b	2.5 ↑	2 b	na	44 ↓a	9.5
Switzerland	na	7–12	na	13–19	na	1.3 ↑	18	na	44	5.0 a
Turkey	100	6–10	42 ↑	11–16	20	0.5 ↑	3	11	42 ↔	2.7 a
UK	100	5–10	83 →a	11–17	na	1.5 ↓a	7 a	na	45 ↑a	5.8 a
Yugoslavia	100	7–10	83 ↑	11–18	18	1.8 ↓a	1 a	17 a	39 ↓a	4.9 a

Source: UNESCO 1983 Statistical digest, UNESCO, Paris

a 1980.   b 1975.   c 1979.   na not available.

↑ rising.   ↓ falling.   ↔ steady.

Note: Where the UNESCO figures clearly indicate approximately full enrolment 96, 97, 98, 99, 101, 102, 103% have been replaced by 100%.

their environment to improve their own comfort. Children do not grow up in isolation: parents, siblings, neighbours and later teachers and schoolmates all leave their mark, and this environment makes an enormous amount of difference to the extent to which natural curiosity and skill develops.

For all sorts of reasons, religious, economic, even linguistic, some periods of history have favoured such curiosity more than others. In Europe the scientific revolution of the sixteenth and seventeenth centuries could be said to mark the beginning of an especially encouraging environment for developing intellectual curiosity. Formal systems of education, however, benefitted only a small proportion of the population. But in this century states have seen fit to provide school places, at both primary and secondary level, for most if not all of their young people (Table 3.1). In theory, then, every child can develop his talents. The brightest and best (though it still helps if your parents are well off too) can aspire to the jobs where they can follow their natural curiosity to make new discoveries at someone else's expense. Or can they? We will look at the system through the eyes of the aspirant natural philosopher. We will assume that he has surmounted the hurdles of primary and secondary education and is now surveying the prospect of higher education. But first a little background . . .

The student boom

The opportunity to study at a university is one that is available to many more young people than before the Second World War. Now between 10 and 20 per cent of the relevant age groups take part in university education. As a result, the characters of many older universities have changed dramatically and many new institutions with distinctive features have come into being to meet the demand. In all the countries we are considering, numbers of students have grown rapidly and the growth in the numbers of teachers has rarely been commensurate. For some statistics on the wide variation in student/teacher ratios see Table 3.1. Later on we will look at the effects of these changes on research, but for the moment let us consider the matter from the student's point of view.

Expansion has been most rapid in countries where access to university requires only a simple school leaving certificate with no further selection procedure. This is the case in Italy, where an enormous student population has to be supported on government funding that is shrinking in real terms. The result is very large universities and faculties, the highest student/teacher ratio in Europe, low morale among both teachers and students, and a frighteningly high drop-out rate.

The situation is similar but not quite so extreme in Spain and

Germany. In France and, more recently, the Netherlands the same principles apply, but the student body is severely pruned after assessment of one or two years' work. In Switzerland and Austria fewer young people are prepared for university entry, so satisfying demand does not place quite such a strain on the system. All these countries have, with some minor exceptions, carefully avoided a concept we take for granted in Britain, the *numerus clausus* or set limit on the number of entrants into each subject or course.

Britain, in spite of recent inroads made by government, still has the most autonomous universities in Europe, and the institutions themselves set the limits and also have complete power over whom is accepted. The Scandinavian countries are gradually changing from an open system to one where numbers are limited: Finland takes the hardest line over this, while Denmark and Sweden, where demand for university education is in decline, take an intermediate position. Europe's poorer countries, by contrast, cannot afford to satisfy demand and so they have to be selective: thus Ireland, Greece, Turkey, Yugoslavia and Portugal all have some sort of *numerus clausus* system.

At the beginning of the 1970s, European governments anticipated steady expansion of their higher education systems: the expansion continued in most places at least during the first half of the decade. Most growth came in social sciences and humanities. Demand for medical studies also grew rapidly, but it was not always satisfied. Natural sciences and engineering fared relatively badly until the last years of the decade. In the 1980s expansion is already levelling off. One reason is the fall in the birth rate in the late 1960s and early 1970s so that there will be fewer eighteen-year-olds around in the late 1980s. Another factor is the failure of mass higher education to deliver on its promise of greater economic productivity: at a time of financial stringency, governments are re-thinking their strategy of throwing money more or less blindly at the system and wondering how their spending can be more effectively focussed.

Faced with gloomy warnings about the relatively new phenomenon of graduate unemployment, students too are reassessing their priorities. In France and Germany particularly there are distinct trends towards more vocationally orientated types of learning, whether inside or outside the higher education system. In the Netherlands the government is trying to guide a larger proportion of students into vocational studies by requiring them to complete degrees more quickly and reducing the opportunities for doctoral work. Our prospective natural philosopher may not be put off by such mundane considerations, but the atmosphere in which he studies may well be affected.

The new pressures affect institutions in different ways. In many places the nation's need for graduates in a particular discipline has begun to filter through to university planning. The subjects concerned often depend on local conditions, though there are a few skills that now seem to crop up almost everywhere as examples where demand from employers outruns (or will shortly outrun) supply. Computer science and electronic engineering are typical examples. So is biotechnology, though what sort of training to provide, and indeed how many trained people are needed, seem to be more open questions.

Universities may be unwilling for various reasons to provide courses that are so blatantly vocational, regarding this as detracting from their role in the all-round development of the individual. Even where university authorities are keen to change their approach, either through their own initiative or in response to external pressures, they may face competition from other parts of the higher educational sector which are already more focussed and can be more flexible in devising and setting up new courses and demanding different entry qualifications.

At the same time the demand for other subjects may fall because of student choice or national policy. The consequences of this may be to spread equal misery among the affected faculties at each university: alternatively a pecking order of departments may well emerge, with only the strongest and most popular surviving. Some see the latter trend as a serious threat to the concept of a 'university' and, in the long run, to the potential for multidisciplinary research. Others will see it as an inevitable symptom of a dynamic and flexible system. The latter perceive the benefits such changes could bring to all aspects of university life, including research. New priorities and disciplines could supplant old patterns too deeply embedded in the structure to die naturally within the old hierarchy.

Moving into research

Whatever the impact of these fairly major pertubations, the basic business of the university is to transmit knowledge and teach the means of applying and extending it. Let us assume that our student chooses to attend a university (under which I subsume all institutions that both teach and undertake research) and gains a place. The chances are that his first two or three years will be mainly concerned with absorbing knowledge, and will be punctuated by some form of annual assessing of progress. By the fourth or fifth year (often the third in the UK), the student will usually have some idea of his or her abilities and preferences, and will use this insight to develop long-term aspirations.

These aspirations do not, of course, develop independently of external factors, ranging from the general state of the economy to responses to the individual's performance within the university. In particular, students of outstanding ability are often singled out by teachers and encouraged to think in terms of a research career. Opportunities for a fairly long practical project in the last year or years of undergraduate work, which are common throughout Europe, often provide the ideal occasion to pursue such encouragement. While academics still gear much undergraduate teaching to the needs of the potential researcher, and sometimes make this seem the most natural progression from undergraduate studies, they are quite pleased to know that most graduates, with any luck the less bright ones, will go off somewhere else.

A number of factors have combined to make the real situation facing graduates in the natural sciences and engineering a far more complex one. Let us assume for the moment that we can make a simple division between high fliers and, for want of a better word, 'plodders'. We will leave flounderers, who have not gained significantly from university education, to fend for themselves.

For a high flier, postgraduate work leading to a doctorate may at first seem an attractive option. He or she will be welcomed by the department of his choice and will look forward to the opportunity of learning from and stimulating a team of high intellectual calibre: a congenial arrangement. Some of them may go overseas to broaden their experience. In some countries such as Portugal and Greece, this is almost compulsory, since there is little provision made at home for PhD training. In larger countries many are discouraged from leaving their country in case it reduces their chances of being around when a suitable opening occurs. He and the department now attempt to raise the necessary funds. In some countries, such as Sweden, universities have special posts (usually temporary) for postgraduates. Assuming the candidate can win one of these (and demand usually considerably exceeds supply) the first battle is won. But an increasingly widespread system is for postgraduate support to be provided nationally, often by bodies such as research councils which have to incorporate national priorities such as special research areas or manpower needs in their planning. So the prospective student and his department may find they have to modify their original research plan. They may have to change the content or approach, or it may be a matter of, say, collaborating with a company. In fact, this latter course may prove quite attractive to the student, who may by now be weighing up his chances of an academic career and seeing that, even for the brightest it is not very bright.

Often this consideration takes the high fliers out of academic life altogether. They may opt for a technical or research job in government science or industry (where pay for those with certain skills can be very high indeed), they may seek an administrative or executive post (particularly in Britain and France, where research jobs offer relatively low prospects for advancement), or they may retrain for a high status profession such as accountancy, the law or even medicine. The high fliers often find it relatively easy to find backing for expensive further training.

What of the 'plodders'? Some of these may believe that they also could make good researchers and endeavour to stay in a university department to prove it. If they cannot obtain funding for doctoral research they may succeed in entering a taught postgraduate course. Increasingly, though, such courses are taking on a mainly vocational emphasis. Nevertheless, the project work in such a course can help a student demonstrate his work. Sometimes universities can benefit from such ambitions: they can take on such aspirants as technicians, thus providing valuable support for the research of the department. Where a department has not a sufficient reputation to attract high fliers it can use such willing workers to build up a substantial research programme.

More usually, though, today's 'plodders' will be deterred from research careers, seeing that the hurdles that daunt brighter colleagues will be even greater obstacles to them. They will seek careers outside the university, either entering jobs immediately or seeking vocational types of postgraduate training: for teaching or for skills in information technology for example, where many countries are trying to meet industry's demand by retraining graduates with degrees in non-relevant disciplines.

Employers' attitudes to first degrees have changed too. Fifteen years ago a degree was a passport to a job, often a well-paid and secure civil service post or an elite profession such as medicine or law. As more graduates came onto the labour market, employers in industry and commerce as well as the state sector could raise their aspirations and graduate entry became the norm for an expanding range of careers. Over the last five years employers have become dissatisfied with some kinds of graduate, and they can afford to be more choosy. In Italy and France, companies often provide extra training for graduates to give them the right skills; in Germany many companies have rethought their recruitment policies, preferring more adaptable and less demanding school leavers to graduates who may be seven or eight years older. More generally, where graduates and vocationally trained people come into direct competition, the latter are beginning to have the edge.

In the 1980s some graduates have failed to find any reasonable training or employment option open to them, and the phenomenon of graduate unemployment has entered the statistics books. Countries consider this in different ways. In the Netherlands, for example, the graduate unemployment figures include those who cannot find work of the standing thought to be appropriate for graduates. In the UK, Sweden and Switzerland, the figures are balder, concerning only those who are actually on the dole. In Germany the high level of graduate unemployment (in 1983, 8.4 per cent for natural science graduates, 10.3 per cent among those with engineering degrees, compared with a national average of 8.6 per cent) is considered an argument against shortening university courses: young people are better off in universities than on the streets, some think. It's impossible to get any figures for graduate unemployment in Italy, because a large population of graduates and near-graduates stay on at university in various temporary, and even unpaid, positions, hoping for better times. This is partly because, for bureaucratic reasons, Italy did not have a proper PhD programme between 1972 and 1984.

Another rapidly growing group consists of those who get a job after their first degree and then take up doctoral studies part-time. These students are cheap because they do not have to be supported, but for various reasons they are less likely to make a substantial contribution to the work of a department. The falling of completion rates for doctorates is now causing concern in many European countries, though some would argue that non-completion in itself does not really matter: it is the underlying problems in the research system that need to be tackled.

Whatever the underlying factors at work, the number of doctoral graduates has fallen in almost all European countries over the last decade. This has been one factor among many in the general malaise in university research in Europe.

The postdoctoral job gap

Once upon a time the acquisition of a doctoral degree was a sufficiently unusual and prestigious achievement to command universal respect. Its award was a right of passage worth working hard for. As we have already seen, the accolade no longer automatically confers immediate benefit. Just as many are discouraged from embarking on doctoral studies, those who do take them on often see little incentive to complete them. Probably the major factor is that the student realises that a PhD will not guarantee him an academic job. If he wants to continue doing research, he may have to make do with some kind of temporary post-doctoral post. This can either be a university post (as is common in Italy and France) or associated with a research project funded by an external agency. The conditions of such posts are often less attractive in the short term than those of their recent studentships with the tasks more narrowly specified. Another problem is that external constraints often limit the periods people are allowed to spend in such posts. Wage scales, for example, may make the older contract-holders too expensive or alternatively employment laws may give such people redundancy rights if they are allowed to stay beyond a certain time limit.

Many, of course, do complete their PhDs successfully, and come to another decision point in their careers. The brightest will have a number of options. They can look for a job in industry, either in r&d, or, eschewing their research aspirations, in management of one sort or another. In some countries, such a transition can come later in their career, but in the UK it becomes increasingly difficult as a researcher ages. Jobs in government laboratories or in other parts of the civil service may come up, though often attempts to curb public expenditure as well as shortage of openings conspire to make such posts few and far between.

For many this will be the last chance of a good job outside the academic system. By this time our erstwhile research student may be quite old – over 30 would not be unusual in Germany. Those who prefer to opt out of the system to find jobs in industry will increasingly find that what they have actually done is of more interest to the company than the proper qualifications, and where important skills are at stake it will scarcely matter at all. External employers may well opt to employ a less qualified person than to pay a high salary for a postdoctor PhD with more skills than they require and who maybe less adaptable and will almost certainly be more demanding.

Nonetheless, many stay inside the academic system, either from choice or because no alternative comes up. Very few new PhDs will immediately find a permanent academic job. Some systems preclude this possibility anyway. Early appointments to such posts were more common during the rapid expansion of the 1960s and early 1970s. The lucky beneficiaries of this job bonanza were not particularly outstanding intellectually, and now, in their forties and fifties, are holding on to the permanent jobs the next generation would like.

So the usual next step is for a PhD to join a rapidly expanding and increasingly significant section of the university research community: those who occupy the 'grey areas' between research students and permanent staff. Exact conditions for such people vary enormously: some teach, others do not; some enjoy wide freedoms, while others have to fulfil sometimes quite onerous and demanding tasks, occasionally even doing work that might in less stringent times have been entrusted to a technician; some are reasonably well paid while others do badly, sometimes, through the vicissitudes of bureacracy, going for months without being paid at all. In some countries, such as France and Italy, such people actually have a reasonably good chance of being consolidated into the system one way or another regardless of merit: in others, the UK and Germany, for example, they do not. The latter system reduces morale while ostensibly maintaining standards: the former system, obviously, does the opposite.

Whatever the local variations, it is this part of the research system that warrants most concern during the 1980s. It lumps together in almost uniform misery the extremely bright youngster eager to prove himself, the older researcher who by now has a very good track record, an international reputation but no job, and those researchers, both young and old, who through lack of either opportunity or talent, have failed to distinguish themselves.

Some countries have become aware of these problems and tried to tackle them in various ways. Germany, the UK and the Netherlands all have schemes to give outstanding young researchers some security as they establish themselves and wait for a permanent post to come up. In each case the schemes are administered by national research councils and guarantee a salary for five years, with the prestige of winning a rare place an added incentive in itself. Britain and Sweden have national schemes to provide tenured posts for talented researchers. The Swedish scheme provides permanent jobs immediately, while the British one involves interim funding with a commitment on the part of the university to provide a permanent job within five years.

Beyond the gap: an ageing and pressured academic community

The lean years for university recruitment have had adverse effects on the quality of teaching and research within faculties, and on those who did manage to find jobs. As we have seen, a large cadre of academics were recruited in the late 1960s and early 1970s. These are now in their 40s and 50s, and set to stay in the system for the next twenty years or so. Future generations have not been able to find jobs so easily: financial constraints have slowed expansion of faculties even when growth in student numbers continued. Nowadays many countries foresee declining student numbers and most are anyway concerned to cut costs. In the Netherlands and the UK the number of permanent posts has already declined. All these factors make it difficult to bring young academics onto the permanent staff, although some special schemes like those mentioned have helped.

The 'age profile' of academics is a problem for a number of reasons (Figure 3.1). It discourages bright youngsters from even trying to enter the profession, so general standards go down. New knowledge and ideas take longer to penetrate through to undergraduate teaching. Senior academics lack the stimulation provided by younger faculty, and their developing ability to advise on rather than carry out research is frustrated because they have no one to inspire. In general the age problem is seen as a greater threat to research than teaching, and attempts to deal with problems often involve the creation of posts for young researchers. This is usually because academic job hierarchies have been very much based on the teaching role of academics. Although academics are usually free to pursue research and often contracted and funded accordingly, their teaching role comes first.

This didn't matter much while student numbers were small, and research was a relatively simple activity. But now teaching and administration duties are more onerous and research is increasingly delegated to doctoral students and postdoctoral researchers of one kind or another described earlier. The result is often that research quality declines because the best equipped to lead it do not have enough time to do so properly. Some countries have tried to restructure their systems entirely to provide openings for young researchers and teachers that have

Figure 3.1 Age structure of academic staff (all subjects)

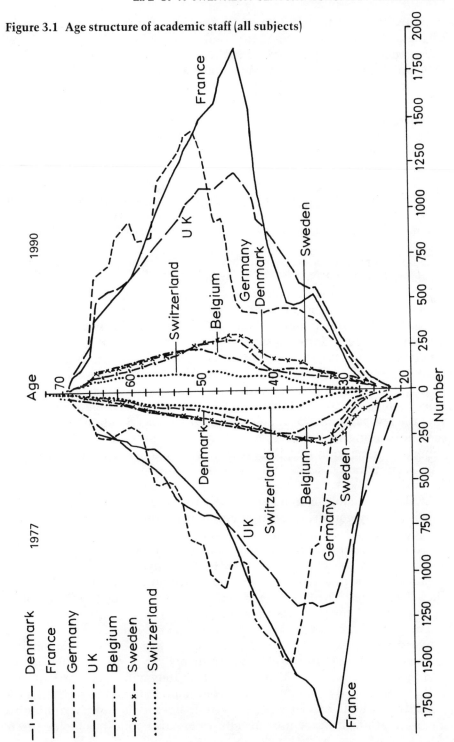

Source: Employment prospects and mobility of scientists in Europe 1980 p13

permanent rather than temporary status. Italy has done this and similar changes are planned in the Netherlands.

Another reason for the age structure problem is that once attained, an academic post is usually easy and comfortable to hang on to. Although in some countries minimal duties, such as teaching hours, are laid down, there are very few specific demands made on academics. In most countries academics are civil servants with permanent tenure of one kind or another and good pension rights. This makes it particularly hard to persuade them to leave or even to retire to make way for 'fresh blood'. Such an operation was, however, fairly successfully managed by a very expensive scheme in the UK. Selected universities are allowed to appoint a few young researchers of their choice who are paid from a central fund for five years, on the understanding that the university will find a job for them during that time. Similar proposals in Germany have not been implemented.

On the other hand it would be wrong to conclude that European academics in the 1980s enjoy a carefree and pampered life style. The freedom academics once enjoyed has been increasingly eroded by pressures from a number of sources.

The most obvious, and perhaps the most serious, is the increasing burden of teaching duties as student/staff ratios have grown. In countries where student intake is declining for demographic or financial reasons, academics can hope for some relief from this. However, this is likely to be patchy: demand for vocationally relevant subjects such as computer science and electronic engineering is increasing so fast in some places that the few academics available to teach them can hardly cope. One new idea is to bring in engineers and scientists from industry to help out, though in some countries, local rules or laws make this difficult. Sweden has been notably successful in making the most of industry professorships.

Student demand for more say in the running of universities has resulted in many countries creating different boards and committees with jurisdiction over some aspect of university life. This has had quite far-reaching effects on course content and examination procedures in the social sciences, though natural scientists and engineers do not in general regard it as a seriously destructive influence on intellectual progress in their disciplines. The latter are, however, more concerned by the amount of time they spend on such procedures.

The new decision-making structures are usually imposed on universities via parliamentary legislation. In most European countries, universities are state institutions and in theory can be quite rigidly controlled by the appropriate ministry. In France, Italy and Spain curricula are laid down centrally, and the finances of each institution negotiated individually with the ministry, though in Spain this is now beginning to change. Although academics usually resent this kind of outside interference it can be a powerful agent for countering inertia: bringing beneficial reforms that a system with more autonomy cannot achieve on its own. This may well prove the case with the reforms the Dutch government is imposing on its universities.

External pressures have also eroded the academic's freedom to pursue the research of his choice, especially if the applications of the work are not obvious. When their research funding comes from within the university, academics usually have quite a large say in what they do with it. Such budgets often expanded in proportion with staffing levels during the 1960s and early 1970s but are now levelling off or even declining because of overall cuts and the increased cost of teaching. This has been the case in France, Italy, Austria, Sweden and, until recently, the Netherlands.

In other countries, such as Germany and the UK, research councils play a significant part in funding, particularly as the necessary equipment has become more sophisticated and expensive, and some facilities are provided by research councils and shared by university groups. Where this is the case governments have sometimes tried to steer university research by directing the research councils to concentrate on certain priority areas. Sometimes the research councils have taken the initiative in providing such direction: the Science and Engineering Research Council in Britain, the CNR in Italy and, more recently, the CNRS in France have all worked hard to promote areas they considered to be priorities, usually because the results could be applied in one way or another.

It is less usual, although by no means unknown, for other government agencies to sponsor work in universities, and this is beginning to be a significant source of income in some countries. Usually such projects have specific aims in view and can affect research programmes of departments. The same is true of projects sponsored by industry. With declining internal support, academics cannot afford to turn away such funds, even though the research involved may be more applied and short term than they would regard as ideal. There is a distinct danger, though, that too great an emphasis on short-term work will destroy the universities' capacity to innovate in basic research and to maintain a fairly long-term view of strategic disciplines that underlie important technologies.

Sweden and Norway have both noted such trends and in its 1984 research bill Sweden has taken steps to reverse it. In the Netherlands, strenuous efforts have been made, particularly with the national biotechnology programme, to ensure that basic strategic and applied research get a fair share. Hopes are high that the UK's Alvey programme in information technology will do equally well. Nevertheless, the structural threat to basic and strategic research in Europe could well be one of the most important issues in university planning in the 1980s, and it is certainly one that concerns many academics.

Table 3.2 R & D in the higher education sector 1979

Country	Contribution of r & d in higher education: As a percentage of national r & d		As % of GDP	Sources of funding for r & d in higher education: Public			Private	Other national sources (eg. industry)	Overseas
	Expenditure	Researchers in science and engineering		As % of	As % of public funding		Private higher education		
					Direct govt. funding research councils	General university funds			
Austria [a]	37.4	48.3	0.34	96.7	5.7	94.3	0	2.9	0.3
Belgium	20.6	59.8	0.28	89.0	29.7	70.3	7.0	2.2	1.8
Denmark	26.2	39.9	0.26	97.2	12.5	87.5	0	1.5	1.2
Finland	18.3	37.4	0.20	93.3	19.5	80.5	0	5.2	1.5
France	15.5	32.6	0.28	96.1	62.0	38.0	0	3.2	0.7
Germany	16.0	23.7	0.38	98.0	20.0 (est)	80.0 (est)	0	2.0	0
Greece	13.9	48.2	0.20	100.0	na	na	0	0	0
Ireland	18.4	53.4	0.14	86.1	17.5	82.5	1.9	6.3	5.7
Italy	17.7	43.3	0.15	98.5	na	na	0	1.2	0.3
Netherlands	24.9	33.4	0.49	98.1	6.8	93.2	0	1.8	0
Norway	31.3	39.8	0.43	95.9	15.3	84.7	0.8	2.9	0.4
Portugal [b]	17.8	50.1	0.06	97.1	na	na	1.7	1.2	0.1
Spain	6.2 [c]	26.9 [d]	0.02 [c]	100.0 [c]	na	na	0	0	0
Sweden [e]	21.7	23.7	na	96.2	32.9	67.1	0.6	2.6	0.6
Switzerland	17.7	45.3	0.43	83.7	20.4	79.6	0	16.3	0
Turkey	16.3	na	0.06	100.0	na	na	0	0	0
UK [b]	11.4	16.5 (est)	0.25	79.8	22.0	78.0	9.8	8.4	2.0
Yugoslavia	18.3	28.7	0.16	na	na	na	na	na	na

Source: OECD 1984 *OECD Science and technology indicators.* OECD, Paris

[a] 1975.   [b] 1976.   [c] 1976.   [d] 1974.   [e] Natural science and engineering only.

Research inside and outside the university

Some European countries rely almost totally on the universities to carry out basic research (Table 3.3). Others maintain substantial networks of laboratories where scientists can concentrate on research without being interrupted by teaching duties. The most substantial networks are the Max Planck Institutes in Germany, the Consiglio Nazionale delle Ricerche (CNR) in Italy, and the Centre Nationale de la Recherche Scientifique (CNRS) and the Institut National de la Santé et de la Recherche Médicale (INSERM) in France. Spain's Consejo Superior de Investigaciones Científicas (CSIC) operates similarly. Switzerland also has a number of institutes where substantial amounts of basic research are done; often these are based around expensive and larger types of equipment, particularly for nuclear physics. The same has happened in Denmark, where the Risø national laboratory, originally formed to develop the use of nuclear power, now undertakes a large proportion of basic science, partly because the country has decided against a nuclear power programme. Turkey is now increasing its investment in such centres. In the UK the government owns central laboratories such as the National Physical Laboratory and the National Engineering Laboratory both paid for by the Department of Trade and Industry. There is, however, no cross-disciplinary network. In agriculture, the institutes are largely autonomous and work independently of the university system; in medicine, laboratories are often sited at universities, while in natural science the central laboratories now concentrate on making complex and expensive equipment available to university groups. Germany has a separate organization which looks after a dozen or so such facilities where work ranges from basic to applied. Often in-house researchers work alongside university groups in these laboratories. In the Netherlands and Norway the main government research networks are more applied in character: the trend is to make such work more, rather than less, directed and short-term.

Compared to university groups, scientists at such laboratories may enjoy a relatively privileged existence. They have no teaching duties, though they often supervise doctoral students, and they usually enjoy civil service status with job security and healthy pensions. They often find it easier to obtain funding for research they want to pursue, and equipment is more likely to be ready to hand. If they can draw on an annual budget their work is likely to be less subject to severe scrutiny than those who regularly compete for short-term funding. That said, many of their problems are the same. Personnel at the labs show a similar age profile to academics, and jobs are now almost as hard to come by as permanent university posts. Because of their centralized funding they are probably under more pressure to bow to government directives, for example, to do more applied work, to research more closely with industry, and even, particularly in the UK and the Netherlands, to shed staff.

Table 3.3 How basic research figures in the national research effort (1981 or latest available figures)

Country	Basic research as % of total r & d in each sector					National basic research effort in natural sciences and engineering in each sector			
	Higher education	Govt.	Private non-profit	Business enterprises	All sectors	Higher education	Govt.	Private non-profit	Business enterprises
Austria	45	17	27	19	37	84	6	3	7
Belgium	na	na	na	na	na	na	na	na	na
Denmark	62	17	55	1	18	72	22	3	3
Finland	na	na	na	na	na	na	na	na	na
France	90	19	40	3	21	67	20	10	9
Germany	72	40	22	5	20	54	24	1	21
Greece	na	na	na	na	na	na	na	na	na
Ireland	57	6	31	3	14	56	25	0	18
Italy	52	25	0	1	13	54	37	0	9
Netherlands	na	22	22	13	na	na	na	na	na
Norway	53[a]	14[a]	23[a]	2[a]	20[a]	79[a]	15[a]	1[a]	6[a]
Portugal	37[a]	6[a]	30[a]	3[a]	12[a]	58[a]	33[a]	6[a]	3[a]
Spain	65[a]	33[a]	43[a]	3[a]	19[a]	79	15	1	6
Sweden	71	51	1	1	18	88	4	0	8
Switzerland	51	na	na	na	10	76	26	0	0
Turkey	na	na	na	na	na	na	na	na	na
UK	98	18	28	3	16	60	24	2	14
Yugoslavia	na	na	na	na	na	na	na	na	na

Source: OECD Data Bank, Paris

[a] includes social sciences and humanities.

Note: Basic research = experimental or theoretical work undertaken primarily to acquire new knowledge of the underlying foundations of phenomena and observable facts without any particular use in view.

In France, Germany and Italy the research networks often attract the country's best researchers and set a standard that university groups rarely aspire to. Nevertheless, there are drawbacks in too much isolation from university life: a shortage of fresh ideas; a lack of the stimulation provided by teaching; and the dangers of losing touch with developments elsewhere. In France and Italy the national networks support quite a lot of centres at universities in an attempt to combine the advantages of both worlds – the same is true in Spain. In Germany the national research council provides extra support for selected university groups under several schemes: for the moment the Max Planck institutes have eschewed formal links with universities.

For both structural and financial reasons, governments are likely to encourage better contacts between universities and research labs in future. Again this involvement is a double-edged sword. Crudely applied, it can be used to cut funding indiscriminately; but if the scientists coordinate their efforts sensibly they may be able to secure protection for vital strategies and basic parts of research programmes.

This is particularly true where governments have become disenchanted with the progress made by scientists in solving the country's problems, as happened nearly all over Europe in the 1970s, and have responded by identifying priority areas where efforts are to be intensified. At first the objectives tended to be social: topics such as environment and health care were favourites. Here the partnerships were really between government agencies, research institutes and universities. Later, the emphasis shifted to industrially exploitable topics such as microelectronics and biotechnology. In these projects the idea is to encourage better links between industry and the basic researchers, often an even more complex business than intragovernmental enterprises.

In some countries, scientific organizations have seized the initiative on these priority programmes: examples are the research councils such as Comissión Asesora de Investigación Científica y Técnica in Spain and Consiglio Nazionale delle Ricerche in Italy. In Sweden much of the impetus comes from the National Board for Technical Development (STU). Britain's lack of focus for technical strategic planning has resulted in rather a different spectrum of initiatives, some being defined within the scientific community and others outside it. The outstanding exception is the Alvey programme to promote developments in the information technology industries, which is beginning to show signs of success in coordinating research in industry, government labs and universities. Germany has a sophisticated mechanism within government for planning such enterprises, and in recent years France has tried to mobilize its governmental structures to do a similar job, with some success.

The new emphasis on collaboration and coordination across the spectrum of industry/government university/research has highlighted other structural problems. Many of these can be subsumed under the heading of mobility. Bureaucratic reasons such as non-transferability of pensions and different salary scales often make it difficult for people to cross from one of these three domains in to another. Alternative part-time arrangements whereby an academic spends a day in an industrial lab or an industrial scientist teaches lectures and supervises at a university are also difficult to set up. Of more concern to basic research are the difficulties associated with spending short periods at universities or institutes overseas. Apart from financial and language problems, an issue of increasing importance is finding appropriate work for spouses.

Mobility of ideas is a slightly vaguer concept. One symptom of the difficulty here is failure to turn useful inventions into marketable products, which seems to be a peculiarly British failing. It may well be linked with additional factors, with difficulties in the relationships between institutions and rules about who can work there, and with industry's consistent reluctance to invest in its own r&d.

The (not so) gentle art of research

In describing a researcher's life in terms of the pressures imposed from outside, we have come a long way from the bright starry-eyed youngster determined to pit his wits against mother nature. At least some of that ambition must, of course, remain if an individual is to make good as a researcher. But it must be overlaid with some mastery of the mechanics of the academic world. As we have seen, research is increasingly a matter of teamwork, and the gift of being a team player, and eventually a team leader, is a valuable one.

Research that no one else knows about is near-worthless however good it is, so it also helps to be a good communicator, both orally (for conferences and seminars) and on paper (for articles in journals). In competitive fields one also needs the skills of a diplomat in trying to work out how much to give away about research in progress: too much, and a bright colleague will pick up a good scent; too little, and no one else will hint at his own results, which could have saved you much wasted time and effort.

In many cases practical skills are important too: working with animals or plants; manual dexterity in fitting, adjusting and adapting equipment. Where research groups are building complex innovative machines that cannot be bought, excellence at designing and engineering such instruments can be enough to guarantee a successful career. In less sophisticated projects, ingenuity can often help to alleviate the effects of temporary cash shortages. Talent at writing computer programs and handling statisics are skills that are rapidly becoming part of the essential armoury of the aspirant researcher. And as increasingly sophisticated techniques yield novel and exciting information, accepted borderlines between old disciplines vanish. Researchers with different backgrounds then have to join forces and learn something of each other's languages.

Research that either straddles the traditional subject disciplines or is unfamiliar and innovative work, often presents insuperable challenges to funding systems. The problem is bad enough when money is solicited from a university department or research committee: it is rather worse when application is made to a national research council with individual subject committees whose members often have enormous vested interests in the way resources are allocated.

Even in the scientific world, the individual who manages to master all or even most of these skills is a rare bird. The important question is what the individual can draw out of his or her portfolio of skills and abilities, adapted to meet the prevailing external constraints, in order to come up with new ideas, test them, and interpret the results. The notion of scientific creativity is a complex and controversial one: yet it is reasonably easy to say who possesses it and who does not. And in spite of many a long hour wasted in discussing the relationship between creativity and age, it is usually easy to spot an individual who has run out of steam. Eager and ambitious youngsters will be quick to recommend pensioning off and putting out to grass an unfortunate who has reached this point.

But there are useful jobs that such an individual can do if he is honest enough to accept his limitations (and a fallow period may not last for ever). He can concentrate more on teaching and devising new courses. He can serve on various committees and boards inside his university or in other forums where science is planned or discussed, often making a crucial difference to the success or failure of younger people and sometimes even in saving or salvaging a threatened research group or even a whole department.

Another option open to scientists in both 'active' and 'fallow' stages of research careers is to take more interest in the world outside the cloistered gates of the scientific community. Scientists of all ages are beginning to come forward to either talk or write about their work for a wider audience in magazines, radio and television, and in books. In the past the scientific community has discouraged this kind of activity and tolerated it only among a few outstanding elder statesmen. Now it is becoming more acceptable. This is partly because public opinion needs to be wooed in order to keep the cash flowing into research. Often the outside world needs to be reassured that what goes on behind the laboratory doors does not pose a threat to public health or moral sensibilities. In thinking through these issues for themselves, some scientists come to the conclusion that a particular type of research does constitute such a threat: research on nuclear weapons is one example, unnecessary experiments on animals is another. They may choose to keep their opinions to themselves or join with lay campaigners to change things.

Scientists with outstanding track records are often elected to national or local academies. Apart from the prestige attached to such elections, fellows often have a direct say in planning research. The fellows may also be called upon by government, formally or informally, for advice. Such outstanding scientists may become quite involved with giving advice on this basis or in taking part as experts in public enquiries on matters of general concern. Disillusionment and frustration may set in when expert advice is not taken, but on the other hand public exposure can be exploited when it comes to airing important general issues concerning the scientific community. More generally, since science has become largely a public enterprise, researchers have come to see themselves and their work as an important part of the social system to be fought over and justified like any other. However, this healthy development is not yet complete: nor should the scientists agree to emerge fully from the academic cloister until the bureaucrats come to appreciate that science which is fully planned and programmed will very soon cease to be worth funding at all.

CHAPTER FOUR

Public perspectives of the scientific world

Everyone needs doctors

Of all the sundry faces of research, medical science is probably the one uppermost in the mind of the man on the Clapham omnibus (or Paris metro, or stuck in a Roman traffic jam). Probably the first 'scientist' the European encounters in his lifetime is a physician and his first unconscious gropings towards his image of a 'scientist' may well be connected with the medic's white coat and unfamiliar equipment, not to mention an impressive filing system, calm concentration and attention to detail. Could the contrast between the immediacy of the patient's pain and the apparently dispassionate touch of indifferent instruments be the source of the widespread perception of scientists as cold and detached?

Leaving such idle speculation aside, doctors do seem to be, as a group, the scientists most exposed to public approbation and censure. They are also often the best rewarded financially and among the most highly respected members of the community. Medicine, therefore, attracts many aspirants, but demand is usually set by what the state can afford to pay for health care. Over the last twenty years Europe has consistently overproduced doctors. This is an expensive luxury, for medical training is extremely costly and unemployed doctors can be a difficult social problem. For this reason medical training is providing an interesting test case in many countries of Europe. In Germany, for example, it is one of only a tiny group of subjects where the authorities apply a fixed limit on the number of students and the details of a selection procedure (an idea unfamiliar to the rest of the university system) are the subject of continuing controversy. In the UK selection procedures are the norm, but (at least until recently) manpower planning is not. Nonetheless, in medicine (and a small number of related subjects) the state does lay down precise limits on the number of entrants.

Of course, not all doctors are researchers. Nevertheless, the intellectual world of medicine is a rapidly changing one, and patients expect their practitioners to have the latest results at their fingertips, or at least to know someone who does. Research in medicine does come through to the 'consumer' fairly quickly and efficiently in Europe, although of course standards vary a great deal. This is partly because the institutional framework is sound: in the past twenty years there has been much capital investment in hospitals. In big cities especially, the main hospital will also be a medical school and a research centre where students, non-medically qualified researchers, such as biochemists, and practising clinicians regularly come into contact. Within the limits of time and money, these prove to be excellent sites for research, particularly the testing of new approaches to treatment. Sometimes even poor states are willing to make larger investments in health care: and their medical researchers can often make international reputations where their counterparts in the physical sciences lag well behind. Spain is a good example of this.

Modern hospitals need to maintain a whole battery of scientific support services. These include laboratories for biochemical tests of many sorts, and also, increasingly over recent years, medical physics departments that supervise diagnostic techniques and treatments based on X-rays, radioactive materials and ultrasound. A recent newcomer on the scene is a rather complex physical technique called nuclear magnetic resonance. Much medical research today concerns the testing and improvement of this type of equipment – work which involves an increasing number of physicists and electronics engineers in medicine. These techniques, in spite of their potential risks and high costs, are generally welcomed by doctors and enthusiastically accepted by patients. Often groups of local citizens will actively campaign for a hospital to have a particular piece of equipment, either by collecting money themselves or by putting pressure on the appropriate funding agency.

There are some groups who protest against high tech in medicine. They say its expense denies simpler treatments that would benefit more people in the long run; that it forms part of the state's apparatus for social control; and that the doctors use it to reinforce their view of the patient as a passive mechanism with no say over his own destiny. But these critics remain on the fringe.

That is not to say that medical research does not inspire any public controversy. The widespread and sometimes not strictly necessary use of animals in experiments has led to public demonstrations, sometimes violent. So august a body as the Council of Europe has highlighted the problem and brought together much factual information and comment in an effort to reduce the scale of such work. Another active controversy surrounds the science of *in vitro* fertilization, a technique now beginning to become available in major European hospitals. Everyone feels they have the right to comment on when life begins, and emotional and philosophical issues soon become inextricably interwoven with scientific 'facts'.

Much basic science underlies the mainly patient-related research done in hospitals. Biochemistry, biophysics, genetics, immunology, epidemiology: all these topics are pursued in university departments or research institutes. Many of them have received a boost recently because of the industrial potential of biotechnology. This has to some extent counteracted the general decline in funding for basic research. In some areas, such as determination of molecular structures of important biomolecules, there is often little to distinguish research in a university laboratory or public institute from that done within the research department of a pharmaceutical company (except that the latter is more generously funded). Much greater controversy surrounds another aspect of research in the drug industry: the testing of drugs and monitoring their use, with a view to identifying and limiting unwanted side effects. Drug companies come in for periodic vilification for concealing research results that would cast doubt on their products.

There are some widespread cavils about failures of communication between doctors and patients, the doctor's lack of concern with mental as well as physical problems, and overuse of prescription drugs. Nevertheless the medical profession, including research, is usually credited with having the interests of patients at heart. Some doctors indeed take their concern outside the strictly professional arena. An example is the various medical organizations that publicize the possible effects of nuclear weapons and campaign against their construction and use.

Food research: often ignored when most successful

Once life itself is assumed, the next basic necessity is to gather resources to support it. The most important of these is food: other demands on the living world include raw materials such as wood, cotton, wool, leather. Expertise in exploiting such products has been developing since the dawn of recorded time, and its practitioners are generally considered to be craftsmen rather than technocrats. The idea of applying the scientific method to improving agriculture has arrived rather late on the scene, and made a relatively small impact on the concept of husbandry. However large or small a particular holding, the farmer maintains control over the processes and activities that take place there, and insofar as he needs technical advice he will seek help from outside agencies rather than employ his own experts. (Where agriculture is a state enterprise, as in Turkey or Yugoslavia, the situation is somewhat different.)

Since the Second World War governments in all the European countries have responded to this need to provide technical back-up for their indigenous agriculture. All our eighteen countries have networks of laboratories where scientists maintain and develop stores of knowledge about particular crops and animals. Almost invariably these are funded by government and staffed by civil servants, often coming under the jurisdiction of agriculture ministries. In the larger countries there may be two networks, one with the general objective of providing advice to farmers, and the other with more emphasis on research and development. Usually, however, it is extremely difficult to separate the two, since research topics often arise from specific local problems.

That is not to say that the practice and productivity of agriculture have not been radically transformed by scientific and technical advances. In a sense agricultural science in Europe is becoming a victim of its own success. There is more than enough food in Europe to feed the population; agriculture employs fewer people each year, and the lower the proportion of GDP provided by agriculture, the more economically advanced a country is considered to be.

This is the background behind the lack of spectacular changes in the scale of spending on agricultural science in Europe during the 1970s. In some ways it makes agriculture a particularly vulnerable sector for public spending cuts in r&d, though the sheer numbers of farmers combined with the vital importance of food could become a powerful lobby in most countries if support services reach a seriously low level. And there are still places where agriculture needs to become more efficient; Ireland and Denmark devote a particularly high proportion of r&d spending to agriculture for this reason. In the Netherlands spending is still fairly high although most of the efficiency savings have probably now been achieved. The countries around the Mediterranean tend to be the poorest and most dependent on agriculture: in some places there are attempts at exploiting local advantages, for example Spain and Italy are looking carefully at the potential of agriculture.

Meanwhile there are new challenges to be met. Rapidly emerging as a significant threat to several types of agriculture are environmental hazards such as acid rain and other toxic waste products of civilization. Sometimes the boot is on the other foot: farmers are blamed for damaging natural habitats, polluting the atmosphere and causing health hazards, for example, by burning stubble. Often it is the more 'scientific' tools of the farmer – such as fertilizers, weedkillers and growth-promoting chemicals added to animal feeds that are identified as health hazards to humans and other animals. Arguments about the quality of food have also become rather jumbled with moral and aesthetic arguments against factory farming techniques and the cruelty they involve. People who actually alter their eating habits for such reasons are still few and far between.

Europe's citizens, particularly in the more developed countries, are beginning to change their eating habits for a different reason: because of the purported links between obesity, consumption of saturated fats and heart disease. In spite of the heated controversy generated over the interpretation of experimental results in this area, national governments are beginning to commit themselves to advising their citizens to take more exercise and reduce their consumption of saturated fats. Research into such links has been a national priority in Sweden, for example, since 1982.

Such concerns may well influence trends in the food packaging and food processing industries. These are far more akin than farming to manufacturing industry in general in that they can easily be centralized and mechanized. As might be expected, r&d, particularly in the form of product and process development and testing, can play a more important role. Food industry interests are increasingly using scientific research, mainly medical, in propaganda wars between such formidable adversaries as butter and margarine makers. The outcome of such battles may well affect the health of every citizen, but the very size of the interests at stake make it almost impossible to be sure of a fair outcome.

In the richer countries particularly, foodstuffs packaged and precooked or frozen form an increasingly larger part of the diet, and it is often difficult to tell exactly what has gone into a pork pie or an ice cream dessert. Health experts warn that processed food often contains large amounts of saturated fat, not to mention synthetic colourings and preservatives that could be hazardous. Food manufacturers are beginning to exploit these concerns by introducing special product lines advertised as low in calories, sugar, salt or saturated fat, or possibly even free of preservatives. Products boasting high fibre content are also making their way onto the market, and wholemeal bread in one form or another is no longer just for 'cranks' but available in many high street bakeries and supermarkets.

While trying to cope at home with diseases of affluence, many European countries spend at least some of their r&d resources in helping developing countries with very difficult problems: developing suitable crops and fitting them in to some viable microeconomy. Some of this work is in the hands of charities and international agencies. More commonly its expense makes it expedient for governments to demand some political kudos in return, which comes more readily from a bilateral or national programme, often favouring countries where there are historical links as in the case of ex-colonies. Such aid can also be in the form of training or collaborative research for non-European nationals based either in their home countries or at institutions in Europe. Now that some underdeveloped countries are rich, exporting expertise can in some circumstances be turned into a financially profitable business too.

Science for defence – and offence

When human beings can feel relatively sure about perpetuating their own lives it never seems to be long before some of them at least turn their attention to taking away those of others. Scientists have been involved in this from Thales onward, and even when there was no one to explain why weapons worked, there were surely those prepared to show how. For the need to subjugate one's neighbours, take their goods or avenge slights, often seems to be a more pointed and urgent objective – and one justifying a greater intensity of personal or national investment – than any other. The threatened party's natural urge for self-defence obviously escalates the process.

No honest scientist – or citizen – can deny the strong impetus such aims and investments have given to science and technology at many turning points in history. In our own time 'r&d: objective defence' (being civilized we prefer to think of ourselves as defenders rather than aggressors) has been the context of many important breakthroughs in our understanding of and control over the natural world, particularly in the physical sciences. It has also changed the public view of how scientists work. After the development of radar and the breakneck construction of the atomic bomb, there is now no denying the view that throwing money at a problem can yield results, though the range of sensible application of such a tactic can still be debated. And in the wake of Hiroshima and Nagasaki, the scientific community cannot continue to parade either an unworldly altruism or a detachment from the needs and demands of the state.

The experience of the Second World War showed, however, that only the biggest nations could afford to stay ahead in the weapons research game. Indeed it has well suited the superpowers, both economically and politically, to play the game this way. In many ways, then, the pressure is off the countries of Western Europe, particularly members of NATO, and many of the smaller countries get along quite happily with hardly any investment in defence r&d, as, incidentally, does Japan. The Allies disbarred Germany from carrying out defence r&d until the formation of the Republic in 1950: it has never caught up. France has withdrawn its troops from the NATO military command structure: like non-member Sweden it continues to carry out its own defence r&d. The UK still invests heavily in defence r&d, although it is an active member of NATO and contains many American bases and a growing volume of sophisticated US weaponry. In Britain (as in the US) the efforts to win the Second World War left a large chunk of industry dependent on the state for subsidies (including funding for r&d) and for orders. In the UK this cycle of dependence has not yet been broken and the military industrial complex is less an outgrowth of a state with a desperate lust for power and violence and more a (not altogether successful) effort to keep a fair number of people in jobs by supplying warring nations as far away as possible with aircraft and conventional weapons of medium sophistication.

That said, in the US and the UK the sheer scale of defence funding for r&d has provided 'fat' funding for basic science with actual or at least potential civil spin-off, at a time when basic science in the civil sector has been under considerable pressure to cut spending. Some of this investment is now being recouped, in the US by the electronics industry and in the UK through the participation of defence laboratories in civil r&d programmes. The same is true of computer hardware (in the US) and software (a speciality for the UK).

During the Second World War the scientists of free Europe rallied to offer their services to the allied effort and this was almost universally considered the natural and patriotic course of action. Yet today many young people wish to avoid defence r&d at almost any cost. Obviously they are put off by the distastefulness of using their skills to develop agents of death, whether the effect is brought about by physical or more recently chemical and biological means. But there is another disincentive. There is an artificial barrier placed between defence scientists and their colleagues in the civil sector by the need to comply with security regulations, and in general to avoid any kind of political or social involvement that is in any way related to their work. They are therefore in no position to form a counterweight to the increasingly vociferous groups of academics in Europe who, like representatives of many other professional groups, work to oppose the very existence of certain types of weapons. The scientists among them, from climatologists to geologists to biophysicists to doctors, apply their assorted expertise to assessing the global consequences, say, of nuclear war.

Before the 1940s the objective that came closest to uniting scientists was their collective mission to provide a materially improved and more democratic life for humanity at large. Now that aim is too threadbare to merit anything more than occasional fond memories. For many scientists its only replacement has been a sense of collective guilt and responsibility about the changes science has and could in the future unleash on the world and today this is the issue most likely to prompt one of the rare collective public statements made by national or scientific organizations. Meanwhile, the public must look on with some bafflement at a community of which one part claims that its professional ethos gives it a special right to deplore, condemn and outlaw the work carried out proudly by other scientists under the same (or a very similar) code of professional ethics. On the other hand, most members of the public are sensible enough to realize that scientists have no more special hold over governments than any other group: a fact that the scientists themselves have been slower than most to grasp.

The dream of cheap energy and the nightmare of too little work

The concept of energy took scientists several hundred years to get to grips with. Once they did, it very soon transformed European society completely as the harnessing of energy for manufacture drew thousands away from the land and into the cities to find work in mills and factories. It took another two centuries or so to discover that energy might be controllable, but it would not necessarily be available. Warning signs were already perceptible in the 1960s, but it took the oil crisis of 1973 to drive home the message that the Western world could never again rely on a plentiful supply of cheap energy.

Thanks partly to nuclear power programmes and discoveries of offshore oil and gas, Western Europe's production of energy has increased steadily since 1950, but its demand for energy has increased much faster. In 1950 Western Europe produced 88 per cent of its total energy consumption: by 1978 it needed to import just over half (54 per cent) of total consumption, though by 1980 the proportion had fallen just below the halfway mark (47 per cent).

The picture varies from country to country of course. Norway is a net exporter of energy and so profits from the high prices: a situation which is likely to continue for some time. The Norwegian government spends little on energy r&d – it even plans to insist that oil companies base at least some r&d locally and also contribute to improving the nation's basic research effort. The Netherlands is a small net exporter of energy, but this is unlikely to last long: spending on energy r&d has fallen since 1970. The UK is relatively well off, its energy production is equivalent to about 90 per cent of internal consumption, though again exploitation of natural oil and gas will pass its peak in the late 1980s.

Elsewhere the situation is generally gloomy. Italy has virtually no natural resources of energy and Germany is also heavily dependent on imports. It's not surprising then that both governments spend over 20 per cent of their r&d outlays on energy r&d. In Italy over 80 per cent still goes on nuclear forms of energy, while in Germany the proportion is nearer 70 per cent.

France also has few natural energy resources, but spends rather less on r&d. It has, nevertheless, successfully executed an ambitious nuclear power programme which, along with imports of gas from the Netherlands, Algeria and the USSR, will reduce its dependence on oil imports. Sweden has adopted an almost diametrically opposite approach: popular opinion has led to a brake on the building of nuclear power stations after 1990, and over half of energy r&d is now non-nuclear, with a serious effort going into energy conservation, especially in buildings. Austria and Denmark, also rather short on natural resources, have completely forsworn nuclear programmes for the moment.

Public opinion about the dangers of nuclear power (along with downward revisions of future energy demand) have limited the size of nuclear programmes almost everywhere. The substantial number of scientists needed to develop, build and maintain power stations, not to mention those working on the disposal of nuclear wastes, find themselves in a similar position to their colleagues working in the defence world. Particularly in the UK, where up to now at least indigenous industry has built the power stations, there is a powerful lobby to proceed with programmes even when risks seem high and need low. The scientists are constrained in one way or another from 'whistle-blowing' even when they think public safety is in question.

Of the poorer countries, Yugoslavia is relatively well off for natural resources while Spain has already developed a fairly sophisticated policy for energy and a matching r&d programme that includes research into photovoltaics, hydroelectricity, wind power and agroenergy. Portugal, Greece and Ireland, short of natural resources but with as yet no great energy demand from industry, have so far put little money into energy r&d.

Europe's energy r&d efforts have not increased nearly as fast as those of the US or Japan since the oil crisis of 1973. Nonetheless, the energy question has united Europe in a common goal more than any other, with the possible exception of space. It is not surprising then that collaborative r&d and particularly that sponsored through the EC has concentrated particularly on energy, and especially on the nuclear option. The usefulness of these programmes has been questioned, though Europe's demonstration project for thermonuclear fusion, the Joint European Torus at Culham in the UK, is well respected.

But concerns about energy now seem to have taken second place to prospects for employment or, to use another term shared with the physicist, work. In the early 1980s work seems to be another rapidly diminishing commodity in Europe. Even Europe's healthier economies are set to live for at least another five years with millions of active able-bodied citizens who produce nothing and merely consume the bare essentials of life. Two decades of materialism have turned the European worker into an expensive commodity, one that is often pricing itself out of the market. Automation may require even larger capital investment, but it can be offset against long-term and continuous recurrent outgoings on personnel, where costing has to include state overheads such as national insurance, expensive legal obligations such as maternity leave and the ultimate resort of redundancy pay. On the other hand, the unemployed individual is also a drain on the country's economy and industry will have to pay for him, albeit indirectly.

Attitudes to this dilemma vary widely in Europe, and the diversity is cultural as well as political. In Sweden unemployment is low because the state sponsors special work schemes. Sweden also has a state-funded institute to study aspects of work and a national r&d priority is to look at effects of and alternatives to unemployment. The Netherlands is also keen on this type of socioeconomic research but seems to have had little success in relieving the symptoms.

In spite of these efforts no European country seems to have adopted one of the most obvious tactics in the war against unemployment: sharing jobs by reducing the number of hours in the working week. Some studies show that younger Europeans are becoming less materialistic, but it will probably be a long time before unions and employers can agree about how much people would be paid for less work.

The dream – and the reality

In the last two decades, then, the European social contract with science has considerably changed in character. The economic successes of the 1960s prompted almost boundless optimism that Europe would at least be able to harness science to raising standards of nutrition, health, transport and communications. New science-based technologies would be harnessed to provide the necessary financial growth, and science-based approaches to social planning would help to distribute the pickings with due regard to the needs of young, old, weak and inadequate. The darker side of the new technology, such as the military-industrial complex and environmental pollution, seemed relatively minor and short-term problems.

Against this background, it made sense for European states to invest massively in producing citizens who would be capable, physically and intellectually, of acquiring a range of knowledge and skills and applying them – hence the expansion of education at all levels with a new emphasis on the importance of the sciences. Some of the brightest would find work in productive industry, but most would go to populate the knowledge factories and operative arms of the state in universities or government institutes of one sort or another. So began the growth of research. Science was expected to earn its keep indirectly as a servant of the state.

The 1970s proved a disappointment in three ways. Firstly, it showed that the new prosperity was extremely fragile and that without it the state could hardly afford to fuel its basic necessities, still less to invest heavily in future changes and growth. Secondly, it showed that there was no simple or short-term pay-off for state investments in science and technology: Italy and Germany invested far less in education and research in the 1960s than Britain and France, yet their economies grew much faster. Thirdly, the worms in the scientific apple showed a distinct resilience to short-term treatments and, what was more, a highly educated generation was becoming all too aware of them. Health risks from fertilizers, weedkillers, lead in petrol, hazardous chemicals and noise in factories, and nuclear power stations were all subjects for protest. In the minds of a growing and vociferous minority, the state's hold over science threatened to turn from a democratic instrument of benevolence to a sinister tool of manipulation and exploitation.

In the early 1980s the relative poverty of the state has weakened science's absolute right to resources, though the state cannot withdraw so easily from its responsibilities as an educator. A vague collective entity called industry is now thought to be a far more important customer for highly educated people than the state, and the putative needs of this entity are beginning to play a more important part in planning the education of all, including the brightest.

Up to now the education of the most able has been based on a set of ideas that are inextricably woven into European thought patterns. Vocational training including craft and technical skills has been widely available for the less academically gifted, but intellectual ability has been rated more highly and its possessors indulged with considerable freedom of access to and choice in often very expensive forms of higher education and training. Teachers at all levels have striven to maintain traditions of the value of knowledge for its own sake, and of science as applied curiosity in intellectual rather than a practical sense. Physical skills and considerations of material usefulness have been consistently played down. For the sake of simplicity I propose to take my life in my hands, throw caution to the winds and call this the 'European scientific ethos'. Society has accepted self-selection as teachers by people who subscribe to such values. And so in successive generations they become more and more firmly enshrined in the education system.

What do I mean by the 'European scientific ethos'? While I feel rather unqualified to develop this idea, being by profession neither a scientist nor a historian of ideas, it seems to me to be so central to the theme of this book that it would be cowardly for me to shirk at least a tentative elucidation of the idea.

Let me enumerate a number of relevant themes. A primary element seems to be the opportunity for people to develop their natural curiosity about the world around them, with enough confidence and self regard to trust their perceptions even when they differ from those of others. A certain detachment is also necessary: the natural philosopher must be able to subjugate his own immediate physical and emotional needs in order to consider and reflect. Patience is another essential quality, along with the strength of mind to maintain a belief that progress is possible in spite of frequent setbacks. And yet there must be a sufficient dose of scepticism and self-criticism to allow ideals to change in the light of experience.

In addition our enquirers must attempt to impose a pattern on their observations and experiences. He (or she!) can do this in a number of different ways. The most abstract is to relate events and phenomena by means of logic: a procedure for manipulating objects and relations. Some assume that the rules of the game are self-evident and will be acceptable to all thinkers. Others explicitly discuss and justify their particular tactics. Aristotle was perhaps the first thinker we know of to have developed a logic for scientific discussion in detail, though later on the use of deductive logic came to be more closely associated with mathematicians and geometers.

A less intellectually demanding way to impose pattern is to look for events that are always related closely in a time sequence – in other words to look for simple chains of cause and effect. The trick here is to pick out the relevant detail from the enormous number of possible facts and observations surrounding a particular sequence of events. It helps if the observer can stage and manipulate the events so he can get a better idea of which factors are relevant and which are merely incidental. Hence the idea of a controlled experiment.

Once the searcher after truth begins to take an active part in devising and performing experiments, his interests come closer to those of the craftsman whose expertise is precisely to dominate at least part of his environment by imposing his own sense of design and beauty on formless raw materials. Keen experimenters through the ages have sought out craftsmen in order to benefit from their skills: craftsmen, who have often improved their techniques by conducting informed experiments, have also gained insights and new ideas from such contacts.

Medical men usually need to combine both scientific and craft skills to be successful healers and investigators. They, and more recently their associates the physiologists and the biochemists, are faced with a paradox: to learn to cure they must often violate the flesh of human cadavers and live animals. The church initially fought the dissection of cadavers but soon gave way to the pressures of would-be anatomists aided and abetted by lawyers determined to find out how death had been brought about. The church had no problems at all with dissections of and experiments involving animals, since God had not endowed them with an immortal soul. In modern times, though, people are so uncertain about the soul, and indeed, about religion in general, that the clear-cut dividing line has become blurred. To such people it does not seem absurd to protest against experiments that unnecessarily inflict pain on animals, and they even resort to illegal and violent forms of protest.

A third approach is to look for pattern in space rather than time. There are those who proceed by listing a very large number of objects and making intelligent guesses, based on careful observation, about which characteristics might be useful for dividing them into classes. With the modern dominance of sciences that rely heavily on deduction of one sort or another, such 'stamp-collecting' activities have sometimes been despised; nevertheless they lie at the heart of such rigorous disciplines as astronomy and high energy particle physics.

A natural philosopher who applies any or all of these methods to topics which particularly interest him will not, if he is patient and determined, find it too difficult to develop new insights and approaches. The chances are that he will realize that there must be others who share and have shared his interests – and seek out their works, usually in written form. It seems natural that an aspirant researcher should read everything that has gone before and indeed that was Aristotle's method.

However, there comes a point in time at which such a procedure is no longer practical. And there are sciences, where skills as well as knowledge are imparted in which words and images on paper or stone cannot always tell all. Hence the need for a young enthusiast to seek out a teacher who can encapsulate and communicate what he believes to be worth knowing, doing and considering in order to build on what has gone before. And the teacher will be grateful not only for a captive audience that will carry his work into posterity, but also to share the tasks involved in making further progress. The idea of the unity of teaching and research has a long tradition: it was for example embodied in Aristotle's Lyceum with its ambitious research programme.

It was the need for such mutually beneficial transfers of knowledge and skill that led to the association of research with particular buildings that housed libraries, instruments, and lecture halls. Once the scientific enterprise is based at institutions, all sorts of other possibilities arise. Resources can be provided that transcend the means and abilities of the individual: libraries, instruments, and craftsmen (or rather technicians, to use the modern word). Experts can collaborate and exchange ideas; students can receive broad training and personal tuition.

But there is a price to be paid: such institutions usually require support from outside the circle of natural philosophers, so they have to perform some function that has meaning to the sponsor. It could be based on altruism, or a sense of duty or responsibility; equally it could be a function related to prowess in war or other forms of technical engineering, agriculture or medicine. At one time astrology and magic provided an equally good incentive, and the traditions of these two related attempts to predict and control the world have had close links with the development of what we now think of as the most rational of intellectual pursuits.

We can distinguish such institutes, which usually have specialized objectives, from universities, where the whole point is to teach anything and everything to students who have a fairly free choice of what they study. Individual university departments may boast substantial research efforts, and research institutes have often been situated at or attached to university faculties. Nevertheless, since the first universities grew up in twelfth century Europe, their primary role has been teaching; there is no such thing as a 'research university'. Academics have always been expected to teach a much wider group of students than they ever hoped might join them as seekers of truth or developers of new ways of thought.

Universities usually receive the bulk of their income in support of their teaching function, and any additional funds they need to pursue research often come from a wide spectrum of sources and in relatively small chunks. As a result they are fairly independent of direction from outside in devising their research programmes. They also have a reasonably good record of freedom of thought and conscience, a characteristic often associated with the idea that academics cannot be sacked except in the grossest of circumstances. But history has shown that such freedom can also result in stagnation, sometimes to a degree that would not be tolerated in an institute which had closer connections with the outside world.

Even so, many, perhaps most of the people we now revere as top scientific achievers have been trained and taught at universities, managing one way or another to find the time, space and resources to pursue the research for which they are remembered. Many also selected the pick of their students to build fine research teams and hand on their enthusiasm and expertise.

On the other hand, particularly in the early days of modern science, neither of these two types of organization proved to be suitable homes for many natural philosophers. This is particularly true of the many amateur scientists engaged in commerce, agriculture or manufacture who could not abandon family or business responsibilities. Many clerics, too, practised science as a hobby. Nowadays it is more difficult to make a significant contribution as an amateur scientist. On the other hand, there are far wider opportunities for those trained as scientists. Many would argue that the job opportunities attract those who in previous eras would never have become natural philosophers at all, and who regard their profession as just one of a number they could have chosen, rather than a special calling to seek out the truth of things. Many who are now described as 'scientists' are not in fact researchers, but rather those who have acquired technical skills that enable them to practice a particular competence.

Mutual respect and above all free communications between thinkers based anywhere in Europe, irrespective of paper credentials, financial and social standing, and religious beliefs, fostered the rise of science in Europe. For some centuries members of these 'invisible colleges' shared a common scholarly language: Latin. Often their elementary education – in the classical syllabus laid down by Boethius and revived by Charlemagne, shared many similarities. And many had reasonable opportunity to travel, especially when young, and visit those with similar interests.

The manner in which the business of the natural philosophers was conducted owed much to a common European culture. The ideals of Christianity – of piety, humility, value of, and respect for the individual and awe in the beauty of nature as a manifestation of God's grace to man – shine through classic texts of modern science. There are, of course, some less edifying aspects, such as acrimonious disputes over priority and some crushing critiques of colleagues' work.

The record of the various churches in promoting science has been mixed. At several crucial points in the history of science in Europe, organized religion has seen free thought as a threat, and reacted strongly to defend itself. On the other hand, there is much to be said on the credit side. Monasteries kept alive the light of learning in the middle ages, and it was monks who developed the ideas embodied in the earliest forms of education in Europe. It was largely those educated by the church who disseminated Greek and Arabic learning as manuscripts trickled through into Europe via Spain and Italy. And later on it was the church that took the initiative in education as the Jesuit colleges pioneered the teaching of modern science throughout Catholic Europe.

Religious ideals and aspirations have also helped to promote the pursuit of science for improving the human condition. More recently secular institutions such as the state have taken over this role almost completely. Nevertheless, making life easier for human beings has been an important part of the stated motivations of many scientists, particularly physicians. It is however a relatively new idea for specialists in other disciplines to have the direction of their work guided by such considerations. And the widespread pursuit of knowledge for profit or with war in mind has made it clear that the opposite can just as easily be the result. The moral value of knowledge and its associated power over the environment no longer has an obvious credit balance.

But since the age of Voltaire and Descartes it has become more difficult for scientists to reconcile inquiring and sceptical spirits with the ideological demands of formal religions. In the nineteenth century Darwin's theory of evolution make it well nigh impossible for scientists to make an honest and conscientious intellectual reconciliation between belief in a personal God and an openness to persuasion by scientific argument. It is unfashionable today for scientists to make a show of theistic belief. Nevertheless many scientists play an active part in church life in Protestant countries; and the Vatican runs an observatory and regularly arranges scientific conferences.

There are many other apparent contradictions, or perhaps we should say tensions, behind the creativity of the scientific enterprise in Europe. Natural philosophers have traditionally been loners, forswearing ordinary hobbies and pleasures in order to focus their energies on their researches. They have often failed to develop – or even despised – the social and empathetic skills that would ease collaboration and discussion. Until very recently it has not been necessary to collaborate in experiments; so this didn't matter too much. Certainly theorizing has usually been lonely work. But even the most independent researcher wanted to pass on his ideas and discoveries in written form and in teaching.

Recent developments have changed this somewhat. For all disciplines the conference, where oral presentations are made to one's peers, is a common mechanism of reporting one's own work and learning of other people's. Many academies have to teach large classes and also to spend a significant amount of time in administration and democratic decision making procedures in universities, and the latter tasks also accrue to senior scientists in academies and institutes.

But the change that represents perhaps the most serious challenge is the growing necessity to work in teams on complex experiments that use very sophisticated and expensive equipment and techniques. In particle physics experiments and also in many types of astronomy, the young researcher has to take on a very small part of a grand plan devised by much more senior research staff. This grand plan may determine the tasks of dozens or even hundreds of scientists over four or five years. Will the qualities of obedience and discipline required in such an enterprise be compatible with the quirky originality and flair assumed to be the mark of an original scientific thinker?

So far theorists have not had to contend with the problem to the same extent: no one has yet found a way of forming a 'group mind' to tackle the solution of an intractable equation (though more and more sophisticated jobs of this nature are being taken over by computers). The folk image of the shock-headed, absent-minded scientist who scribbles earth-shattering formulae on the backs of envelopes is still with us, strongly reinforced within living memory by the example of Albert Einstein. Up till quite recently scientists in many disciplines could be both theoretician and experimenter. Practical scientists are still often responsible for devising theories that they then test. Where they often need help is in expressing and working through the detailed mathematical implications of their ideas – hence the separate role of the theoretician, who must have a good training in mathematics and now too a good mastery of computing. So far this separation has been most evident in physics and chemistry. Now the same thing is happening in biology, which has reached the stage where some theoreticians use techniques akin to philosophy to help them interpret the strange results that genetics and molecular biology have combined to throw up, and to find a way of making progress in devising a coherent framework of theory. Until quite recently most parts of biology have been descriptive and qualitative: biologists have been able to do without all but the simplest mathematics. This is now changing rapidly. Biologists are becoming more numerate and also attracting professional mathematicians to contribute to their literature.

The beauty and symmetry of mathematical ideas and their

embodiments in nature have held an endless fascination for European scientists since the Italians came upon the mathematical treatises of the Arabs and Greeks. Mathematicians have been able to do without science, but very rarely has a scientific advance not been connected with some kind of new mathematical insight. Mathematics has also been closely associated with art and poetry, and it is when attracted by a new mathematical conceit that even cold-hearted scientists have become lyrical about the beauty of nature and the power of structure and pattern. Sometimes these conjectures acquire religious or even mystical over-tones, a throwback perhaps to the mysteries of the pagan and alchemical traditions that are intertwined with the rise of science. In some peculiar (even mysterious!) way these reflections satisfy some extremely deep human need and endow their begetters with almost ecstatic gratification. Often though, too great a fascination with a beautiful theory has held up a more powerful idea that fits the facts more exactly and hence has better predictive power. Nevertheless the primacy of theory and the search for deeper meaning is part, perhaps an indispensable part, of the European scientific ethos.

While the state was the major customer for graduates, industry was glad to pick up a smattering of high flyers trained with these ideals in mind, often to add prestige as well as skills to the company. But now this has all changed. There are far more graduates and so a much larger chunk of a company's key posts are filled by them. They also encompass a far wider range of intelligence and ability. And the state has fewer jobs to offer. In many countries in Europe, industry is beginning to be the major customer for graduates and very often it does not like the product.

To some extent industry can vote with its feet, leaving graduates jobless, but in the long run industry wants the talent that university study attracts. There are a number of things it can do to change the product: it can provide its own retraining (often expensive) or it can try to influence the kind of education the state provides, either by direct lobbying or by using its power over the market place to change the aspirations of young people.

Such influences have had substantial effects on education systems in the last decade, encouraging a change of emphasis towards a positive view of industry and its role in the economy, a higher value placed on understanding and manipulating objects rather than facts, and a more down-to-earth approach to choosing a career and aiming towards the necessary qualifications. Within limits this kind of approach can interact constructively with 'the European scientific ethos': basic principles and laws of science can be exemplified through descriptions of technological processes; mathematical ideas can be reinforced by the use of computers. But beyond a certain point conflict can arise. This is a very complex issue. I will limit myself to two gross generalizations which should be regarded as starting rather than finishing points of the discussion.

Firstly, some teachers object to the assumption that education of the individual is the same as the requisite training of consumers and producers: in other words they object to the encroachment of a materialist ideology on their own more idealistic approach to life and culture. Secondly, they argue that their job is to teach children basic ideas of science (for example) and the scientific method, including a critical approach to information and an understanding of logical deduction. Learning the details of specific technologies and the workings of industry can distract their efforts from laying this essential foundation. Too strong an emphasis on the former rather than the latter could, some would argue, erode that special quality of 'the European scientific ethos' whose erstwhile expression led to the birth of modern science itself

Resolving these tensions will play a major part in the development of education in Europe in the next century and in determining Europe's future in contributing to world culture and enterprise in the 21st century.

CHAPTER FIVE

Science: cornerstone of culture or foundation of wealth?

We have seen how the public perceives the practical fruits and activities of science. Its results have also radically changed our view of the world, particularly over the last century. Scientific theories such as Darwinian evolution, powerful mathematical structures such as relativity and quantum physics, and theoretically based techniques such as psychoanalysis, joined and threatened to displace such previously un-assailable competitors for human loyalty and attention as religion and nationalism. These currents of thought had provided and altered all aspects of life and culture. Gradually a similar influence came to be expected of the new ideology. The multiplicity of cultural spin-offs has been dazzling, but anyone who expected them to provide a clearer or more convincing view of the human endeavour has probably been sorely disappointed.

One of the crudest of these enterprises has been the attempt to turn disciplines such as philosophy, politics, theology, economics, sociology – even art – into 'sciences' with axioms, procedural rules and a battery of techniques. At least as far as the Western world is concerned, not one of these attempts has succeeded to the point where given measures can be guaranteed to produce a set of desired results.

Slightly gentler attempts at cooperation have, however, been extremely fruitful. At the purely technological level, computers have revolutionized the collection and processing of information of all kinds. Along with sound synthesis techniques, holography and lasers, they have made possible new forms of visual art and music. They have also made it possible to contemplate compiling enormous data banks about citizens and their activities. These could lead to better understanding of the aetiology of disease or other social problems; but the line between comprehension and unacceptable control may be a difficult one to identify. Less controversially, techniques based on scientific knowledge have helped archaeologists to discover and pursue ancient artefacts and to make increasingly accurate estimates of their age.

Scientific ideas and vocabulary have penetrated deep into philosophy. The use of consistent symbolisms for logical quantities and operations has probably not hastened the solution of general philosophical problems such as the nature of the soul, but it has at least established some ground rules about the type of statements that can and cannot follow from a particular set of axioms. Limitations on proofs, along with uncertainties shown to be inherent in physical processes, have incidentally sown doubt about the predictability of the world, an idea closely bound up with the scientific approach. Nevertheless, logic can help with hitherto intractably complex problems such as analysing the structure of human discourse.

Meanwhile, new brands of scientific mysticism have grown up, based largely on two sets of comparisons. The first is the similarity between elegant patterns generated by modern physics and the symbolisms of ancient religions. The second is between the conceptual difficulties of some aspects of modern physics – the relativity of time, the uncertainty principle – and the mysterious and sometimes contradictory tenets of some Eastern religions.

Such discussions often refer to a long tradition of closeness between scientists and mystics such as that embedded in the ancient astronomical priesthoods of Babylon or the long tradition of alchemy.

The roots of alchemy can be traced back to a corpus of writings in Greek, probably dating from the second century, which were ascribed to an almost certainly legendary figure called Hermes Trismegistus. Astronomy, medicine, sacred rites and magical formulas were all jumbled among the hundreds of manuscripts ascribed to this author. Later writers often drew on these works in forming their own world views. Until as late as the seventeenth century it was often difficult to distinguish between an alchemist and a natural philosopher, although both Christianity and Islam officially shunned magic and superstition. Sir Isaac Newton, in many ways the founder of modern science, is also paradoxically famous for the amount of time he spent on a serious study of alchemy and its links with theology.

Modern attempts to analyse the links between magic, alchemy and the roots of the scientific revolution make fascinating reading. That the tradition of discussing magic and mysticism in connection with science still persists seems strange to many thinkers, who consider it merely a branch of intellectual history. To others it seems very natural. Theoretical physicists, for example, sometimes find such ideas a fruitful source of inspiration and metaphor. Others would like to exploit such links to develop a more compassionate or 'life-enhancing' view of a universe that science, or so it seems to them, threatens to reduce to sheer mechanism.

As science has become a force to reckon with in modern society, practitioners of other disciplines have also applied their own techniques to study its principles and practices and practitioners. The philosophers are, perhaps, ahead of the game. The question of how we can know anything for example, is one that has puzzled natural philosophers for centuries, especially those we now think of as pioneers of science. More recently philosophy of science has become a subdiscipline in its own right. Modern philosophers of science seem to agree that scientists can 'know' the world in the sense that they can develop theories about how it works and apply them. Where they differ is in their descriptions of how theories are formulated and what makes scientists abandon one theory or set of theories for another.

One of the most famous names in the game is Sir Karl Popper. As secondary school teacher of mathematics and physics in his native Austria he wrote his first classic work on the philosophy of science, *the logic of scientific discovery*. This book launched his academic career in philosophy during which he wrote a long line of seminal works that span many branches of the subject from metaphysics to social and political commentary.

In this first major work, published in 1934, Popper rejected a common assumption of the time (still widely promulgated today) that science proceeds by induction, that is the passage from single or particular statements – about observations for example – to universal statements which may be construed as hypotheses or theories. Popper could find no logical basis for induction. He described an alternative procedure: to start by proposing universal statements with one indispensable property – that they could be proved wrong. If such hypotheses survived severe testing against facts or experimental results, then they grew in status and eventually became accepted as truth. Of course, such theories could never be absolutely proved: but the eternal possibility of falsifiability or refutation was an insurance policy against mistaking theory for dogma.

This is a reassuring position for the scientist – and many scientists like the new solidity Popper's approach appears to give to the output of their efforts. But for those who demand more from a philosophy of science, those for example who seek to develop some conceptual framework for the history of science, it is unsatisfying. In particular it fails to highlight the very intimate links between prevailing theories and the concepts on which they are based. These in turn will affect the nature of the new hypotheses that scientists will develop and the precise details of the way they choose to test them.

Thomas Kuhn, a physicist turned historian of science and philosopher, attempted to come to terms with these problems. In his *Structure of scientific revolutions*, published in 1962, he painted a less abstract picture of the growth of science, widening the focus from each individual advance of theory to that of a group of scientists all engaged in developing definitions and concepts and a whole range of theories that purported to link them. During some periods in the development of a discipline, Kuhn observed, a reasonably well-defined group of thinkers could agree at least on the ground rules for the formulation of concepts, theories and experiments to test them. This implicit area of agreement constitutes what Kuhn calls a paradigm, and the scientists are engaged on what Kuhn calls normal science.

Such science produces results whose significance can be more or less non-controversially interpreted within the paradigm. If this state of affairs were to persist for long, however, the work would become repetitive and of little subsequent interest, for the paradigm would be confirmed in all respects and there would be nothing more to discover. A more likely outcome is that as the scientists attempt to test more and more powerful theories within the paradigm, its internal weaknesses come into focus. Eventually some of the basic assumptions of the paradigm come under attack. As these attacks build up, a period of crisis or revolution ensues during which concepts are redefined and theories are formulated in a correspondingly new way. The alternative paradigm that results forms the basis for a new period of normal science, and so on.

In Kuhn's opinion, his outlook and Popper's do not radically conflict: it is largely a matter of a difference of perspective. Nevertheless, Hungarian philosopher Imré Lakatos felt it necessary to come up with a third picture that spelt out exactly how the falsification approach to testing hypotheses could bring about the growth of a discipline.

Lakatos expressed his ideas in the framework of research programmes. He strongly objected to the apparent arbitrariness and lack of laid-down procedures in Kuhn's description of science: he attempted to replace this with a well-defined methodology that is supposed to clarify exactly how scientists develop a theory, and thereby prove that their work proceeds along predictable and even necessary paths. In constructing their research programmes, Lakatos maintains, scientists choose a hard core of theory which, they agree, cannot be falsified. Around this hard core is a protective belt of auxiliary hypotheses which are invoked to bear the brunt of the attacks. In addition, the programme embodies a partially articulated set of suggestions or hints on how to modify and refine the protective belt. Lakatos further states criteria for deciding when the programme thus defined is progressing: for example, it must point towards a coherent course of future development, and it must occasionally result in the discovery of novel phenomena. Lakatos has applied his model to a number of episodes in the history of science, notably Newton's gravitational theory and Bohr's theory of the atom.

This brief outline may make the philosophy of science sound dull and irrelevant, and indeed there are many texts on the subject that are well nigh impenetrable to any but the specialist: scientists may find the purported descriptions of their activities and thought processes totally unrecognizable. Fortunately there is a joker in the pack who keeps his colleagues on their toes. Paul Feyerabend is a journalist turned philosopher who argues against any and all of the pretensions of science to a special place as a way of describing the world, as a driving force in society and, in particular, as a source of authority and dogma. Anarchy, unorthodoxy, humour, joy: all these are elements Feyerabend would like to be allowed to liberate science from the serious and central position that it now, he asserts, occupies in our society.

Is it a coincidence that the European philosophers tend to take a more rationalist and, dare one say, pompous view than their transatlantic colleagues? Whatever the ins and outs of this, European sociologists have not been slow to acknowledge Kuhn as a pioneer sociologist of science (though by no means the first of the great figures in the field) and develop his ideas through detailed studies of how individual sciences have grown and what structures underlie the various communities involved.

Sociologists of science produce works in a wide variety of styles. Some are essentially historical studies of a whole discipline, looking at the contributions of individuals, geographical or intellectual groups, and the interactions between them. External factors such as availability of funding, travel and political upheavals may also play a part. The participants' own views about his work and sometimes also his political or social attitudes may also enter into the discussion. Alternatively the sociologist may isolate one aspect − such as journal publication or refereeing − and look at what part this plays in the development of ideas.

When one expert has built up a satisfactory picture of many such processes he may attempt to describe the structure of the scientific enterprise as a whole. There is also a place for more theoretical discussions, sometimes involving lengthy analysis of specific examples which look at topics such as the devising of a particular experiment or the testing of a particular theory. Here the work of the sociologist sometimes comes quite close to or even overlaps with that of the philosopher.

For many sociologists such storytelling about science as a human activity suffices to meet their professional and personal aspirations. Others spread their net more widely, looking at the web of relationships by which the scientific enterprise is linked to other activities in society. One of the most pressing issues of the day, as we have seen many times, is the relationship (usually within a political unit) between resources devoted to science and technological innovation in industry and subsequent economic growth. Here the sociologist (or economist) may have unorthodox views to contribute. We have seen the kind of assumptions OECD made about this relationship in the 1960s and early 70s in formulating its guidance for member states. But in 1970 Michael Gibbons could sum up a study of the development of the transistor as follows:

> This case study suggests that the relation between science and technology is symbiotic rather than that technology is applied science, which seems to be the prevalent view . . . the important problem is . . . the mechanism whereby new concepts . . . diffuse into existing practice and stimulate not only technology but science itself.

Fourteen years later the discussion is couched in different terms, as we might expect from what we have already discovered about the development of science policy. The vocabulary is more sophisticated but the same idea underlies the discussion, again by Gibbons (and Gummett 1984):

> Science aspires, when it can, to the freedom of universities while technology usually evolves within the social framework of industry in general and the business enterprise in particular. But of course there are scientists in universities who have contributed to technological projects and, conversely, technologists who make contributions to the scientific literature. The upshot of all this is that the traditional language which distinguishes science clearly from technology is beginning to break down. When we attempt to distinguish between pure and applied science, between short-term versus long-term research and between curiosity-oriented and mission-oriented research and development we merely bring to light the cognitive, institutional and psychological dimensions of two closely related activities . . . the ideal of completely disinterested research, . . . is itself a product of the way science used to be (or at least how we thought it to be) in the eighteenth and nineteenth centuries and, alas, may be disappearing.

Politicians are just now beginning to realize the importance of pinning down such relationships more finely so they can devise ways of distributing resources for r&d most effectively, whatever the particular result they want to bring about. So sociologists of science who are prepared to address these issues are now following the more mainstream economists in the public and political arena.

A recent fashion is the quantitative assessment of scientific output, for example, by counting the score of a particular individual or institution in terms of the number of times the papers produced are cited by other scientists. This research often produces violent reactions from the scientists involved, but it can often yield vital insights. Two pioneers of the European science policy scene, John Irvine and Ben Martin, have used such studies to show that:

> areas of previously pure science are being transformed into strategic research . . . moreover this transformation is comparatively rapid – the time delay between publication of scientific results and their citation in patent applications is currently as little as one or two years in certain biological and electronics specialities.

Quantitative methods are currently joining the more traditional sources of advice and information in the scientific community, distinguished elder statesmen of science, and the views of the two groups, formulated as they are from rather different perspectives, do not always dovetail neatly. The sociologists can sometimes gain a neat advantage by making expert advice to government a subject of study in its own right. Such studies are based on interviews and statistics as well as more conventional sources such as memoir, autobiography and biography.

Such expert advice has concerned not only the pay-off from science but also wider issues such as energy policy, environmental pollution and industrial safety standards. Sociologists of science have also begun to provide external commentaries on these issues and the way decisions involving essentially technical factors are taken and implemented. They have studied, for example, the nature of protests by the public and investigations undertaken on its behalf. They have also looked at the roles played by the law, the state and other specialist groups such as doctors and civil servants.

There is often a rather narrow and blurred demarcation line between detached observers of this type of activity and those who write with a particular political perspective in mind. (Some would say that this is necessarily true of all sociologists; I think it is possible to make important distinctions at least of degree.) There is, for example, a substantial corpus of publications by scientists and sociologists of science who aim to develop a socialist critique of science, in the tradition, perhaps, of Bernal and his contemporaries. The best of these works (for example, *Science and Society* by Hilary and Steven Rose) have done much to inform and stimulate public debate.

For some groups of science watchers informing the public is the primary motivation of their work. This group includes the new and growing breed of science journalists and science writers. It also encompasses the scientists who for reasons discussed elsewhere want to promote a wider knowledge of science. Laying the foundations for a sophisticated public understanding of science is also the job of science teachers, whose work is also discussed elsewhere. It is worth mentioning here, though, the work of small bands of teachers who devise science courses that incorporate facts and analyses related to the social and political issues that surround science and technology. Until recently such courses have had a rather limited following. Now that governments are becoming interested in scientific literacy for all, they may become more popular as a tool for making science seem more relevant and interesting. Even this topic, though, is not without controversy. For there is a narrow borderline between constructive comment and inquiry and criticism that may challenge the intentions and implications of the state's involvement with science and technology.

The price of governmental patronage for science

Our excursion into science's interactions with culture has led us to concentrate on intellectual preoccupations that, while not exactly timeless, are certainly long term. We must now return to the more mundane and often shorter-term demands made on science by what in most European countries is its major patron: government.

In principle the government's role as patron allows it to exert very strict controls over what research and development is done. Nevertheless in Western Europe at least researchers in universities and institutes normally have a certain amount of freedom to choose interesting projects and pursue lines of investigation that seem promising. While individual situations vary enormously, those involved in fundamental research are generally less restrained than their counterparts working in laboratories set up to work closely with industries such as agriculture.

There are a number of reasons why governments should wish to finance fundamental research, but not to control it too rigidly. In an attempt to formulate the principles behind science policy for the Western world, a group of scientists convened by the OECD came up with the following rationale for a *laissez faire* approach:

> The starting point for this survey is our deep conviction that the well-being of and security of the peoples of the Member countries require a rapid, balanced and sustained growth in the strength and quality of scientific activity, that science can provide a dynamic and progressive element to contemporary society and that fundamental research is a creative force behind all scientific development.
>
> But in fundamental research. . . . the very notion of planning seems to be a contradiction. Experience shows that the great discoveries of science, which open up new lines of advancement of man's mind towards the unknown as well as leading to significant practical applications, have nearly always been made by individuals of out-standing ability and scientific intuition. It is universally agreed that such research leaders should be allowed and encouraged to follow the lines of their own genius, and that research constrained by prede-termined plans is frequently sterile. . . .

These circumstances clearly rule out any narrow approach to the selection and planning of research. In fact, it is often suggested that the policy of an enlightened government towards fundamental research can only be to provide and respect the environment of research so as to maximise its creativity, and finally to leave science to run its own affairs without interference.

While the OECD encouraged its member states to develop their fundamental research efforts and slightly change their focus, it is clear that development in this category was not its primary concern. Europe was seriously falling behind the US and even Japan not in fundamental research but in exploitation – technological and ultimately commercial – of that research. In some European countries the point got through better than in others. Germany and Sweden were, perhaps, the most enthusiastic takers, with both industry and government rapidly increasing their hitherto low investments in research. Less-advanced countries could not afford such high investments, but nevertheless tried to make the best of what they had by setting reasonably sensible structures for planning, often in line with OECD recommendations. In some countries such as Switzerland and the Netherlands governments followed national traditions of leaving industry to its own devices and concentrated on research designed to benefit the community at large. Institutional patterns of funding in the UK changed hardly at all. Nevertheless, it was in the UK that planners first began to work out how to marry up defined government objectives with existing structures for fundamental research.

Radical proposals for action along these lines were drafted in 1971 by Lord Rothschild, a distinguished scientist familiar with research in academia, government and industry. Rothschild proposed that 'applied r&d, that is r&d with a practical application as its objective, must be done on a customer-contractor basis': the customer, in most cases, being a government department, and the contractor a research council. He recommended that a quarter of the research councils' budgets should be transferred to government ministries to be spent in this way: in the case of agriculture the proportion was almost 80 per cent. The 'Rothschild principle' was eventually implemented, though in a slightly toned down form.

Another British study provided some new vocabulary for discussing these issues. In reviewing the work of the research council system as a whole, a working party led by Frederick Dainton distinguished three categories of science: Gummett (1980) summarizes them as follows:

a) *Tactical science* – the science and its application and development needed by departments of state and by industry to further their immediate executive or commercial functions.

b) *Strategic science* – the broad spread of more general scientific effort which is needed as a foundation for this tactical science. It is no less relevant in terms of practical objectives of the sort we have mentioned, but more wide ranging.

c) *Basic science* – research and training which have no specific application in view but which are necessary to ensure the advance of scientific knowledge and the maintenance of a crop of able scientists.

This report, published as an annex to the Rothschild document, achieved far less notoriety. The concept of strategic science, though, has made a lasting impact on the debate. For such work is vital in ensuring a healthy approach both to basic science and to its follow-through to exploitation. It is rather ironic then, that, as a recent report designed to review the workings of the Rothschild principle has pointed out, strategic science is at risk in Britain in the early 1980s, perhaps more at risk than almost anywhere else in developed Europe.

Strategic science

What is strategic science, or rather strategic research, as the phrase is more commonly used today? I want to describe a programme whose objectives and structures, as attributed by its organizers, come fairly close to bridging the gap between basic research and industry with a fairly substantial middle ground of interest to both sides. I refer to an outline of the programme by R. A. Schilperoort and R. R. van der Meer entitled 'The innovation-oriented programme on biotechnology (IOP-b) in the Netherlands'. (This document is unpublished but an edited version appears in *Biofutur*, May 1984, No. 24 p. 62.)

> The basic idea behind the IOP-b is to establish an r&d infrastructure for biotechnology that is optimally organized to achieve innovations (ie the frequent generation of new discoveries), and ensure their application in practice as soon as possible. It implies a reappreciation by the government of the importance of research and development for a productive and constructive industry.
>
> The IOP-b rests on two elements. One concerns the protection and stimulation of high quality basic research in the four scientific disciplines on which biotechnology relies. [Listed elsewhere as biochemistry, molecular genetics, microbiology and process technology]. It should be accepted that free development of basic research in these areas is essential for the generation of new disciplines in biotechnology. The development of new scientific principles and methodologies, which eventually turn out to have an important impact on industrial innovation, has occurred because of the freedom given to scientists to exploit their creativity and inquisitiveness. These have rarely been predictable.

The other element on which the IOP-b is based concerns bridging the gap between the scientific world and the industrial world so that new developments that could be of commercial interest will be tested and applied rapidly in practice. The framework of the IOP-b will have a stimulating impact on the conversion of results from basic research into applied research. It is obvious that these objectives can only be worked out effectively if the (biotechnological) scientific world embraces the opportunities offered by the IOP-b and thereby protects itself against the severe general cutbacks in budgets for scientific research now being experienced in the Netherlands. To safeguard funding for their basic research, scientists must be willing to address their work as far as possible to areas that are also of considerable value for the Dutch biotechnological industry. To create a bridge between itself and universities and insitutes, the Dutch industry, including agriculture and environmental protection services, must participate enthusiastically and actively and help to guide the scientists. Participation of several leading representatives of industry in the PLBB [the IOP-b's programme committee] should guarantee that this will occur.

So much for the ideology, noting in passing the golden opportunity offered by general cutbacks in scientific research to hold out the carrot of 'safeguarding funding for their basic research'.

Three other aspects of the planning deserve attention. The first is the impressive review of relevant work already in progress at universities, research institutes and in industry. This information has been essential in identifying topics where there is already deep research experience on the one hand, and, on the other product areas likely to be of particular economic significance because of particular natural resources or markets in the Netherlands. Such insights in turn have been used as pointers to suggest new directions for all the participants.

Secondly, the resources of the project (400 million Dutch florins between 1983 and 1988) have been strictly divided between three types of project. The first consists of basic research projects of high scientific quality:

primary financial aid should come from existing governmental money flows for basic research. Additional funding can be made available from IOP-b.

The projects are carried out at universities and institutes. Four 'accent' areas for

multidisciplinary and applications-oriented biotechnological research form the second type. These have more emphasis on methods, techniques and systems rather than basic knowledge, and they must have practical relevance for one of the appointed areas of biotechnological applications. Again, universities and institutes (with more emphasis on the latter) will host the projects. About half the projects funds will go on the first two categories. The rest will break up industrial support for 'integrated applied projects' where the initiative comes from industry itself:

> projects consist of both basic and applied research on a theme that is of interest with regard to the market the industry in question already occupies or is planning to exploit . . . industry will have to seek as its partners in the project those scientists who are qualified and willing to perform basic or applications oriented research that is in line with applied industrial research.

The third point of interest is that the programme's funds will also be needed to support the organization of seminars, workshops and symposia, invitations to foreign biotechnologists to give lectures, participation in international conferences, filing of patents development of culture collections, gene banks, data systems and even 'public relations-activities relating to Dutch biotechnology'.

Like many other such schemes, this programme was planned by a committee made up of academics, government scientists and industrialists. But a rather unusual feature was the involvement of a professional consultancy which has wide experience of advising government and other funding bodies on how to select projects to fund. Although it operates on a non-profit basis, it charges fees based on hours and days of work done. Working almost always on a multidisciplinary basis, its staff look at the organizational, economic, scientific and technological aspects of projects.

It may seem perverse to pick out a scheme in a small country when similar efforts are now gathering momentum in France, Italy, Germany and even, in a small way, in Britain. Smaller countries too, from Sweden to Spain, have their own versions, normally associated in one way or another with 'priority areas'.

Small countries are in some ways at an advantage in arranging such programmes. Obviously they cannot span as wide a range of projects or draw on such a diverse scientific or industrial community. But members of the respective communities tend to know each other well already and it is easier to gather information and select participants. Often the smaller countries are far more conscious of the need to develop a particular identity on the international scene and to keep up-to-date with what other countries are doing.

The Dutch example is also outstanding in its sophisticated approach to encouraging basic research within the framework of the programme. A concern to safeguard basic research to some extent has informed the drastic changes that are now occurring within the Dutch research system. But Dutch planners, like their counterparts all over Europe, have failed to crack the problem of how to ensure that the madcap scheme that does not fit into any particular framework still receives some support.

It is generally accepted that the best way of allowing for this possibility is to give each researcher a small amount of money to do what he likes with. As money for research (particularly in universities) dries up and a higher proportion of what is left is 'programmed', this opportunity becomes available to fewer and fewer.

The next best method of encouraging basic science, so the conventional wisdom goes, is to allow committees of scientists to select from applications according to criteria of scientific merit alone. Such peer review systems are the traditional *modus operandi* of research councils, both inside and outside Europe. Again, though, the trend is to restrict the funds available on this basis, or to pollute the peer review system by assigning priorities to certain topics for other than scientific reasons.

This process is almost inevitable because peer review is just not an adequate philosophy in a time of declining real budgets or even serious financial heart-searching. Nevertheless, strategic science and basic science will find it hard to live comfortably together until these problems have been satisfactorily addressed and resolved.

Putting over the scientist's point of view

Public knowledge (Ziman 1968) is about the internal workings of the scientific community and the crucial role of communication and consensus in the development of science. Up to now scientists have in general paid little attention to the state of public knowledge about their craft in the wider sense. For the scientist, especially at the peak of his creative life, research and its dissemination, among the scientific community brings far greater rewards than talking or writing a textbook.

With some notable exceptions – T. H. Huxley, Sir James Jeans, Sir Arthur Eddington, Erwin Schrödinger, Henri Poincaré, Santiago Ramon y Cajal come to mind – European scientists have not been keen to emerge from their ivory towers to try and put over to the general public the importance of their work and why it exercises such compulsion over their souls. Such enterprises have been discouraged – except for the greatest and the best – by the unspoken code of the craft, which fears rather than welcomes the prying eyes of the uninitiated.

This code has not basically changed, but a number of outside influences are making divulgation of scientific information for public consumption both desirable and expedient. An important element in this is the need to account for public monies spent and to keep before the taxpayer the importance of maintaining the flow. Fortunately the scientists who write or broadcast are not completely mercenary and they do manage to put over some of the fun and excitement important for another worthwhile objective; inspiring young people. In a high tech age, scientists, governments and industrialists generally agree on the need to encourage the brightest and the best to at least consider scientific or engineering careers. And scientists in Europe are beginning to play an increasing part in workshops and holiday activities for schoolchildren. Tapping the intellectual potential of groups who have traditionally played a smaller part in science – such as women – is another tactic here.

In the 1980s, however, a new element has entered the game. Recent developments in science have made it possible to envisage completely new ways of satisfying basic needs and of organizing modern industrial life. Robots, computers, artificial food, genetically cultured drugs are just the most obvious of these. It is not yet clear whether the populace of the twenty-first century are to be workless and mindless proles or highly sophisticated technocitizens, but at the moment it seems that governments are keen that their citizens should acquire at least some of the skills associated with the new technologies such as computing. So there is a trend towards establishing some kind of minimum standard of scientific literacy and understanding for a much larger part of the population than was hitherto considered necessary. The topics that would form part of such a programme are often the same or at least closely related to a state's strategic or priority areas of science and technology. Just as with strategic science itself, the motives for pursuing such topics are not purely scientific: they are tempered with economic and possibly social and cultural overtones. The 'European scientific ethos' could come to have a wider influence – or it could be obscured.

While the scientists are in general becoming keener to cooperate in efforts to popularize the scientific content of their work, they are still rather reluctant to talk about the way their own communities are organized. Apart from the traditions of the closed order, the scientists fear public scrutiny precisely because it may encourage interference with their hitherto almost complete control over their internal affairs, at least as far as fundamental research is concerned. As I mentioned above, the conventional wisdom (which should not always be mocked) is that such research cannot be planned and its supervision is best left to the scientists.

The problem is that in neglecting to discuss their affairs more widely the scientists are in grave danger of letting this point go by default. It is not one that is well understood outside the scientific community, and there is a lot of lost ground to be made up before the basic research lobby can enter into a sensible dialogue with European governments.

However quick they are to make up for lost time, the scientists will have to compromise to some extent. As I pointed out above, peer review is not an adequate strategy when times are hard. The development of other mechanisms – 'parliaments of science', grand national committees, quantitative assessments of 'outputs', using data from citation indices – is still in its infancy, but will not go away. The best chance for the scientists is to engage in a dialogue with the planners to make sure their views are sensibly formulated and put across cogently. After all, that is the way both science and democracy are supposed to work – though both, of course, have failed to live up to their ideals from time to time.

CHAPTER SIX

Science goes international

Table 6.1 Membership of European organisations, July 1985

	OECD	NATO	CERN	EMBO	ESO	ESA	ILL	NHO	ESF	Council of Europe	EC	Western summit
Austria	√		√	√	a				√	√		b
Belgium	√	√	√	√	√	√			√	√	√	b
Denmark	√	√	√	√	√	√		√	√	√	√	b
Finland	√								√			
France	√	c	√	√	√	√	√		√	√	√	√
Germany	√	√	√	√		√	√	√	√	√	√	√
Greece	√	√	√						√	√	√	b
Ireland	√					√			√	√	√	b
Italy	√	√	√	√		√			√	√	√	√
Netherlands	√	√	√	√	√				√	√	√	
Norway	√	√	√	d					√	√		
Portugal	√	√	√						√	√	√	b
Spain	√	√	√			√			√	√	√	b
Sweden	√		√	√	√	√		√	√	√		
Switzerland	√		√	√		√			√	√		
Turkey	√	√							√	√		
UK	√	√	√	√		√	√	√	√	√	√	√
Yugoslavia	d								√			

[a] observer.   [b] represented at the summit by the EEC.   [c] France is a member of the Atlantic Alliance but not of NATO's integrated military structure. It sends a full member to NATO's science committee.   [d] associate.

The first stage of postwar collaboration

Back in 1945 the scientific world was a much simpler place, and its aspirations rather freer of the complexities of profit and loss accounts. Nevertheless, the dropping of the atomic bomb tarnished both the public image of science and the scientists' images of themselves. A not insignificant factor in this was the lingering necessity for secrecy about some of the most exciting and central ideas of the new physics. Meanwhile, the politicians were keen to show that Europe could forget the past and move forward in unity. By regarding science as a purely cultural activity, following the lead of French Nobellist Louis Victor de Broglie in 1949, politicians and scientists alike could proceed quickly and with a minimum of controversy.

One of the results was the birth of the European Organization for Nuclear Research (CERN) in 1954 (three years before the Treaty of Rome founded the European Economic Community). CERN's convention provided for collaboration between the twelve member states (founder members were Belgium, Denmark, France, West Germany, Greece, Italy, Netherlands, Norway, Sweden, Switzerland, United Kingdom, Yugoslavia) in nuclear research of a pure scientific and fundamental character, excluding work concerning military requirements. All results, moreover, should be published in the open scientific literature.

By the late 1950s CERN's first particle accelerators, the synchron-cyclotron and the proton synchrotron, had been completed at CERN's site near Geneva, on the French-Swiss border. The laboratory soon became established as a centre for European research and acted as an important stimulus for nuclear physics in the smaller member countries. At the beginning, however, its scope in terms of cost and demands on manpower formed only a small part of the national effort in the larger countries, notably Britain and France. This began to change in the early 1960s, when discussions began for a new collaborative project, the super proton synchrotron. The scientists convened a new committee, the European Committee for Future Accelerators (ECFA), to specify what such a project would involve. Wranglings over siting and finance led to much acrimony, including Britain's temporary withdrawal from the project in 1968. But it was a British physicist, John Adams, who came up with a solution that eventually commanded the support of all the members (except Greece) – to site the SPS at the existing Geneva laboratory.

By the time CERN completed the SPS in 1970, there was only one European country that could afford to plan any serious work in particle physics in its own national laboratories. That was Germany, whose Deutsches Elektronen Synchroton laboratory at Hamburg had plans for PETRA. Just as the UK shut down its two accelerators NINA and NIMROD in the late 1970s, ECFA was contemplating the next big project at CERN: a Large Electron Positron. Agreement on this finally came in 1981, at the price of closing down some of CERN's other installations and reducing the running time on others so that the total CERN budget would remain constant from 1981–86. LEP is expected to begin work in late 1988 or early 1989.

In 1984 CERN boasted a total staff of just under 3500 and a budget of 701 million Swiss francs. Another 2500 university students from all over Europe use CERN, and some hundreds of fellows and students work there at any one time. There are many who would agree with a statement by French physicist Louis Leprince-Ringuet printed in a recent publicity brochure:

> CERN is the largest, finest and most modern research centre in Western Europe, as a European organisation CERN has helped the continent's laboratories compete with the most important laboratories in the United States and the Soviet Union . . . the organisation has also been responsible for fostering a common consciousness and a sense of unity amongst European scientists . . . the brain drain [presumably among nuclear physicists] has been halted and many of the best scientists from East and West now come to work with us.

CERN makes no claim to any application for the fruits of its research, but is proud of the way that its demanding contracts for equipment placed with European companies have helped to encourage technological advances and open up new markets. A survey published in 1975 indicated that suppliers of computers and precision electromechanical devices had done particularly well.

Nevertheless, CERN's enormous expense at a time of stagnating (at best) research budgets makes it a subject of continuing controversy. Britain's participation has recently been reviewed again (see pp 72, 163).

NATO muscles in on the act

Postwar Europe was also concerned with military as well as cultural alliance, and the wartime Allies enshrined their continued interdependence as a military unit in the North Atlantic Treaty, signed in 1949. By the mid 1950s the enlarged alliance recognized the need for wider cooperation, including that of promoting recruitment, training and employment of technical personnel including scientists, engineers and technicians.

Remarkably, NATO took a very broad view of the steps needed to encourage such activities and when its Science Committee was formed in 1958 its brief was to increase the effectiveness of national efforts through the pooling of scientific facilities and information and the sharing of tasks.

From the beginning the Science Committee, which has always included scientists with distinguished records in basic research, has supported collaboration and information exchange across the whole spectrum of science, with emphasis on the long-term.

NATO also decided that the whole question of the 'effectiveness of Western science' needed more thought, and in 1959 it set up a study group under the chairmanship of Louis Armand, president of the council of the French École Polytechnique. The 1960 report of the Armand committee proposed that

all western nations should have one or more science councils responsible for the support of fundamental and applied science and for the maintenance of quality and breadth of scientific education.

It also recommended that countries should aim to spend 0.2 per cent of GNP on basic research and 2.0 per cent of GNP on applied research and development. The Armand committee added a whole series of other measures to promote scientific and technical developments in universities and industry and international exchanges.

The NATO Science Committee had already devised its own tactics to promote such ends. Its first mode of action (which still accounts for more than half of its budget) was to set up science fellowships, to enable scientists and engineers in member countries to continue their research or training at

the most prestigious laboratories and institutions in other countries.

Later it began to sponsor advanced study institutes and grants for collaborative research, with some special areas designated for particular attention.

In 1973, the NATO Science Committee could report that

in a world which demonstrates a growing tendency toward rigid economic justification of efforts in science and technology, and even an animosity toward continuing basic research for knowledge, the science committee is a staunch supporter of the long-range value of pure research guided by individual ingenuity and curiosity.

Throughout the 1970s, the NATO Science Committee continued this apparently unlikely role of defending basic research. The early 1980s saw a number of new departures. One was the 'science for stability' pro gramme which began in 1981 and was intended to run for five years. The idea is to

> strengthen Greek, Portuguese and Turkish national scientific infrastructures by means of applied r&d projects.

The Science Committee got this programme off the ground, but from 1981 the bulk of the NATO funding will come from the NATO civil budget, though it is intended that the support (for international aspects of the work) should be more than matched by investments by national governments.

The 1980s also saw NATO's reentry onto the science policy scene with messages to member governments. It was the major sponsor of a workshop held in June 1981 on 'international mobility of scientists and engineers' and out of this workshop arose a message on international mobility on research. According to its own summary,

> the NATO Science Committee stresses the fundamental value of interactions between the different elements of the r&d system and its fear that artificial barriers will progressively grow up between the various sectors in the system, as well as between the various nations of the alliance. The Committee concludes by appealing to governments, funding and management authorities to support a policy of research mobility between nations and between sectors.

As if to set a good example, it set up a 'double jump' programme to fund fellowships and research projects that involve scientists from different sectors (government laboratories, universities and industry) in a number of countries. This began in 1982, the same year as the Science Committee came out with its second message, this time on research management and zero growth.

> The NATO Science Committee notes the fact that the present research system, which was built in a context of very rapid growth, is finding it very difficult to adapt to the abrupt stabilisation of its means . . . the present scientific structure will be seriously threatened unless some relatively moderate financial measures are rapidly put into practice. These include careful establishment of a balance between salaries and equipment expenditure, and reasonable financial contribution to procedures promoting international mobility.

The economists step in

In spite of considerable efforts in specialist areas, research efforts did not figure significantly in postwar economic development. The Organization for European Economic Cooperation (OEEC), the body that administered the Marshall Plan, opted to re-equip European industry with mainly traditional plant and machinery. In 1949 the OEEC set up a working party on scientific and technical information. In 1961 OEEC became the Organization for Economic and Cultural Development (OECD). Referring to the early 1950s, Scientific Affairs director, Alexander King, later commented,

> at that particular period of European reconstruction, when capital was exceedingly short, scientific research and even technological innovation had little to offer immediately.

Nevertheless, the OEEC foresaw that in the long run spending on r&d would have to increase substantially, perhaps growing out of the reach of smaller countries. It therefore attempted a few experiments in international collaboration. One was a European low-shaft blast furnace later taken over by the European Coal and Steel Community. The others were generating electricity from wind power and desalting of brackish water. Throughout the OEEC sought only a promotional role, wanting to hand over projects as soon as they had got off the ground. This was later to prove a difficult exercise.

Later on (though not in fact until 1958) the question of r&d personnel became a sufficiently important issue to merit its own OEEC working party. The scientists and educators who made up this group persuaded the OEEC council that it should actively stimulate member countries to increase the numbers and quality of scientists and engineers, and the council set up an office of Scientific and Technical Personnel to take on the job. The US (an associate member of OEEC) offered half the cash. OECD played an important part in planning the expansion of science education during the 1960s, particularly through the Mediterranean project, which drew in the economically most backward members: Greece, Italy, Portugal, Spain, Turkey and Yugoslavia.

In OECD's first year its secretary general set up an *ad hoc* Advisory Group on Science Policy. In a report published in 1965 it set out a philosophy of science policy, that, without much alteration, was to inform OECD's approach for the next decade or so:

> A nation needs a comprehensive and consistent policy for the support and advancement of science, because there are more opportunities to advance science and technology than there are resources to exploit them all . . . government authorities need guidance on how to allocate their funds and trained manpower . . . the purpose of a national policy for science is to provide such guidance.

How will this affect the scientists?

The scientist . . . has not only his age-old responsibility to guide his work according to his lights, but also the opportunity to cooperate with the educator, the economist and the political leader in deciding how science as a social asset can be furthered, and how a nation and the human community can best benefit from its fruits. Science, in a word, has become a public concern.

It adds:

The existence of a national science policy implies no abridgement of the scientist's autonomy in the conduct of research.

And what will it do for society?

In association with sound policies, [science and technology] can contribute essentially and increasingly to national safety, physical health, adequate nutrition, economic growth, improved living standards, and more leisure for the populations of the world.

What factors must be considered in formulating a national science policy? The report lists the following: manpower problems, including training and mobility; funding mechanisms such as research contracts, tax concessions and provision of expensive facilities; scientific communication; and the need for r&d statistics.

Provision for compilation of such data is an indispensable prerequisite to formulating an effective national policy for science.

It also notes

the danger that exclusive policy attention to urgent near-term problems will result in failure to maintain adequate financial and institutional support of basic research activity,

and it warns that

no failure could be better calculated to bring all scientific advance to a stop within a very few years . . . it becomes a primary concern of policy thinking to arrive at the appropriate sum for each nation . . . errors in this calculation should be allowed only on the generous side.

Finally, what needs to be done to formulate a country's science policy, and who exactly should do it? The report favours the idea of a national science office to formulate a national science policy and coordinate a country's various scientific activities. A third task – integrating science with a general policy – could also be done within such an office, though the OECD accepts that this could be done outside.

During the 1960s and early 1970s the OECD Committee for Science Policy, under the guidance of its leading lights Jean-Jacques Salomon and Alexander King, masterminded a series of very detailed reviews of national science policies. In the case of the larger countries these were mainly descriptive, but for smaller and particularly economically backward countries the reviews often contained frank comments about specific weaknesses and advice about the action needed to rectify them. As we have seen this advice was sometimes heeded.

A particular difficulty was the day-to-day vicissitudes of political upheavals, which would throw governments into turmoil at short notice, often upsetting the essentially long-term planning necessary for science policy.

The fickleness of governments was also an apparently insuperable barrier to the OECD's experiments in encouraging international projects.

> Governments, and their representatives on international bodies are generally impatient with regard to the development of many small technical projects, each of which appears unimportant and even trivial, although the economic importance of some of the problems attacked may be great.

said Alexander King in a seminar held in 1967. He pointed to the example of the OECD's 'barnacle' project on marine corrosion which 'may sound ridiculous to the layman, although such corrosion in fact costs our countries' shipping about three billion dollars a year'. He added ruefully,

> we have always been pressed, therefore, to withdraw from this kind of thing and leave the projects to sink or swim after about one or two years. We have in fact tried very hard to off-load such projects with rather little success.

Nevertheless, he reaffirmed the 'strong economic urge towards international cooperation', and concluded, 'there is, then, as yet no international or European research policy, only the need for one and some striving towards its initial conceptions.

In the late 1970s this gap was being filled in various ways; by bilateral agreements, by joint use of a number of international facilities, and in some rather specialized areas by European communities. But the OECD's interventions in science policy were declining in vigour. In the 1980s its role in the game is as a passive commentator and (very valuably) a collector of statistics. We shall consider later where the new foci of activity lie.

Scientists gradually follow the CERN example

The example of CERN was to prove a powerful force in internationalizing certain types of science in Europe. Even before the CERN convention was signed in 1954, discussions were under way for a European observatory. In spite of help from CERN planners, it was a whole decade before the European Southern Observatory (ESO) convention was signed in early 1964, and another thirteen before its first telescope started work at La Silla in Chile. A southern hemisphere site was chosen because the southern hemisphere sky had as yet received comparatively little attention. Another important factor in the choice of site was, of course, the good weather conditions and clear skies of an isolated site.

> While this may appear as a very slow start, it should be realised that optical astronomy in Europe was in relatively underdeveloped state, partly as a result of the unfavourable weather conditions . . .

ESO literature comments.

ESO's founder members were Belgium, Denmark, West Germany, France, the Netherlands and Sweden. Italy and Switzerland joined in the early 1980s. Today ESO's thirteen telescopes form the workhorses of much of European astronomy, particularly for the smaller countries which cannot afford their own facilities. Until 1981 ESO's European base was on the CERN site at Geneva, but now it has its own rather grand building at Garching near Munich in Germany.

Meanwhile Britain looked more to its Commonwealth and transatlantic connections, collaborating for example with Australia on the Anglo-Australian telescope at Siding Springs. Later it used another site at Mauna Kea, Hawaii, for several other installations for infrared and millimeter work rather than optical astronomy.

More recently it has redeemed itself as far as European connections are concerned, by initiating a multinational optical astronomy project based, not quite on continental Europe, but at least on Spanish territory, at La Palma in the Canary Islands. Britain's main partners in the project are Spain, Sweden and Denmark, with the Netherlands and Ireland as scientific partners. The Spaniards in particular are determined to take advantage of the choice of site to develop their own astronomical community. 'First light' at La Palma observatory was celebrated in early 1984.

The benefits of pooling resources in the biological sciences were not so clear. Nevertheless, the example of CERN was a compelling one. In 1962 molecular biologists John Kendrew and James Watson travelled from the Nobel Prize investitures in Stockholm to visit CERN. It was during this visit that ex-nuclear physicist Leo Szilard suggested that European governments should set up a similar laboratory for molecular biology. According to an article by John Tooze, Kendrew in particular:

> was deeply concerned that the initiative in molecular biology was by 1962 rapidly passing to the USA from Europe, where many of the early key discoveries had been made, and convinced that Europe could only play its accustomed role in the far reaching intellectual movement that molecular biology represented if the individual countries pooled at least some of their national resources in this field of research.

The European Molecular Biology Organization (EMBO) was formed the following autumn and 140 molecular biologists from Western Europe (and Israel) were nominated as members in 1964.

Until 1969 EMBO confined itself to funding fellowships and running courses and workshops, activities whose worthiness was beginning to be doubted by scientific bodies in member countries. But the plans for a European Molecular Biology Laboratory reawakened interest, for by this time the molecular biologists' demands for highly sophisticated equipment were becoming more ambitious and more justified by results. By 1972 the organization had agreed on a main site at Heidelberg with outstations at the Deutsches Elektronen Synchroton at Hamburg as a source of electromagnetic radiation including X-rays and the Institut Laue Langevin at Grenoble, as a source of neutrons. The main laboratory was completed at the end of 1977 and officially opened in 1978, with John Kendrew as its first director general until 1982, since when Lennart Philipson from Uppsala University in Sweden has taken over.

In 1983 a committee appointed by Britain's Medical Research Council drew up a detailed balance sheet of benefits and costs of national participation in EMBO. It noted that Britain's entry into EMBO had been largely a political decision. Nevertheless, it concluded that twenty years later there was a good scientific case for remaining, in spite of the expense (£1.3 million in 1983). On the plus side it recorded the facilities available at the two outstations which are not duplicated in the UK, and would be far more difficult to use without the EMBO stations. As for the central laboratory

> new and potentially important areas of science, not yet strongly represented in this country, are being exploited, and, by international collaboration, a critical mass – and a training nucleus – can be built in a way which would be impossible in any one country's domain.

But the EMBO is far from faultless: a comparison of costs shows that it spends far more money per scientist than Britain's prestigious research centre, the Laboratory for Molecular Biology in Cambridge. The Medical Research Council (MRC) review says that at present the laboratory lacks effective machinery either for those who provide the money to gain adequate information or the value for money its output represents or to allow them to influence the direction of its programmes. Nor is the intrinsic quality of the work, and the value of the science to the scientific community, subjected to the sort of rigorous and objective peer-review that is, in our view, an essential part of the process of accountability for publicly funded science.

This is exactly the sort of criticism that can easily be launched at any well-funded and prestigious laboratory (national as well as international) and more often than not it is justified. When European physicists came to consider their next big collaboration they were careful to avoid the problem as far as possible by setting up a central facility for university researchers rather than an independent laboratory. Thanks to the endeavours of Professors Heinz Maier-Leibnitz and Louis Néel, the Institut Laue Langevin (ILL) was founded in 1967 with an agreement between the French and German governments. Britain joined in 1973, just after the nuclear reactor at the heart of the ILL Laboratory in Grenoble began producing the first useful beams of neutrons for experiment in physics, chemistry and biology, having abandoned plans for its own national neutron source. Now the three countries each contribute one third of the annual cost, and are approximately equally represented among the scientific staff that keeps the machine running and supports the experimental groups.

In 1984 the ILL claimed with some justice to be 'the leading world centre for neutron investigations – that is, elastic and inelastic scattering of neutrons and fundamental physics experiments using neutrons as a primary beam'. It hosts about 850 experiments a year – about 70 per cent of the proposals submitted. These experiments yield about 500 publications annually.

Quality as well as quantity characterize the work done at ILL across a wide range of disciplines, a number of which have been opened up and developed almost entirely by European researchers. By the ealry 1980s, the Americans were becoming distinctly worried that they had lost the initiative. A review sponsored by the US Department of Energy (which runs many of America's neutron sources, which tend to be based on nuclear reactors) reports that the US made most progress up till 1970, but that most of the recent breakthroughs had been the result of work done at ILL. The Brinkman report called for greater investment in neutron sources in the US and better national planning to ensure that researchers would have access to the correct state-of-the-art machines.

Though ILL's useful life is far from over in the early 1980s, demand is growing for other types of neutron source for research. Strangely enough, there are no plans as yet to meet such demands on a European basis. This is partly because the French already have a new source near Paris, and Britain has invested in its own Spallation Neutron Source, with the

Germans too making a plan for a very similar (though technically slightly more advanced) source. It would be a pity if these projects could not become part of an international deal.

Researchers form their own European parliament

By the early 1970s it was high time for the scientists to think about a professional response to two major trends of the 1960s that were already beginning to impinge on their work.

Thanks to the painstaking work of the OECD, governments were developing their own science policies in terms of objectives as seen by society. In some countries this outlook was beginning to compete with the more intellectual approach of the scientist who regarded it as his traditional right to pursue ideas for their purely scientific interest. In most European countries the bodies most concerned with the interface between these two categories of scientific effort were the research councils, and not surprisingly the subject came up at a conference of the West European Science Research Councils at Aarhus in February 1972.

Brian Flowers, then chairman of the British Science Research Council, summarized the conference:

> The duties and roles of research councils are somewhere between the government and the scientists, somewhere between those who are responsible for scientific objectives and those who have to meet them. . . . our task can be described as that of trying to match the horizontal activities (the practice of physics and chemistry and biology and engineering and medicine in the universities and the research institutes) to the vertical needs of government, which are supposed to represent the requirements of society . . . for health, for transport, for defence, for education, for agriculture.

The second important trend was the increasing need for countries to pool their resources to pursue basic as well as applied science. So far this had been done on a largely *ad hoc* basis, but the time was ripe for an umbrella organization to nurture new ideas through the problematic path from conception to technical outline to acceptance by and breaking from national governments.

Broadly speaking these were the two pressures that led to the formation of the European Science Foundation (ESF) in 1974. There were, however, two other ideas that contributed to its birth and exercised an important influence on its self-image and hence its structure. The first was the idea of scholarship. According to Flowers, who was one of those who can take the most credit for the birth of ESF,

research generates new knowledge; scholarship assesses what the knowledge means and where it fits into the scheme of things; and teaching, of course, passes on that knowledge for other people to use.

As we shall see later on, the ESF has kept faith with the idea that it should promote work relevant to contemporary life and thought in Europe.

Not entirely unconnected with this idea was the second stimulus: a call from the Commission of the European Communities (CEC) for the formation of some kind of research council for the community itself to advise the Commission and the Council of Ministers about basic research in the Community. In the event the EC rather lost interest in basic research outside the social sciences until the very end of the 1970s, when the ESF came into its own as one (but certainly not the only) source of information and advice.

Much thought went into the structure and membership of the Foundation, which operates from a couple of floors of a cool and pleasant building (once a convent) on the banks of the ILL in Strasbourg. Its members are not states or individuals, but research councils and academies, usually those which have national responsibilities for promoting basic research and allocating resources. They are from eighteen different countries of western and central Europe, representing a much wider spread of culture and thought than the EC alone. Flowers (1979) writes,

> we are a *forum* within which our member organisations can discuss common policies, collaborative schemes and joint projects on a regular basis, and which can bring to bear when needed the full expertise and resources of the respective countries. This is Europe by consent rather than Europe by compulsion, or by directive as they have it in Brussels.

Within this framework the ESF is now associated with some dozens of research projects (including some training for research) across the natural, medical and social sciences and humanities. Five standing committees monitor the different disciplines: medical sciences; natural sciences; space science; humanities; and social sciences and if necessary set up special working groups to look at specific problems. They also generate ideas for additional activities: projects of scholarships or research that for good scientific reasons need to be done collaboratively across Europe. Once formulated, and passed by the ESF's Executive Council, such plans are put to the ESF's Assembly. This, the main decision making body of the ESF, meets once a year in Strasbourg. With eighty or so participants representing the forty-eight member organizations, this two-day meeting amounts to an impressive parliament of European science.

Proposers of a new 'additional activity' research programme make the case to the Assembly, whose members vote on its adoption. Actually this is usually a formality, any controversies have usually been hammered out within the inner cabinet of the Council. Additional activities are not funded by the ESF: proposers still have to persuade member organizations to come up with separate cash allocations.

What constitutes a genuine need for European collaboration? The ESF has found a wide variety of answers to this question. One of the earliest examples, which goes back well before the Foundation opened its doors, is the European Training Programme for Brain and Behaviour Research (ETP). The German network of research labs, the Max Planck Society, originally set this up in 1969, following an earlier initiative from OECD, and the ESF took it over as one of its first additional activities in 1976. The idea of the scheme is to

> encourage multidisciplinary and multinational collaboration among scientists working in the field of brain and behaviour and also to enable young research workers to travel to other laboratories to gain new experience and skills.

Hundreds of scientists have benefited from its activities.

By 1983 the ETP was the most costly of the ESF's additional activities. As well as running the three regular courses the ETP sponsored long and short-term fellowships, twinning grants, meeting grants and a repeat of a senior scientist training course introduced in 1982. All this cost nearly FF0.9 million, of which the largest share came from the UK, with France and Germany not far behind.

The very success of the ETP has caused the ESF some serious headaches. The ESF sees itself as a springboard for activities: it wants to avoid open-ended long-term commitments. Participating countries found it valuable enough to continue contributing, but no one would undertake to find a home for the administration and the programme's international scientific committee concluded that if the ESF were to withdraw from its involvement the programme would collapse. So the ESF reluctantly invented a new category of activity called an 'associated programme', stating that 'all overheads incurred in the management of the programme after the end of 1984 will be carried by the programme'.

When it comes to the social sciences Europe itself can be the laboratory. This is the case with the three major projects that come under the umbrella of the standing committee of the social sciences. Interdisciplinary research teams from fifteen countries are involved in the study of migration, the only ESF project in which the EC has shown a strong and continuing involvement. In fact the project received the special blessing of Professor Ralf Dahrendorf, who, while EC commissioner for education and culture, played a large part in the birth of the ESF.

After reviewing work already published on 'the human and cultural aspects of migrations in Western Europe' the ESF has organized meetings and published proceedings on 'migrant workers in metropolitan cities', 'cultural identity and structural marginalization of migrant workers', 'psycho-pathology of the transplantation of migrants' and the 'status of migrants' mother tongues'. The second phase of the project which focuses on the cultural identity (sense of belongingness) of second generation descendents of foreign workers is due to end in 1985 with final publications appearing in 1986/87.

Europe can also be the laboratory for projects in the natural sciences. A spectacular example of this is a project to survey the outer layers of rocks on the Earth's crust along a line from Scandinavia in the north to Spain and possibly North Africa in the south. This European Geotraverse project will cost about 35 million Swiss francs, all to be financed by national funding agencies, with the ESF taking on the task of coordinating the various parts of what is already turning out to be an extremely complex project. Similar geographical considerations apply to topics such as atmospheric chemistry and forest ecosystems where the prospects for joint programmes are now under study.

Only a year or so after the birth of the ESF, a very ambitious idea came along. The scheme was for an extremely intensive source of synchrotron radiation to be built as a joint European project. Synchrotron radiation was familiar to nuclear physicists as a by-product from beams of particles travelling round accelerators at relative speeds. Solid state scientists had begun to use these continuous spectra of 'light', with useful intensities from ultraviolet to hard X-rays, as protons of atomic and molecular structure. Not satisfied with 'parasitic' use of other people's machines, they were beginning to build their own purpose-built synchrotron radiation sources. Almost overnight solid state physics, structural chemistry and, later, structural biology turned into big science. By 1975 the planning of a European synchrotron radiation source became an additional activity of the ESF. By 1979 a sophisticated feasibility study and scientific case had been compiled by seventy researchers and machine builders from all over Europe.

But the cost of the project was enormous, and the research councils who made up the ESF could not afford anything like enough money without extra help from their governments. The ESF took the unprecedented step of forming a political committee to try to persuade governments of countries represented within the Foundation to come up with the cash. Progress here was very slow. By 1982 new technical knowledge and experience had made it necessary to revise the original plans. By the end of 1983 an element of desperation was entering into the affair, with appeals to other international bodies to put pressure on member governments. In 1984 the EEC began to show some interest in the matter, and in late 1984 France and Germany officially confirmed their intention to go ahead.

Structural science is not the only discipline that needs expensive facilities. There are a number of others, such as nuclear physics and astronomy, where countries cannot each afford a full range of equipment.

Scientists can considerably advance their own interests by keeping an eye on what is available where, and point out gaps that need to be filled. Often money is not the only constraint: the number of scientists working in each subject, in each country and in Europe as a whole, is another important element in the 'ecology' of a particular discipline. A few ESF working groups have applied themselves to making surveys of resources and manpower in this way, and have come up with very useful directories, data and even some quite acerbic comments about other organizations.

A 1978 study of European astronomers, for example, reported that 60 per cent of European astronomers, were under forty.

> This gives the subject a remarkable vitality but it also implies an increasingly difficult recruitment situation since so many of the available posts are filled by relatively young people. In fact, projections for the future show discouraging figures concerning the employment possibilities for young PhDs in astronomy and the development they predict is a rapid decrease of the population in the younger age groups. This is a serious threat to the whole discipline and can be avoided only by the creation of new positions and such other imaginative steps as allow for necessary continued recruitment of young astronomers.

Thus wrote Reimar Lüst, then chairman of the ESF's astronomy committee and now head of ESA.

Britain had the most astronomers per head of the population – 12.9 per million inhabitants – with the Netherlands next at 10.1. France and West Germany had 8.0 and 7.0 respectively, with Yugoslavia (1.5), Spain (1.3) and Portugal (0.6) trailing behind the average across the ESF countries of 6.5. The number of support technicians varied from 0.3 to 1.8 per scientist, with an average of 0.6. And the funding of astronomy in ESF Europe rose in real terms by about 40 per cent between 1970 and 1976.

The first major study by the Space Science Committee had a different flavour. Rather than looking at manpower, the committee chose to review the whole discipline of planetary science, particularly as practised in Europe. The information was assembled at a workshop held at Strasbourg in 1980 attended by over eighty scientists.

Having noted the lack of previous attempts to draw together the European planetary science community, the report (ESF 1982) points out that:

> Europe had, until the beginning of the space age, a leading position in planetary studies . . . whereas its leading, or at least, competitive role could be maintained in many areas of the 'earthbound' types of investigation, Europe's contribution to exploration from space has been minor, mainly carried out by individual scientists participating in US

146

or USSR space programmes. Although such cooperation has been fruitful, and should be continued, only in a few cases has it given Europeans the opportunity to play the leading role . . . moreover their efforts have remained isolated, giving but little stimulation to the European planetology community as a whole.

Whatever had happened to the highly rated European Space Agency (ESA) (into which the European Space Research Organization had been transformed in 1975)? Well, according to the ESF, not much where planetary science was concerned. In 1978 ESA's Science Advisory Committee reported that

ESRO and ESA have never participated previously either in a pure solar physics or a planetary or cometary mission. This situation bore no relation either to the great efforts made in the USA in this field or the strong interest and ability of European scientists to participate in such programmes.

In an attempt to fill this gap ESA undertook studies that led for example to approval for the GIOTTO mission to fly by Halley's comet in 1986. Nevertheless, the report says:

it may be fairly stated that, while a considerable amount of attention has been paid to planetary and deep-space missions in terms of studies of specific missions and by means of policy deliberations, the success rate has been low. This has been largely due to the fact that the size of the scientific budget of ESA is small in relation to the cost of such missions.

It concluded:

Europe has a sound technical foundation for planetary exploration but has not allocated the resources needed for a significant programme of planetary research. When the justifiable claims of space astronomy and other branches of space science are also considered, and when the trend towards larger and more costly missions in all disciplines is taken into account, the viability of the scientific programme of ESA on the present basis has to be called seriously into question.

Nuclear physics was the next subject for in-depth treatment, and in this case both manpower and experimental facilities were researched in detail in a report published in 1984. This time the scientists recommended that

for the future construction of very large facilities, a consensus of European countries should be sought. In view of the limited financial resources and the rising costs of new equipment, efforts must be coordinated to avoid unnecessary duplication. As examples we can cite the construction of a high-duty cycle, high intensity, multi GeV electron accelerator capable of imparting several GeV/nucleon to the most massive nuclei. Such installations would have great scientific potential. Already plans are being formulated separately by many of the groups responding to our enquiry and these initiatives must be co-ordinated in order not to upset the balance of research in European nuclear physics.

It also suggested closer cooperation between existing laboratories and better communications between European nuclear physicists. And it considered that

> there is a strong case for the European Science Foundation to take the lead in ensuring the future developments in the field are pursued in collaboration.

Incidentally, the report also remarked that Switzerland has by far the highest ratio of nuclear physicists to population, with thirteen per million inhabitants. Denmark comes next with Germany and then Belgium, France and Sweden. The UK with about two nuclear physicists per million population beats only Turkey, Yugoslavia, Greece, Ireland and Spain and falls well below the European average of between four and five.

The ESF's reports on individual disciplines highlighted several trends common to the whole scientific community, and one in particular was noted in the ESF's annual report for 1978. This was the lack of posts being offered in universities and research institutes to young scientists and of the general ageing of research populations. Worries about career prospects also seemed to be discouraging young scientists from moving between different types of jobs (in industry, government or academic life) and also from spending time abroad. One of the EEC's science committees, the European Committee on Research and Development (CERD) also expressed its concern, and asked the ESF to make a detailed study of the situation and come up with some recommendations for concrete action.

The ESF's detailed and thorough report, which covered fifteen countries, published in 1980, confirmed that these trends were general across all countries and all sciences, particularly the social sciences. It reported, for example, that since 1975

> very few new posts had been created in universities and research institutes and the recruitment of university teachers and researchers has almost come to a standstill in most European countries . . . the result is a highly distorted age distribution among university teaching and research staff, the average age of staff is now beginning to increase, clear evidence of a slowing down in the recruitment of personnel.

In the business sector

the number of researchers employed is still increasing in many countries.

Growth in electronics, computing and chemical industries contrasts with stagnation in transport, textiles and steel industries.
As for mobility

the general consensus is that movement between different sectors and particularly between the universities and the business sector is too low and should be encouraged.

And,

regional mobility would seem to have decreased in recent years . . . the few vacancies which do occur tend to be filled from within university departments, thus hindering the flow of ideas and talent.

The ESF also reviewed exchange schemes already available and national programmes to help young researchers and made a number of recommendations for future action. It pointed out that

the scientific community in Europe transcends national boundaries and as these problems exist on a European scale, concerted action is called for as well as decisions at national level.

Most of their suggestions called for action on the part of the European Community and we shall see later how the EC responded.

The European Community looks deeper into science

We have not so far discussed collaborative efforts funded by what is likely to become one of the most influential of European research sponsors because for the first decade at least of its existence, the European Community's (EC) involvement with science and technology was largely confined to the technology of nuclear reactors. Topics tackled broadened out in the 1970s, but it is only now beginning to extend its interests into more basic areas of science with a view to tackling some of the structural problems I have already described.

Today the EC is an umbrella organization for three different 'communities'. The oldest of these is the European Coal and Steel Community (ECSC) which dates back to 1952. From its earliest years the ECSC commissioned basic and applied research on coal, iron ore and steel, though it has never had any research establishments of its own. Much of the EC's research on health and safety, and some substantial programmes in coal and steel technology, still carry the ECSC label.

The first substantial EC research programme was to develop nuclear technology. In March 1957, two days before the Common Market Treaty was signed, ministers of its six signatories put their names to the treaty forming Euratom. The idea was to promote a degree of coordination between national research programmes to avoid wasteful duplication; to stimulate activity in the national centres, private research units and industrial firms in the atomic sector; and to expand the scope of research by investigating new types of power reactors. Belgium, France, West Germany, Italy, Luxembourg and the Netherlands were the founder members of Euratom, and when the organization chose to base its research effort in existing laboratories the work was split between four of them, which collectively acquired the title of Joint Research Centre. The biggest in terms of staff and facilities was (and still is) based on a complete laboratory campus at Ispra in Northern Italy. The other three are offshoots of national laboratories at Petten in the Netherlands, at Geel in Belgium, and at Karlsruhe in Germany.

The Common Market itself initially took little interest in r&d except for a few agricultural projects. But in 1965 government experts from the six community countries came together to identify growth sectors in European science and technology. They came up with data processing, telecommunications, new transport modes, oceanography, metallurgy, environmental protection and meteorology. As it happened, these topics were not however pursued by the six alone: by 1971 a group of nineteen countries had agreed a package of cooperative projects in these areas under the banner of Cooperation Européenne dans le domaine de la recherche scientifique et technique (COST). Coincidentally or otherwise, the nineteen included the eighteen ESF countries and Luxembourg.

In the early 1970s the lack of a common policy for scientific r&d within the community began to be felt. The Commission of the European Communities took the initiative in 1972 (the year that Britain, Denmark and Eire joined the community) by submitting a document on the subject to the Council of Ministers. The ensuing discussions contributed to the birth of the European Science Foundation in 1974 (see p 142) and (somewhat more slowly) to a single community policy for science and technology. A key step in meeting the objective was the formation of the Scientific and Technological Research Committee (CREST) whose members were (and are) 'senior officials responsible for scientific and technological policy in their respective countries'. A separate advisory committee consists of a score of people appointed on individual merit: this is the European Committee for Research and Development (CERD). At the same time the work of the Joint Research Centre laboratories was reviewed. The four year programme for the JRC due to run from 1973–76 outlined a plan for diversification away from nuclear research to include topics such as environmental protection, hydrogen and solar energy.

While the JRC did its best to incorporate the new activities into its traditional framework, the EC worked towards a common policy. The philosophy behind the programme for the period 1977–80 was set down in 'Guidelines for the Common Research and Development Policy'. It came up with four main priorities: long-term security of supply (for energy, agriculture, raw materials); promotion of industrial development to make the Community internationally competitive (data processing, textiles, the setting up of a Community bureau of references); improvement of living and working conditions (medical research, urban planning etc); protection of the urban and natural environment.

In implementing this policy the Community r&d budget grew from 70 to 300 million units of account between 1973 and 1979. The work of the JRC (direct action) came to be complemented by 'indirect actions' carried out under contract by public bodies or industrial firms in member states (EC paying half the cost) and by 'concerted actions' administered and so coordinated by the EC but financed entirely by member states.

Indirect action provided the framework for what is unquestionably the EC's greatest achievement in science and technology in the 1970s. That is the launch of the Joint European Torus (JET) project, based at Culham in southern England. JET is a large steel doughnut that can contain materials in a hot (plasma) state where ions are completely dissociated from their outer electrons. Under these conditions it is possible to promote thermo-nuclear fusion between small atomic nuclei and to collect the energy thus released. The object of JET is to demonstrate that more energy can be extracted from this process than is consumed in setting it up. The scale of the JET project (which no one member country could have afforded alone) puts it on a par with front-rank projects in the US, Japan and the Soviet Union. In order to join in with JET, Sweden and Switzerland have signed association contracts with Euratom.

The late 1970s also saw steps towards better integration of EC programmes with those already in progress under the auspices of COST: today the secretariat of the COST committee (which consists of senior r&d policy officials from the nineteen member countries) is provided by the EC Council of Ministers, and the Commission and its technical and management committees. As an OECD report pointed out in 1981,

> the COST cooperative scheme is a very original one . . . all the countries taking part in it wish to keep it flexible and a strategy is gradually emerging that aims at increasingly intensive scientific cooperation on clearly defined themes between strictly European countries.

I have broken my own rules about the scope of this book in devoting so much space to describing arrangements for what by any definition is mainly applied science. There is, however, a good reason for this. In the 1980s the EC realized that structural weaknesses in training and research in fundamental science were putting Europe's economic and cultural development at risk. And so it is building on its experiences of the 1960s and 70s in order to make some impact on these problems.

One initiative for these new departures dates back to 1979, when the work of the 1970s came under review from the wider perspective of encouraging better coordination of national activities and reappraising the Community's own priorities for the long term.

The same year saw the publication of a remarkable little book called *Science and the second renaissance of Europe* by André Danzin, then chairman of CERD. Danzin outlines and bemoans Europe's shrinking cultural and economic status in the world, and describes a new cultural identity for Europe that would give it a distinct, albeit humbler, position in the modern world.

The basic principles of the new European society would involve serious moves towards making durable and repairable rather than throwaway goods, and to conserving rather than squandering energy. There would be a shorter working week and more emphasis placed on making leisure a more important part of personal identity and fulfilment. Danzin (1979) writes:

> If consumption habits were to change with the ambition to succeed by free personal work triumphing over the illusory accumulation of assets, we would move from a civilisation of waste and envy, of never-satisfied desires, to a civilisation of the self-fulfilled man, responsible and aware of the reward he will receive for his work and his talent, acts and feelings which, in past history, were the privilege of a very small elite.

This vision is bound up with a new spirit of pride in creative achievement, including that in science and technology.

Danzin reports on how the US and Japanese research efforts are out-stripping those of Europe in both size and vigour, and concludes that Europe must drag itself out of the research doldrums.

> Everything militates in favour of a policy reflecting initiative and pioneering spirit. By taking the offensive, we avoid being left behind, sometimes with no hope of catching up; we oblige others to follow us and we preserve our liberty.

Whatever the Council of Ministers thought of this personalized and idealized worldview, they asked the European Commission to assess the possible impact of r&d on 'horizontal' planning such as regional, structural, economic and industrial policies, in particular policies concerning small and medium firms and development assistance. This request was fulfilled through the FAST programme (Forecasting and Assessment in the field of Science and Technology), which had in fact been agreed by the Council of Ministers in 1978. Under this indirect action programme research groups from all over the community competed for grants for forecasting in three problem areas: work and employment, the information society, and the biosociety. These priorities, incidentally, reflect the major foci of interest identified by Danzin. His concerns about the mobility and structure of the research community in Europe were also referred to the Commission, who, as we have seen, were already investigating the problems through the European Science Foundation.

FAST proved to be a remarkable enterprise, with a coordinating team of a dozen or so based within the Commission's Directorate General for Science, Research and Development (DGXII) assessing and collating the work of groups at fifty-four separate research centres. They also pooled comment and advice from colleagues in other directorates of the Commission and the committees already involved in science policy such as CREST and CERD. According to the team's own account of its activities it used

> a scenario building approach, which made it possible to discern 'possible futures', rather than use models too locked into past data. FAST sought only to outline the range of future possibilities, to develop proposals offering the greatest flexibility and adaptability in confronting the uncertainties of the future.

It submitted its two-volume Final Report to the Commission in 1982, and produced a more popular version of its findings published as *Eurofutures: the challenges of innovation* in 1984. This includes a wealth of factual information about work already in progress in Europe, possibilities for the future, and the work that needs to be done to arrive at them. The first three chapters address the three key issues of the biosociety, information and work, an interesting rearrangement of priorities. Out of this analysis the FAST team devised a set of proposals for community r&d.

A major (if unsurprising) conclusion of FAST was that

> if European societies want to retain, over the next 20 years, some autonomy and some control over their own futures, then they have no option but to collaborate in a joint strategy for socioeconomic development . . . such a strategy depends on a coordinated approach in order to derive maximum value from the scientific, technological and industrial potential of the Community countries.

Action on these proposals has been fairly fast by the standards of international bureaucracies, although it has seemed slow to those taking part. The first initiative is the ESPRIT programme (European Strategic Programme for r&d in Information Technologies) to which, after some wrangling, the EC has agreed to contribute 750 million units of account over five years.

The basic philosophy of ESPRIT was formulated well before the end of the FAST project. Here is an extract from the programme objectives as published in 1982:

> There is increasing evidence that a considerable proportion of European r&d resources is directed towards research which is aimed at catching up with that which has already taken place elsewhere. Long-term industrial research, which could in effect provide product leadership, is to a large extent neglected because of resource limitations, and ESPRIT will aim at correcting this situation. The overall objective of ESPRIT is to provide the basic technologies which European industry needs to be competitive with those of Japan and the USA. To achieve this objective ESPRIT needs to be:
> — aimed at precompetitive industry
> — concerted with national activities in the community
> Given that there is a shortage of qualified manpower and other resources, which means that companies or governments individually cannot address all topics on a sufficient scale, the concentration of ESPRIT on precompetitive research will enable the necessary critical mass to be reached in key areas.

The r&d framework for ESPRIT was developed by scientists and engineers from major European information technology companies. They came up with five interdependent subject areas: advanced micro-electronics, software technology, advanced information processing, office automation, computer integrated manufacturing.

The following year, 1983, saw the launch of thirty-eight 'pilot phase' projects. These provide an impressive array of topics and collaborations that promised to transcend traditional boundaries such as those between disciplines, between academia and industry, and between researchers at opposite ends of Europe. Towards the end of 1984 the European Commission announced that twenty-nine of these would continue into the main phase and another ninety new projects would begin: these were finally announced in autumn 1985. The industrial participants (at least two from separate EEC countries in each project) will match the 200 million units of account that the community will provide for the first year of the main phase.

It would be naive to expect that companies and universities would put forward their best ideas for projects that involve such wide disclosure.

Nevertheless, there is no doubt that ESPRIT has stimulated new proposals that could not previously have been contemplated: for example where academic groups work in subject areas not matched by the interests of local companies. Now they can take advantage of industrial contacts (and funds) further afield.

Where are the limits to be drawn, though? This question was brought into focus by the revelation that the main phase of ESPRIT will include collaborations involving American companies such as IBM which have manufacturing and research centres in Europe.

DGXII's next big project will, not surprisingly, be to launch similar collaborations in biotechnology. These will build on existing fairly small scale relevant actions in agriculture and data collection and a 'biomolecular engineering programme' launched in 1982. Here once again the programme will be dominated by r&d and training. Precompetitive or 'horizontal' actions aim at

> the removal of bottlenecks which prevent the application of modern genetic and biochemical methods to industry and agriculture.

The key areas are the

> sequences of events and processes which man must understand and control for transforming and/or exploiting on a large scale the properties of those species, organisms, tissues, cultured cells, genes and gene products essential for new industrial and agricultural developments.

The EC programme will also sponsor databanks, collections of biotech materials and related information/communication networks.

For specific actions

> the targets chosen have been selected on the basis of their intrinsic importance, and in view of the fact that . . . it is unlikely that they can be effectively pursued by industry.

Examples include assessment of raw materials and developing for treatment of common and socially costly diseases.

I have only been able to hint here at the radical transformation the rise of information technology and biotechnology have had on perceptions outside the scientific community of the importance of basic and fundamental research. This applies to many (though not all) national governments as well as the EC.

This change of attitude may well have a lot to do with two smaller initiatives in r&d that DGXII is already actively planning. The first is a project to improve the matching of technical solutions already available in research institutes anywhere in the community to problems that might arise in industry, especially in small to medium sized companies, anywhere else in Europe. In the BRITE programme the focus will be on basic technologies such as welding, corrosion, catalysis, and the money will go to sponsor work to fill the gap between problems that are too applied to be interesting academically and ideas that are too basic for a company to find it worthwhile to explore them adequately.

Basic research figures even more prominently in DGXII's 'stimulation' programme. This is designed to break down barriers to proper exploitation of the European Community's 'considerable' and 'high quality' scientific and technical potential.

> There are obstacles [the planners report] which, all too often, limit the effectiveness of Europe's r&d in various fields of activity (particularly the lack of communication or cooperation between European scientists, the unemployment or insufficient training of young researchers). In the face of these it is generally recognised that the national initiatives which are being taken to stimulate the efficacy of scientific and technical research do not always bring about the desired effects. They are in fact shackled by the national limits within which they operate.
>
> At the same time, and in spite of the quality and variety of the centres and teams at work in Europe, scientists and engineers often seek to maintain preferential links with centres located outside the community, either because they are not sufficiently aware of alternative possibilities or because they cannot find enough opportunities for exchanges and cooperation at the European level. The major national or European facilities remain, in many cases, underused. Very few opportunities are made available by individual countries to make it easier (and none at all to make it cheaper) for scientists to undertake moves within the Member States.
>
> Cooperation with non-European companies or centres often seems to be easier than with Community companies and centres, although the former often involves restrictive conditions which are liable to exacerbate the scientific and industrial imbalances which already exist. Lastly, the initiatives which are taken at national level these days to avoid the under-employment of young researchers remain extremely limited, and this leads to a 'brain drain' which is sometimes irreparable. At Community level, on the other hand, because of its very size, a better match between supply and demand can be arranged.

The remedies that DGXII proposes include a flexible programme of research grants to help scientists collaborate on projects that transcend national and also, where possible, disciplinary boundaries. Young scientists who want to train abroad will also benefit, as will laboratories in different countries who want to set up a twinning arrangement. The first phase of this programme will run from 1985–86 and should involve 4000 people (1 per cent of European researchers according to the EC) by 1988.

A second phase of this programme may from 1987 provide funds for large research facilities. The idea would be to buy rights to participation in such facilities for consortia of small countries who could not otherwise afford to join in.

France stimulates yet more collaborations

With substantial amounts of money behind its efforts – perhaps 2 per cent of the entire spending on r&d in the Community – the EC is beginning to emerge as an important force in European science. In 1982, science and technology entered the French political scene in a big way, as we have already seen. President François Mitterrand also carried his enthusiasm over into international circles.

Mitterrand's first arena was the Economic Summit meeting that heads of seven Western nations attend each year. In 1982 he was on home ground at Versailles. He presented a report stressing the importance of technology and innovation in generating new employment, then as now a key political issue, and stressed the value of cooperation between the Western nations. In response to his remarks the summit set up the Technology, Growth and Employment working group. By the 1983 Williamsburg summit the group had identified eighteen areas where collaboration between the seven (and the EEC as a unit) would be valuable. Many of these involve innovations already at the development stage, but a few concern basic science. These include photovoltaic solar energy (lead countries Japan and Italy), photosynthesis and photochemical conversion of solar energy (again with Japan in the lead), biotechnology (this time with the UK and France in the lead), basic biology (with EC in the lead), high energy physics (with the USA in the lead) and exploration of the solar system (again with the EC in the lead).

In each case the lead countries are joined by a number of participants and observers, and in some cases invited international observers too. All the summit members will participate in the basic biology programme, for example, and EMBO and ESF are among the organizations to be invited on board. Here information sharing through databases of various kinds seems to be a priority, with neurosciences and ecosystems as favoured topics for joint research. No special funds are to be provided for any of these programmes. It will be up to national funding agencies to decide whether it is in their interests to invest existing resources in such collaborations.

In its report to the 1984 summit the Technology, Growth and Employment working group reported that the activities it has initiated

> have both improved the climate of international cooperation and helped to focus national science and technology discussions .. in

looking to the future, the working group is firmly of the view that failure to take up opportunities for international collaboration may be just as prejudiced to the introduction of new technologies and hence to economic growth as the obstacles referred to earlier in the report.

It was in the autumn of 1982 that Mitterrand launched his second initiative. This time he chose the parliamentary assembly of the Council of Europe in Strasbourg as his forum, and his proposal was quite specific: that the Council should set up a network of European centres of excellence in order to improve opportunities for developing Europe's scientific and intellectual potential.

This proposal gave a great boost to an exercise in scientific cooperation launched by the Council way back in 1969 through its Committee on Science and Technology. The Council of Europe is essentially an organization for cultural rather than political cooperation. Nevertheless, it places great emphasis on the involvement of democratically elected representatives in its activities, hence the basic philosophy of the scheme:

it was a question of persuading scientists to combine their efforts and of making parliamentarians and scientists aware of their respective problems.

The first two topics chosen were space biophysics and geodynamics.

In 1972 the work of the 'exercise' was formalized through the setting up of a European Joint Committee for Scientific Cooperation and a small amount of money was set aside for the purpose. Since then the committee has built up a rather strange portfolio of disciplines, including training, where it coordinates scientific activities. These include remote sensing, geodynamics, water resources and science-based archaeology.

This work has been hampered by lack of resources (and also, it must be said a fair amount of indifference from both scientists and parliamentarians). But it has formed a base that has enabled the committee to devise a unique format for a series of meetings designed to 'assist with political decision making'. Recent topics have included problems of Mediterranean agriculture, animal experimentation, optimization of health resources and radioactive waste disposal.

The Council of Europe also has a separate committee on higher education and research which has recently stimulated discussions on the future of tertiary education, academic mobility and other related topics. A three-day meeting held in November 1983 rehearsed many of the factors at work in university life that we have already discussed. The general tone of the meeting (heavily dominated by government representatives) can be gathered from the organizing secretariat's summary of the findings:

The quickening process of western cultural integration and the unifying roles of information systems and science among rising and competing cultures was stressed. A call was made for European universities to establish a new European cultural synthesis as a distinctive contribution to global development.

Ten months later, in September 1984, the Mitterrand proposal for a network surfaced again at a very grand meeting in Paris, this time organized by the secretariat of the Council's Joint Committee for Scientific Cooperation. Senior science policy makers from each of the twenty-one Council member states attended, as did observers from the Commission of the European Communities (CEC), COST, ESA, OECD, CERN, EMBO, ESO and ESF.

It soon became clear that the Council of Europe had been persuaded to give up the idea of a physical network of large and expensive centres of excellence that it would run itself. Instead the research ministers agreed on a declaration designed to encourage the formation of a 'European scientific technical area' open to all the participating states. According to the final communiqué,

> they must proceed mainly by redeploying the resources that are currently available, while making better use of existing institutions so as to avoid duplication.

Two main practical steps were envisaged. The first was to strengthen and promote thematic cooperation networks in a number of areas of research. To this end the ministers called on the European Science Foundation to report within five months on the 'ways and means of strengthening and implementing the different proposals regarding networks'. This will build on the groundwork ESF had already done in preparing a document on existing networks and proposals from member states for new ones. It came up with nineteen existing networks of one kind or another, many of them inadequately supported; seventeen where the existence of an identifiable scientific community would make it easy to set up such networks quickly; and another thirty-five where proposals on the table were not formulated precisely enough to make proper evaluation possible. ESF picked out from these eighteen networks 'identified as being of particular interest': it grouped these under the five headings of earth, ocean, space; health, biology; materials, energy; human development; agriculture, food.

To help the ESF with this mammoth task, and also to help it continue its support of existing networks, the research ministers also recommended that member states (technically speaking, through their academies and funding agencies) should increase the money available to ESF. They also suggested that the Council of Europe and the CEC be consulted about the network proposals.

The second practical step was that member states should 'facilitate dialogue between laboratories and promote the exchange of researchers and their mobility, in particular at doctoral and post-doctoral level'. Once again the ESF is to play a major part: it is to submit a report within two years on steps taken by member states (and presumably international organizations) to improve mobility.

It is worth noting that the involvement of the ESF and the Council of Europe will force this work to be undertaken in the context of a much wider Europe than the EEC's ten member states. It seems that the Council's Europe of the twenty-one or the ESF's Europe of the eighteen may once again determine the boundaries of scientific Europe as it was in the early days of COST.

> The CEC and the Council of Europe will also collaborate in devising ways of improving the dissemination and management of scientific and technical information, and the development of a European information system regarding concrete possibilities for organizing exchanges and meetings among researchers.

Other ideas along these lines raised at the meeting included a European researchers' 'card' with entitlement to privileges such as reduced rail fares and – the British contribution – a European academy of science.

To end this chapter with a report of the Council of Europe meeting is not only an unexpected opportunity for neatness but also a welcome excuse for optimism about the future of science in Europe. It is good to know that the message about mobility has penetrated through to research ministers, though as we have seen there are other important practical issues they could also have taken up.

But the major surprise of the meeting was the wholehearted recognition that politicians cannot arrange for good science –

> none of the new initiatives will have any real meaning or real impact unless they are based on the scientific community's expression of its own needs,

the ministers' final communiqué said.

I hope the story told in this chapter demonstrates that for all its imperfections the ESF is singularly well-placed to succeed in this task, and the more substantial bureaucracies are to be praised for recognizing the potential of this hitherto little-publicized organization.

Epilogue

In mid 1985 the topic of European collaboration in science and technology makes headlines almost every day. The main reason for this, ironically, hails from outside Europe. The impetus has been the 'star wars' research programme announced by the United States. More officially dubbed the Strategic Defense Initiative, the plan is to develop a way of defending the US from a nuclear attack. The scheme would include weapons systems based in space that would detect and then eliminate armed warheads aimed at the US. The SDI programme will cost $26 billion over five years.

The US would very much like to tap European expertise. And European companies would love to get their hands on 'star wars' contracts. But governments, with the apparent exception of Britain, are thinking twice about committing their state research efforts to the project. West Germany, after initial enthusiasm, has found cause to reconsider. France, with its own independent nuclear deterrent, has opted out, as have Norway and Denmark. Other NATO countries have yet to commit themselves.

The problem is that membership of NATO has already made European member countries heavily dependent on US technology. Europe spends seven times as much on American arms as the US spends in Europe. The US spends about three times as much on military r&d as European NATO, and contributes two thirds of the NATO budget. European countries are reluctant to increase their dependence by devoting a large proportion of their r&d resources to playing a subsidiary role in a major effort devised in, and orchestrated from, the US.

As we have seen, there is already a widespread realization that Europe's most urgent task is to improve her industrial competitiveness. It is quite likely that many of the 'star wars' technologies will be similar to those that will be needed for future products. But, as the British example has shown, there is a big difference between mastering the technologies because they are needed for defence and making a successful product that will sell in bulk and keep people in work. Also, there is the simple fact that in the war for world markets the US is a competitor rather than an ally. A third factor is a residual European distaste for being drawn yet further into the nightmare world of superpower confrontation. If nothing else, European countries retain the advantages of diversity and strong national identities.

Once again the French have taken the lead in proposing an alternative. Early in 1985 President Mitterrand proposed a joint technology programme for Europe called Eureka. Eureka would be a flexible umbrella that would help companies and academic researchers to collaborate in developing products and technologies that could compete with the scope and standard of those emerging in the US and Japan. Over the next few months European countries, both inside and outside the European Community, began to pledge their support for the project. It seemed a way of getting the best from Europe's good performance in basic research without selling out. Most countries articulated this preference by indicating their correspondingly lower interest in 'star wars'.

By the time of the summit conference of European Communities heads of state in Milan at the end of June, there were two separate plans for Eureka. French planners drew up the first one. The biggest programme concerned computers (Euromatic). One project is a supercomputer based on gallium arsenide chips and another the development of parallel architectures. In both cases Franco-German collaboration would form the core of the project. Many smaller projects, involving Britain, Italy, the Netherlands and Norway were listed. Robotics (Eurobot), agriculture and biotechnology (Eurobio) and communications (Eurocom) were also featured, as was the development of a ceramic turbine (Euromat).

The Commission of the European Communities presented a plan of its own. The CEC plan is called 'Towards a European Technology Community'. It proposes three types of technological r&d programme: research on generic technologies; development and exploitation of joint facilities for basic research purposes; and strategic programmes. The EC would draw on its experience with current programmes to identify new areas and ensure the right approach for each. It makes clear that all member states would have to give a political (and financial) commitment to the idea of a European Technology Community, but that not all states would have to participate in all the projects. Indeed, non-member states would be able to take part in projects that interested them. Without proposing a programme in final form, it mentions ten 'possible mobilizing projects' which include information technology, bio-technology, new materials, lasers and optics, large scientific instruments and broadband telecommunications. To implement these programmes it would need about three times as much money as it gets at present (see below).

At the Milan summit the heads of state achieved a broad consensus of support for Eureka, though each had a slightly different view of what they supported. As a result the idea of European collaboration in science and technology gained wide public attention. Many details remain to be settled however. One is who should run the project – the EC's DGXII would obviously relish the job, but the French think that an independent agency would have a better chance of getting things done. Foreign and research ministers of the twelve EC countries including Spain and Portugal (which joined the EEC on 1 January 1986), Austria, Sweden, Norway and Switzerland will meet to discuss matters further.

DGXII is building up a fairly creditable record. The ambitious ESPRIT programme is still in its early stages. Its activities so far have been praised, but some doubts have been raised about how relevant its projects are to the needs of the market. The other collaborative programmes mentioned earlier are also going ahead during the years 1985–89, though with lower budgets than originally envisaged. At a meeting of research ministers in December 1984 a budget of 1.2 million European Com-munity Units (ECU) was allocated to r&d programmes. Of this more than half will go to research in thermonuclear fusion. Radiation protection and waste management gets 170 million ECU, with 55 million ECU for biotechnology. The stimulation programme gets 60 million ECU, the BRITE programme 70 million ECU (see p 156) and non-nuclear energy 175 million ECU. Since then the research ministers have discussed plans for a new programme of research in advanced communications in Europe (RACE) which would cost 6 million ECU over 18 months.

Whoever ends up running Eureka, there is no going back from the new profile r&d has achieved in Europe, largely through being put on the spot by SDI. Eureka will have none of the diffidence of ESPRIT's cautious approach to 'pre competitive' research – in future projects will go for the commercial jugular. Nobody has yet suggested, however, that basic research will not be involved. Europe seems to have woken up to the fact that it is impossible to develop competitive products and technologies without being totally aware of what is going on at the cutting edge of fundamental research. On the other hand some are warning that Europe's excellent resource of fundamental research may be in danger from the new preoccupation with products.

Efforts to tackle some of the structural problems of fundamental research in Europe have made some progress, though they have not quite achieved the glamour of Eureka. The EC's stimulation programme has received 700 applications for its first, experimental, phase in 1984; 90 per cent of them had to be rejected. Most of the 60 million ECU will go on twinning of laboratories, but some will be set aside for private brainstorming conferences like the Gordon conferences in the US. The BRITE programme has attracted over 3000 expressions of interest from all over Europe including 21 from Greece.

The problem of large expensive laboratories continues to trouble Europe's science policy makers. CERN is under pressure to cut its spending even further following the publication of the Kendrew report in Britain (see p 133). The project to build the European Synchrotron Radiation Source, now formally backed by France and Germany, seems to have become a bargaining counter in a complex international web of trade-offs that the EC is trying to sort out.

Now working closely with the EC, the European Science Foundation has completed its study of scientific networks in Europe and submitted it to the Council of Europe. The new document examines subdivisions of six broad fields: earth, ocean, space; health, biology; materials, energy; human development; agriculture, food; and advanced technologies. The ESF has examined current arrangements for coordination across its eighteen member countries and made recommendations on the topics where links need strengthening.

According to the document

the main idea of a network is to promote mobility and to stimulate mutual awareness ... this would include the organization of workshops in specific fields as well as other kinds of international meetings, and also high level scientific training programmes or schools.

Networks would also help 'peripheral' countries 'where the need for increased involvement in European scientific affairs is indeed a severe one'. Funds for this type of activity could come from a central fund of 1 million ECU which the ESF requests from the Council of Europe.

In some topics it might also be desirable to set up major cooperative projects and research programmes. Funds for these would have to come from other organizations. New networks are proposed for vulcanology; oceanography and oceanology; management of water resources; and informatics.

CHAPTER SEVEN

Pointers towards a new social contract for European science

The natural growth of European collaborations

It would be easy to paint a bleak picture of the state of science in Europe, and it would be just as easy to make such a scenario an excuse for grinding pessimism combined with desperation leading to ill-considered actions. The preceding chapter shows that Europeans can be proud of their scientific achievements in the present as well as the past. In some areas, such as particle physics, neutron scattering and observational astronomy, there is no doubt that international collaboration within Europe has allowed the best scientists access to equipment where they can obtain world class results. The same is true of research into thermo-nuclear fusion.

An important subset of these topics is mainly related to pure research with no obvious end in view. Until recently it was only this type of science that demanded such expensive facilities that sharing and pooling of resources were necessary. Such collaborations are not only a matter of money: it is often also necessary to assemble a critical mass of expertise to design and build large facilities that can rarely be found in one country. When it comes to research, multinational teams often arise automatically, or with only a little extra prompting from committees that select and schedule individual experiments.

This trend goes hand in hand with another change in the way science is done to which we have already referred: the increasing need for teamwork. Often a research team has to build quite complex equipment to house and manipulate samples and to collect data to give them precisely the results they want. They may also have to collect and prepare specimens. Some or all of the group must go to the centre to check and operate the equipment and perform running repairs if necessary. After the experiments are over the data needs to be analysed. There is often work for many hands here: teams from different universities or institutes, possibly in a variety of countries, need to join forces; and people are required at all levels of the scientific pecking order, from undergraduates and research students to professors and academicians. An admittedly exceptional paper, describing research done at CERN, had over eighty signatories: thirty or so is fairly common.

The apparatus needed for laboratories such as CERN makes extremely heavy demands on a wide range of technologies. In the 1950s and 60s, the demands of scientific research had a crucial impact on the development of equipment for computing and control, for example. The same is no longer quite so true today, with process and power engineering highly sophisticated disciplines in their own right. Nevertheless, 'big science' is beginning to build up a closer orientation towards the new science-based technologies. Energy production is one example of this, with the JET project for the pursuit of thermonuclear fusion as an energy source and the large EEC reactor installations to test the efficiency and safety of nuclear power plant.

Another intriguing example is the science of structure, a still un-familiar nametag (for which I am indebted to Dr John Finney of Birkbeck College, London) that covers all attempts to elucidate spatial regularities among the atoms or molecules in solids, liquids and gases. Much of this research is quite close to the realms of useful application: for example, in improving materials, particularly for making microelectronic equipment and helping in the design of new drugs.

Scientists who pursue this type of research may be biologists, physicists, chemists or even mathematicians, and they can select from a wide range of techniques. Some of these are cheap, well established and easily available in their own laboratories: basic x-ray crystallography is an example. Others are more expensive and need to be shared among a number of institutions: state-of-the-art computers and equipment for nuclear magnetic resonance spectroscopy often come into this category. Some types of equipment are entirely beyond the means of small countries and they need to share those belonging to larger ones: at the moment sources of synchrotron radiation are examples here.

In the case of nuclear reactors for neutron scattering, international collaboration has already become imperative and has proved to be extre-mely successful. In September 1985, France and Germany were already talking seriously about pressing ahead with the European Synchrotron Radiation Facility on a similar basis, though a rather wider consortium will almost certainly be needed in this case.

Both the ILL and the ESRF are essentially service laboratories: the idea is to accommodate only a small number of researchers on site, and to concentrate on providing support services for visiting researchers. We have already seen the risks of establishing permanent institutes with tenured full-time staff in the case of many national laboratories and, to some extent, the European Molecular Biology Laboratory and the Joint Research Centre as well. At the beginning there is much pride and excitement at the assembly of a young and enthusiastic team with the latest equipment and facilities; gradually the staff ages and the flow of new ideas dries up; the researchers continue to pursue lines of investigation that may no longer be exciting; and slowly the institute fades off the map of world leaders in a particular discipline. CERN seems to have escaped this syndrome so far; nevertheless, its success continues to come at an extremely high price financially. This lesson has been consolidated by the work of the European Science Foundation, which has carefully and responsibly experimented with other forms of collaboration relevant to basic science.

The trend towards collaboration in areas of science that come closer to everyday experience and even begin to relate to industrial products is powered by (at least) three engines. One is the vision of Europe as an economic entity in competition with the US and Japan, units of comparable size. The second is the changing requirements for and the nature of the science of materials and structures. And the third is the growing importance of information as a shared resource. In biotechnology, for example, the need for libraries of data and samples on the myriad of available organisms may well be more important than the availability of expensive central facilities for experimentation. A fourth factor, of differing importance to the various countries of Europe, is the need to cut costs by avoiding unnecessary duplication; a fifth the perhaps idealistic one of improving scientific standards in the poorer countries with a view to improving their chances of economic independence.

In discussing both the ecology and the content of disciplines that have made a relatively recent entry into the arena of official European collaboration, one is struck by the close relationship between the new approaches and the concept of strategic science. When scientists were imbued with the ideals of pure research, they looked to ivory towers and prestigious institutes for their ideal environment. Such intellectual luxury is by no means obsolete today, but only a privileged few can expect to work out their careers in this way. Most of today's young scientists will categorize their work not only by its coordinates on the map of scientific disciplines but also by its relationship to the everyday world of industry, national and international defence, environment, energy supply and information.

Promoting science of this kind, as planners seem to have recognized, albeit out of expediency rather than acuity, is not so obviously a matter for centres of excellence. It becomes as important for scientists to communicate with many sectors of the world outside their own discipline as to exchange ideas among themselves. And so it begins to make sense to shift the emphasis from tangible institutes to 'invisible colleges' at scientific, industrial and political levels. The new emphasis on strategic initiatives in information technology and biotechnology are examples of this: so in a small way are the calls for stronger networks of scientists and better mobility and career opportunities for researchers. These two directions perhaps enshrine the foundation of a new social contract for the scientists of the twenty-first century: on the one hand to be guided to some extent by the generalized needs of society; on the other, to enjoy relative security and comfort, and not to be pushed too far into work of a very short-term and routine nature.

In late 1984 the point of view of the scientific community seems to be coming across quite clearly in debates at international level. At national level, however, the situation is much more patchy, as we have seen. Most governments are preoccupied with other issues; industries are doing their best to cope with recession. Scientists too are reluctant to become involved in speaking publicly about the structural problems of their profession, particularly if it means exposing to public scrutiny the way they arrange their affairs.

Of course, there are exceptions to this general rule. For example there are those who have written books or articles that address the problems. Without claiming any kind of exhaustive knowledge, I could mention Frenchmen Laurent Schwartz and Pierre Papon, Christoph Schneider of the Deutsche Forschungsgemeinschaft, E. Primo Yufera of Spain, Paulo Bisogno of Italy, John Ziman, Ray Beverton, Michael Gibbons, Stuart Blume and Geoff Oldham of the UK, F. R. Dias Agudo of Portugal. To these must be added the many scientists who have diverted their energies from their work to advise official or parliamentary bodies in private, and those who as heads of research councils or academies have spoken out publicly.

Some countries have institutions that do try to tackle issues of this kind as bodies representative of the scientific community. Germany has its elected Wissenschaftsrat. In France the Centre National de la Recherche Scientifique (CNRS) convenes an elected assembly of researchers. Of the big league, Britain and Italy both lack such parliaments of science. Official efforts to keep the public better informed about scientific issues can create a better climate for intelligent debate about the scientific community itself; Sweden and the Netherlands, where there is already a comparatively positive general view of science, are both working hard along these lines.

There are, then, reasonable grounds for optimism about the future of the scientific community in Europe, but there is no room for complacency. Everywhere governments are making new and more complex demands on their scientists; it is largely up to the scientists themselves to see that these are met at the price of a sensible strategy for support and renewal of the community.

Scientific relations in the developed world

Much of this book has been written as if Europe and her scientific community were completely isolated from the rest of the world. I cannot hope to redress this balance in a short passage right at the end; indeed this would contravene the spirit of the book. But some aspects of Europe's wider international contacts play such an important part in her scientific affairs that they must be at least mentioned to provide a proper perspective.

The Europe of the eighteen (ie the member countries of the European Science Foundation) binds an extremely diverse set of cultures and communities. Mostly it is western, capitalist (even where socialists are in power) and values the freedom of the individual. This description most aptly fits the westernmost parts; Yugoslavia is hardly capitalist, and Turkey, while technically a democracy, has less than average respect for individual freedoms. Austria and Finland, moreover, are fairly dependent on trade with the communist bloc. Ten of the eighteen are members of the North Atlantic Treaty Organization: Austria, Sweden, Switzerland and Finland remain technically neutral and also find it advantageous to stay outside the European Community. Gross domestic product per capita (1984) ranges from 1132 dollars for Turkey to 13 648 dollars for Norway, a factor of more than ten.

This catholicity has enabled greater Europe to avoid the trap of becoming an uncritical bastion of Western values as dictated by the US, even if American military planners think of the European members of NATO as dispensable battlegrounds maintained merely for strategic purposes. European researchers in particular are keen to maintain their ideal of a scientific community with just as few national barriers as possible: they welcome the stimulus of new approaches and ideas even if they have to respect unfamiliar bureaucratic procedures, and so participants from eastern bloc countries are often invited to international meetings. The European Physical Society (EPS), for example, includes a number of Warsaw pact countries among its members, and annual assemblies of EPS have been held recently in Hungary and Czechoslovakia.

Organizations that have a wider than European scope naturally include the USSR and other eastern European states: the prime example is the International Council of Scientific Unions. Governmental and economic contacts are more problematic: nevertheless the Soviet Union has sent a Frenchman into space, and several European countries are working on the Soviet oil pipeline in open defiance of US protests. Such collaborations benefit the East as much as the West, of course – especially if we are to believe the general view prevalent in the West that science and technology behind the iron curtain have continued to suffer from the repressive aspects of communist regimes.

The value the East places on these contacts has several times been used for political leverage: US protests over Soviet actions in Poland and over the invasion of Afghanistan both included restrictions on scientific contacts. Scientists themselves have taken the initiative in boycotts of Soviet research collaborations and researchers in protest against the treatment of political or religious dissidents, and have rallied round to help resettle emigrés. Psychiatrists from the Soviet Union have been expelled from international conferences because of the abuse of psychiatry for political repression.

There are also limits on the type of information that can be shared. The Warsaw pact countries seem unlikely to enter traditional western markets for high technology products, so for once commercial secrecy is not a particularly strong factor in restricting information exchange. Defence technology, however, is another matter and the US has tried to exert strong pressures on European nations not to sell equipment containing advanced computers to the USSR in case it helps them build their own equipment or penetrate the secrets of US weapons. This concern has been one of the factors in the development (still in its early stages) of a science/technology grouping that includes Europe, North America and Japan, but excludes the Warsaw pact countries.

Scientific contacts between Europe and the US have always been particularly free and open. Immigrants from Europe brought science to the American continent, and many of her most senior scientists were born there. Of the new generation, many have European antecedents, though increasingly the great melting pot has brought children of many other cultures and races into the scientific world. We have seen that even by the early 1940s the US could already deploy a much more powerful network of scientific and technical resources than the whole of Europe, though the success of an enterprise such as making an atom bomb still depended on brainpower nurtured on the other side of the Atlantic. Since the war the US has built on these foundations, avoiding some of the pitfalls and problems encountered in Europe. US companies have maintained strong links with basic research, often funding their own laboratories or at least working closely with local universities.

At the same time basic research has maintained its own particular brand of 'gee whizz' excitement without sacrificing professionalism. Without entering into a long discussion, it is worth considering two fairly important ways American universities differ from their European counterparts: firstly there is a far more explicit pecking order of institutions in terms of intellectual standards and research performance; and secondly there is a much larger element of private funding which again keeps institutions in touch with other parts of society.

Many European scientists aspire to work in the US at some time in their careers, and often, especially in the case of poorer countries, obtain US funding to do this. (Take the case of Spain, for example. In 1980 over half of postgraduate fellowships from Spain were taken up in the US;

almost all the rest in Western Europe.) Often such travellers return, to enrich their own countries with new contacts, approaches and knowledge, just as the many Americans who come to Europe return with a larger perspective. All this is fine and friendly. But there is no doubt that in many fields of science there are better opportunities in the US. Salary and job prospects play an important but not usually overriding part in this: the level of funding for projects, stimulation of exciting departments, opportunities for working with or even within industry, and even social status are often more important. Hence the net 'brain drain' from Europe to the US which caused enormous concern during the early 1970s and continues to do so. There is, then, a low current of bitterness about these plum pickings that come at Europe's expense. In some countries this bitterness is counterbalanced to some extent by a perception of the US as a source of funds: in Spain, for example, scientists have access to cash for research supplied as a *quid pro quo* for the use of land for military bases.

A different kind of ambivalence underlies Europe's scientific relations with the new *enfant terrible* on the scientific and technical map: Japan. Japan's Ministry of International Trade and Industry (MITI) is the world's prime example of governmental leadership in investment for strategic research with well-defined priority areas and centrally planned programmes. Its no-nonsense approach to exploiting science for commercial ends – without even worrying about investment in defence r&d, an enormous millstone round the neck of the US and the UK – has acted as a further spur to European thinking on the subject of research and innovation. Whether Europe will ever be able to staunch the apparently never ending flow of cameras, videos, cars and now even computers from the Far East is another matter. As far as scientific exchanges go, Japan seems to be less interested in attracting bright Europeans (though this does sometimes happen) than in sending its own scientists to learn on the spot, through research at postgraduate or postdoctoral level.

Catalysing technological development

One of Europe's main historical claims to fame is the shamelessness with which she has exploited and despoiled other parts of the world that her citizens have chanced upon. Of the eighteen states we are considering, perhaps only the Swiss and the Irish can claim national innocence here. European economies have just about learnt to manage without the easy access to cheap raw materials her colonies afforded (in some cases, such as the Netherlands, lost only very recently). In spite of the misery of high unemployment, they are materially far better off than the citizens of the countries they have given up.

Out of a mixture of altruism, concern for world peace and stability, and a fair measure of historical guilt, almost all of them give aid of many kinds to third world countries, and this objective is an almost universal element in national science policies. Part of the aid is provided in the form of free and cheap opportunities for education and research in Europe; part is in the form of plant and equipment to be shipped out with experts to help install and use it; part is in the form of teachers to provide training and stimulate research on site. Much of this work is at the very applied end of the scientific spectrum: nevertheless, basic science does figure, particularly when it concerns local diseases, crops, geological features or weather conditions. Individual European centres often tend to build their strongest links with countries that share common cultures including especially language: usually these correspond precisely to former colonies.

Much of the more basic work is now the province of international organizations such as the United Nations Educational and Cultural Organization (UNESCO) and the World Health Organization, which coordinate plans and to some extent fund programmes to encourage better education and good practice in science technology and medicine. The International Council of Scientific Unions (ICSU) is also taking an interest in stimulating basic science in underdeveloped countries. As in Europe, new initiatives tend to eschew the idea of setting up new laboratories. Instead ICSU set up a series of International Bioscience Networks, whose aim is (ICSU 1982)

> to help the countries of the Third World to build up their research capability in the biological sciences so that they are better equipped to take advantage themselves of recent advances in biology, and to be in a better position to participate in such advances . . . the IBN organises networks of existing research centres that will establish priorities for each region and arrange training centres and joint research programmes. These will help mobilise the resources of the international scientific community and enable the scientists of the developed world and the countries with a more advanced scientific infrastructure in each region to help their less fortunate brethren.

Three regional networks are now operating, in Latin America, Asia and Africa, with plans for a network for the Arab world well in hand.

There is already one centre, in the heart of Europe, where third world scientists can make contact with some of the most abstract science there is. That is the International Centre for Theoretical Physics (ICTP) at Trieste, which dates back to 1964. Its major sponsoring agency then was the International Atomic Energy Agency: since then contributions from Unesco and the Italian government have played an increasingly important role. ICTP is based on the idea that the poverty from which the developing countries suffer is not just material, it is intellectual also. And the first of these evils can never be eradicated until the second is effectively relieved ... The centre organises research sessions, workshops and extended courses on advanced topics in the physical and mathematical sciences and encourages scientists, especially from the developing countries to visit the ICTP for extended periods. It forms an international meeting point for scientists from all countries and provides its visitors ... with facilities for original research at the highest international standards of excellence.

Closely associated with the ICTP is its director Nobel prize winner Abdus Salam, a Pakistani who also holds a professorship in physics at Imperial College, London. Salam's wide ranging interests also include a deep interest in Muslim history and culture and in the scientific traditions of Islam, which are closely linked with the Western renaissance. Now that many Muslim countries come into the relatively new category of rich but underdeveloped nations, much time and money has been spent on clarifying the history of Islamic science, and working out a new way forward for the Islamic scientific tradition. Western science and technology naturally play a part in developing the Arab states, and European companies can repatriate some of their petrodollars with a clear conscience as they set up ambitious civil engineering projects and hospital complexes with x-ray scanners.

Geographically close but worlds away in culture, the State of Israel also enjoys a rather strange relationship with Europe. While not a member, Israel participates in some European Science Foundation activities in the humanities and social sciences. (It has recently also been granted observer status on the European Medical Research Council.) Many of its scientists are refugees or emigrés from Europe, or descended from such immigrants, and their contacts with European centres remain strong. Germany in particular is still fairly keen to redress its antisemitic past by providing funds for research and favouring Israel when it comes to fellowships and participation in collaborative projects. Israel has many more trained scientists and engineers per head than her Arab neighbours. In fact in the early years of the state (founded in 1948), Israel pursued a deliberate policy of exporting technical experts to a number of African countries to help in development and education programmes that they hoped would lead to political alliances and general regional friendship and goodwill.

But the fact remains that Israel is a small country with relatively meagre resources, and many new sciences have failed to achieve the critical mass of brainpower needed to form world class centres, so it is at least as vulnerable as Europe proper to the brain drain to the US.

Perhaps the most interesting area to watch in the next few years will be

Europe's scientific relations with China. In spite of the very recent repression of scientists and intellectuals under Mao Tse Tung, China now has an enormous government infrastructure designed to exploit science and technology in the interests of the state. Like Islam, China has an honourable scientific tradition, which has been painstakingly conveyed to the West through the works of Cambridge biologist Joseph Needham. Today it desperately needs western ideas and techniques to help solve its major problems – that of feeding its enormous population – and to develop its military and industrial strength. It will be fascinating to see how far the Chinese will be prepared to adapt in order to acquire this expertise. Already it has made a major step forward in agreeing to recognize the patenting system for technological innovations. But copyright on written material still remains an alien concept and textbooks officially photocopied from one master original circulate freely in universities and research institutes.

The challenge of the future

Europe is far from being a spent force in science. Clearly, though, the scientific world is changing and European science must keep pace with the new developments, notably the new central emphasis on strategic rather than pure research. As we have seen, there is a close relationship between assumptions about the structure of science and the organizational arrangements that arise to support it. European countries, working jointly and individually, must pay a great deal of attention in future to making sure of a good fit between the two.

I have so far deliberately avoided being too specific about what an ideal future structure might be, if indeed such a concept has any meaning. The main purpose of this book is to paint in the backdrop to what promises to be an exciting period of reassessment, and to remind those involved – politicians, scientists, and industrialists alike – that there are central questions of principle and practice that deserve urgent thought and consideration and, in the not too distant future, action.

Nevertheless, I will stick my neck out once again to the extent of drawing together a few threads from the preceding chapters and seeing how they might figure in such a debate.

We started by seeing how Europe came to be the centre of the scientific world, through a special blending of idealism and practicality, religious and secular, a sense of community and thrusting individualism, continuity and revolution in thought, class distinction leavened by opportunities for advancement through personal endeavour. The achievements of science in turn played a large part in forming aspirations towards political democracy. Once achieved, government on behalf of all (or at least most) citizens gradually demanded a far greater say in activities such as science that previously had been organized more or less spontaneously. At first the state provided support without seeking to change the basic structures and assumptions of science. Education too received extra support without excessive interference, at least with teaching of the natural sciences. This *laissez faire* approach preserved the European scientific ethos largely intact into the second half of the twentieth century.

The rest of the world had by this time moved on: colonies, an important source of cheap raw materials and therefore economic wealth, gained their independence; the US and later Japan became centres of hard-headed economic initiative, leaving most of Europe far behind with her principles, scholarship and not so genteel poverty. Some European countries have managed a successful response. Germany is one example; Sweden and Switzerland too have done well in maintaining economic performance; Norway and to some extent the UK have profited from unearned windfalls in the form of oil and gas. But in general Europe has not taken a particularly aggressive approach to harnessing new science and technology to economic ends and the shape of the science system largely belongs to a bygone age.

In the middle of the 1980s we can now see that this inertia of the science system has brought some rather substantial benefits. In the science underlying the new technologies – biotechnology especially, but also computing and materials science – Europe has maintained and developed its expertise throughout the twentieth century. In retrospect there was no particularly good reason for this beyond good scientific instincts.

This experience reinforces the view that Europe did the world a great favour in handing over its own particular 'packaging' of science and should be very careful to avoid tinkering unthinkingly with the European scientific ethos. We have seen how in different countries more or less crude approaches have developed; and also some recent marked swings back towards basic research.

Nevertheless, some changes are necessary in order to ensure that innovative science eventually benefits the community, whether in economic, social or even environmental terms. I will not venture into the unfamiliar territory of the management of technological innovation, which has been widely discussed and documented in recent years, but I think it is worth pointing out that governments and scientists in Europe both need to think extremely hard about hammering out a new 'social contract' for science.

It is no use governments demanding the instant appearance of thousands of well-trained information technologists at the drop of a hat, while paying no attention to the resources and career opportunities available to their teachers and research supervisors. Equally the scientists cannot expect to go on developing new and increasingly expensive areas of research without explaining their strategies and philosophies to a wider audience and being seen occasionally to put their own houses in order. These are the essential first steps on the road to a healthier European scientific community.

References and bibliographies

For each chapter a bibliography lists most of the books I have used in the preparation of this work, and many of them will be appropriate for further reading. This applies particularly to Chapter One. Much of the information in Chapter Two is difficult to obtain in published form; nevertheless I have noted my sources so the reader will have some idea where to start in pursuing a particular interest. Chapters Three, Four and Five are based on a wide range of reports and reviews, each in itself rather specialized. I have listed as many as I think might be useful to assist to browse in the peripheral literature of the scientific world: autobiography, sociology, works of popularization. For Chapters Six and Seven I have adopted the same approach as in Chapter Two.

Chapter One

Bibliography

Baker F W G 1982 *The International Council of Scientific Unions: a brief survey* 2nd edition. ICSU Secretariat, Paris
Barber C L 1982 *The story of language* 2nd edn. Pan books
Bernal J D 1939 *The social function of science*. Routledge & Kegan Paul
Beyerchen A D 1977 *Scientists under Hitler*. Yale University Press
Blackett P M S 1947 *Science and the nation*. Pelican
Bush V 1980 *Science – the endless frontier* 2nd edn. National Science Foundation, Washington
Butts R F 1955 *A cultural history of Western education* 2nd edn. McGraw Hill
Cardwell D S L 1972 *The organisation of science in England* 2nd edn. Heinemann Educational Books

Casimir H B G 1983 *Haphazard reality*. Harper and Row, New York

Childe G 1982 *What happened in history* 2nd edn. Penguin Books

Clarke R 1971 *The science of war and peace*. Jonathan Cape

Crombie A C 1969 *Augustine to Galileo* 2nd edn (two vols). Penguin Books

Crowther J G, Howarth O J R, Riley, D P 1942 *Science and world order*. Pelican

Crowther J G 1942 *Soviet science* 2nd edn. Pelican

Dawson C 1956 *The making of Europe*. Meridian Books, The New American Library, New York

Gummett P 1980 *Scientists in Whitehall*. Manchester University Press

Jungk R 1960 *Brighter than 1000 suns*. Penguin

Jungk R 1963 *Children of the ashes* 3rd edn. Pelican

Kinder H, Hilgemann W 1983 *The Penguin atlas of world history* (two vols) trans E A Menze. Penguin

Kirk G S, Raven J E 1971 *The Presocratic Philosophers* 2nd edn. Cambridge University Press

Koestler A 1972 *The Sleepwalkers* 5th edn. Pelican

Lasby C G 1975 *Project Paperclip*. Atheneum, New York

Lloyd G E R 1970 *Early Greek science: Thales to Aristotle*. Chatto and Windus

Lloyd G E R 1973 *Greek science after Aristotle*. Chatto and Windus

Lloyd G E R 1982 *Aristotle: the growth and structure of his thought*. Cambridge University Press

Mandrou R 1979 *From humanism to science 1480–1700* 3rd edn trans B Pearce. The Harvester Press

Mason S F 1962 *A history of the sciences*. Collier Books, New York

McCormmach R 1983 *Night thoughts of a classical physicist* 2nd edn. Penguin

Papon P 1983 *Pour une prospective de la science*. Seghers, Paris

Pritchard J B (ed) 1973 *The ancient near east Volume 1: an anthology of texts and pictures*. Princeton University Press

Pritchard J B (ed) 1975 *The ancient near east Volume II: A new anthology of texts and pictures*. Princeton University Press

Reid R 1970 *Tongues of conscience* 2nd edn. Readers Union/Constable

Reid R 1975 *Marie Curie* 2nd edn. The Quality Scientific Book Club and the Scientific Book Club/William Collins

Russell C A 1983 *Science and social change 1700–1900*. The Macmillan Press

Sanderson M 1972 *The universities and British industry 1850–1970*. Routledge and Kegan Paul

Schacht J, Bosworth C E (eds) *The Legacy of Islam* 2nd edn Oxford University Press

Science in war (anon.) 1940 Penguin

Spiegel-Rösing I, de Solla Price D (eds) 1977 *Science, technology and society*. Sage Publications

Waddington C H 1942 *The scientific attitude* 2nd edn Pelican
Wechsberg J 1967 *A walk through the garden of science.* Weidenfeld and Nicolson
Werskey G 1978 *The visible college.* Allen Lane/Penguin Books
Williams T I 1982 *A short history of twentieth century technology c. 1900–1950* OUP.

Chapter Two

General references

Daalder H, Shils E (eds) 1982 *Universities, politicians and bureaucrats.* Cambridge University Press
Employment prospects and mobility of scientists in Europe 1980. European Science Foundation, Strasbourg
Europa year book 1984. Europa Publications
OECD Science and technology indicators 1984. OECD, Paris
Policies for higher education in the 1980s 1983. OECD, Paris
Spiegel-Rösing I, de Solla Price D (eds) 1977 *Science, technology and society,* Sage Publications
Tisdell C A 1981 *Science and technology policy.* Chapman and Hall

Austria
Completed questionnaires from:
Dr Eva Glück, Secretary General, Osterreichischer Rektorenkonferenz
Dr Raoul F Kneucker Secretary General Fonds zür Förderung der Wissentschaftlichen Forschung
Brunner W 1980 Universities and art academies. *Austria Today* **3**: 43–4
Firnberg H 1980 Science and research. *Austria Today* **1**: 27–8
Osterreichische Forschungskonzeption 80 1983. Bundesministerium für Wissenchaft und Forschung Vienna
Research Organisation in Austria 1982. Federal Press Department Republic of Austria

Belgium
La politique scientifique 1984. Service de programmation de la politique scientifique, Brussels.
Walgate R 1984 Low countries science. *Nature* **309**: 502–10

Denmark
Interviews conducted March 1984 in Copenhagen, Aarhus, Aalborg, Roskilde *New forms of cooperation between industry and the universities* 1982. Denmark National Survey/OECD
Risф between the past and the future 1983. Risф National Laboratory, Roskilde

Technical-scientific research: status and perspectives 1983. Danish Technical Research Council

Finland
Completed questionnaires from:
Professor Anto Leikola, Helsinki University
Professor Pekka Jauho, Director General, Technical Research Centre of Finland
Action plan for the Academy of Finland for the near future 1981. Academy of Finland, Helsinki
Isopuro J 1983 Research expenditure in the state budget for 1983. *Science Policy in Finland – studies and documents* **1**: 3–12
Klinge M 1983 *University of Helsinki: a short history.* University of Helsinki
Räty, T 1983 Supply of and demand for Ph.D's in universities. *Science Policy in Finland – studies and documents* **1**: 13–27
Research and development work in Finland in the 1980s 1981. Science Policy Council of Finland, Helsinki
Science policy review: research and development in Finland in the 1970s 1979. Science Policy Council of Finland, Helsinki

France
France Informations 119 (no publisher or date given)
Friedman A S 1983 Science and technology in France. *Physics Today* June: 24–28
Papon P 1983 *CNRS: un bilan et des perspectives pour 1984.* Centre National de la recherche scientifique, Paris
Papon P 1983 *Pour une prospective de la science.* Seghers, Paris
Recherche et technologie: actes du colloque national 13–16 janvier 1982 1982. Ministère de la recherche et de la technologie, Paris
Schwartz Laurent 1983 *Pour sauver l'université.* Editions du Seuil, Paris

Germany
Interviews conducted January 1983 in Bonn, Munich, Berlin
Completed questionnaire from:
Dr Eberhard Böning, Ministerialdirektor, Bundesministerium für Bild und Wissenschaft, Bonn
Geimer H, Geimer R 1981 *Research organisation and science promotion in the Federal Republic of Germany.* K G. Saur, Munich
Herman R 1983 What's wrong with German science? *New Scientist* 5 May: 277
Massow V 1983 *Organisation and promotion of science in the Federal Republic of Germany.* Inter Nationes, Bonn
Peisert H, Framhein G 1978 *Systems of higher education: Federal Republic of Germany.* International Council for Educational Development New York

Schneider C 1983 *Forschung in der Bundesrepublik Deutschland*. Verlag Chemie, Bonn

Greece
Interview conducted November 1983 with George Carayannis, Secretary, European Joint Committee for Scientific Cooperation at the Council of Europe
Information on the state of research and technology in Greece. Ministry of Research and Technology Bulletin No.4, Athens

Ireland
Completed questionnaires from:
Dr B Finucane, National Board for Science and Technology, Dublin
Dr M J McGuin, Director of the Cooperative Education Division at the National Institute for Higher Education, Limerick
Declan Lyons, National Board for Science and Technology, Dublin
Diarmuid Murphy, National Board for Science and Technology, Dublin
Research Programmes 1983/4 1983. National Board for Science and Technology, Dublin
Science Budget 1983: state investment in science and technology: analysis and commentary 1983. National Board for Science and Technology, Dublin (also equivalents for 1981 and 1982)
Young scientists and technologists employment programme 1984, 1984. National Board for Science and Technology, Dublin

Italy
Completed questionnaire from:
Professor Paolo Bisogno, Consiglio Nazionale delle Richerche, Rome
Bisogno P 1979 *Il ricercatore oggi in Italia*. Franco Angeli Editore, Milan
Bisogno P 1982 *Promoteo: la politica della scienza*. Arnoldo Mondadori Editore, Milan
Granelli L 1983 Speech delivered to the assembly of the Consiglio Nazionale delle Richerche
Herman R 1984 The Italian experiment. *New Scientist* 15 March: 39–46
Italy: a science profile 1983. The British Council, Rome
Stato della ricerca scientifica e technologica in Italia per il 1983 1983. Consiglio Nazionale delle Ricerche, Rome

Netherlands
Herman R 1984 Can Dutch science hang on to its ideals? *New Scientist* 3 May: 17
Schwarz M 1984 The Netherlands: towards a national science policy. In Goldsmith M (ed) *UK Science Policy*. Longman/Science Policy Foundation
Science Policy in the Netherlands 1976. Ministry of Education and Science, The Hague

Taakverdeling en Concentratie Wetenschappelijk Onderwijs: Beleidsvoornemens (recommendations on the concentration of scientific education) 1983. Proceedings of the Second Chamber of the States General, The Hague

Walgate R 1984 Low countries science. *Nature* **309**: 491

Wetenschapsbudget (science budget) *1984* 1983. Proceedings of the Second Chamber of the States General, The Hague

Norway
Information supplied by:
Svein Kyvik, Oslo.

Portugal
Completed questionnaire from:
Professor F R Dias Agudo, Lisbon

Dias Agudo F R 1983 *Scientific Research in Portugal*. Council of Europe, Strasbourg

Grilo E M and Ehnmark E E 1983 *Development and future trends in the functions of higher education, two case studies: Portugal and Sweden*. Council of Europe

Spain
de Miguel A (et al.) 1976 *Reformer la Universidad*. Euros, Barcelona

Herman R 1983 Spanish science tries to grow up. *New Scientist* 29 September; 933

Nieto A (et al., eds) 1982 *Apuntes para una política científica*. Consejo Superior de Investigaciones Científicas, Madrid

Yufera A 1981 *La investigación: un problema de España*. Cajo de Ahorros de Valencia

Sweden
Herman R 1984 Swedish science turns back to basics. *New Scientist* 1 November 1984 p 30

National Swedish Board for Technical Development (STU) 1980. STU Stockholm

Research in Sweden 1982. Swedish Ministry of Education and Cultural Affairs, Stockholm

Research planning and organisation in Sweden 1983. Swedish Institute, Stockholm

Towards better knowledge: public understanding of science in Sweden 1984. Swedish Council for Planning and Coordination of Research (FRN), Stockholm

Higher Education and research in Sweden 1984/5 1984. National Board of Universities and Colleges (UHÄ), Stockholm

Switzerland
Completed questionnaires from:
Andre Vifian, General Secretary, Swiss Council of Science Policy, Berne
R Deppeler, Secretary General, Swiss University Conference, Berne

Turkey
Completed questionnaires from:
Professor Dr Mehmet Nimet Ozdas, Faculty of Mechanical Engineering, University of Istanbul
Professor Dr U Büget, Deputy Secretary General for Technical Affairs Tübitak, Ankara
The Scientific and Technical Research Council of Turkey (undated). Tübitak, Ankara

United Kingdom
Gummett P 1980 *Scientists in Whitehall.* Manchester University Press
Pile W 1979 *The Department of Education and Science.* Allen and Unwin

Yugoslavia
Petak A (ed) 1980 *Science in Yugoslavia* Jugoslovenska stvarnost, Zagreb

Chapter Three

In tackling the general issues raised in this chapter I have drawn on a number of reports that document, compare and analyse the situations in different countries. These are as follows:
Employment prospects and mobility of scientists in Europe 1980. European Science Foundation, Strasbourg
The Future of University Research 1981. OECD, Paris
Policies for higher education in the 1980s 1983. OECD, Paris
OECD Science and Technology Indicators 1984. OECD, Paris
The university and the community: the problems of changing relationships 1982. OECD, Paris

General discussions of this nature are important but inevitably reduce some very subtle issues and experiences to the lowest common denominator of interest and argument. There are many ways that a more demanding reader can delve deeper into how the issues affect the working lives of scientists.

One is to read what scientists themselves have had to say about the scientific enterprise. Sometimes this kind of comment is contained in works that are essentially autobiographical, ranging from James Watson's classic *The double helix* to Werner Heisenberg's far more philosophical reflections in *Physics and beyond*. The life of a scientist working towards a specific objective of vital importance to the world of politics is illuminated by R V Jones' *Most secret war*. A less dramatic but rather more thoughtful scientific autobiography is D W Budworth's *Public science – private view*, an account of the author's education, life as a university scientist and transfer to an industrial laboratory. A similar transition was made by H B G Casimir, but not before his early career had brought him into contact with much of the prewar network of brilliant theoretical physicists in Europe. He outlines his life and reflections on science in *Haphazard reality*. Sir Bernard Lovell has combined experience in policy making for pure science with thoughts about theology and science in three works for the general reader: *The Story of Jodrell Bank*, *Out of the zenith*, and *In the centre of immensities*.

Direct comment based on personal experience by scientists with access to the corridors of power is hard to come by, but some interesting observations are provided by Lord Rothschild in *Meditations of a broomstick*. These days scientists tend not to make lengthy and exhaustive analyses of science planning: some recent partial exceptions are Sir Harold Himsworth's *The development and organisation of scientific knowledge* and Pierre Papon's *Pour une prospective de la science*. Freeman Dyson, a Briton who emigrated to the US, has commented frankly on his view of a number of occasions when science confronted policy in *Disturbing the Universe*. Sir Peter Medawar maintains a more philosophical and sociological approach to the scientific enterprise in his writings, conveniently collected recently in *Pluto's republic*. His *Advice to a young scientist* is also relevant to some of the issues here, and particularly for those considering a career in research. John Ziman has been even more ambitious in describing the intellectual frameworks of science in his books *Public Knowledge* and *Reliable Knowledge*. He has gone, perhaps, the furthest towards the ground now mainly occupied by the professional philosophers and sociologists of science (see bibliography to Chapter Five).

I apologize to non-British readers for the inevitable bias of this list: no doubt they will be better placed to track down examples of writings by home-grown scientists.

Budworth D W 1981 *Public science – private view*. Adam Hilger
Casimir H B G 1983 *Haphazard reality*. Harper and Row, New York
Dyson F 1979 *Disturbing the universe*. Harper and Row, New York
Heisenberg W 1971 *Physics and beyond* (trans A J Pomerans). Allen and Unwin
Himsworth H 1970 *The development and organisation of scientific knowledge*. Heinemann
Jones R V 1978 *Most secret war*. Hamish Hamilton
Lovell B 1968 *The story of Jodrell Bank*. Harper and Row

1973 *Out of the zenith*. Harper and Row
1978 *In the centre of immensities*. Harper and Row
Medawar P 1979 *Advice to a young scientist*. Harper and Row
1982 *Pluto's republic*. OUP
Papon P 1983 *Pour une prospective de la science*. Seghers, Paris
Rothschild V 1977 *Meditations of a broomstick*. Collins
Watson J D 1968 *The double helix*. Weidenfeld and Nicolson
Ziman J M 1968 *Public knowledge*. CUP
1978 *Reliable knowledge*. CUP

Chapter Four

Jungk R 1960 *Brighter than 1000 suns*. Penguin
Jungk R 1963 *Children of the ashes* 3rd edn. Pelican
OECD Science and technology indicators 1984. OECD, Paris
Reid R 1970 *Tongues of conscience* 2nd edn. Readers Union/Constable
Scientific potential and policies in the EEC member states 1982. Commission of the European Communities, Luxembourg
Walton J, Binns T B (eds) 1984 *Medical education and manpower in the EEC*. Macmillan
Yergin D, Hillenbrand M (eds) 1983 *Global insecurity* 2nd edn. Penguin

Chapter Five

General references

Ben-David J 1968 *Fundamental research and the universities*. OECD, Paris
Fundamental research and the policies of governments 1966. OECD, Paris
Gummett P 1980 *Scientists in Whitehall*. Manchester University Press
Tisdell C A 1981 *Science and technology policy*. Chapman and Hall

Science and mysticism

Of the available books I have come across, by far the most fun is Robert Pirsig's *Zen and the art of motorcycle maintenance*. For a rather wild and controversial approach to modern physics try Fritjof Capra's *The tao of physics*. The author has since turned his attention to 'green' politics. Gregory Bateson and Arthur Koestler have both developed intricate theses linking patterns in nature and thought to creativity and life: essentially these point out the inadequacy of logic to provide a complete explanation for these phenomena. It is fascinating to compare these modern discussions with thinkers in the alchemical tradition. Frances

Yates's writings on the subject are unusual in being reasonably clear to the non-specialist. Frank Manuel has explored Newton's interest in alchemy in *A portrait of Isaac Newton*, while Morris Berman in *The re-enchantment of the world* has combined an essay in the history of ideas with some steps towards a new synthesis.

Bateson G 1979 *Mind and nature.* Wildwood House
Berman M 1982 *The re-enchantment of the world.* Cornell UP
Capra F 1975 *The tao of physics.* Wildwood House
Koestler A 1973 *The roots of coincidence.* Random
          1976 *The act of creation.* Hutchinson
          1976 *The ghost in the machine* Hutchinson
Manuel F 1980 *A portrait of Isaac Newton.* Frederick Muller
Pirsig R 1974 *Zen and the art of motorcycle maintenance.* Bodley Head
Yates F A 1969 *Giordano Bruno and the hermetic tradition.* Random
          1979 *The occult philosophy in the Elizabethan age.* Routledge and Kegan

Philosophy of science

An easy way of learning more about this extremely complex subject is to read an excellent introductory survey which forms most of Alan Chalmer's book *What is this thing called science?* An alternative that will give a bit more of a feel for the way the practitioners of philosophy of science write is to look at the essays collected in Ian Hacking's *Scientific revolutions* which includes up-to-date papers from the main figures in the field. If you insist on dipping into some classic works, Kuhn's *The structure of scientific revolutions* remains fresh and readable. Popper followed up his *Logic of scientific discovery* with a number of other works – David Miller's *A pocket Popper* might help you to find your way round these. Kuhn's work was critically discussed by Popper and others at a colloquium in London in 1965: the proceedings were published as *Criticism and the growth of knowledge;* Imré Lakatos's major paper appears in this volume.

Chalmers A F 1984 *What is this thing called science?* 2nd edn. The Open University Press
Feyerabend P 1975 *Against method: outline of an anarchistic theory of knowledge.* New Left Books, London
          1978 *Science in a free society.* New Left Books, London
Hacking I (ed) *Scientific revolutions.* OUP
Kuhn T S 1962 *The structure of scientific revolutions.* Chicago UP
Lakatos I, Musgrave A 1970 *Criticism and the growth of knowledge.* CUP
Miller D 1983 *A pocket Popper.* Fontana
Popper K R 1959 *The logic of scientific discovery.* Hutchinson

Sociology of science

For a wide-ranging selection of readable and up-to-date essays try Barry Barnes and David Edge's selection *Science in Context*. An interesting full-length study of the development of a scientific discipline in modern times is *Astronomy Transformed* by David Edge and Michael Mulkay. Jerry Ravetz's *Scientific knowledge and its social problems* is a pleasant and plausible overview of the workings of the scientific community. A representative selection of the enormous opus of American Robert Merton (*The sociology of science*) also includes a brief history of the subject in its introduction.

Science policy studies place less emphasis on the process of science and more on its implications for and interactions with the outside world. In *Science, technology and society today* Michael Gibbons and Philip Gummett round up some interesting work of this nature. A more detailed historical study of science planning in government is Gummett's *Scientists in Whitehall*. The Roses' *Science and society* is now a little dated but has not yet been replaced as a sensible socialist critique. John Ziman takes a more liberal approach: his mission is educational rather than polemic. His most relevant work is *Teaching and learning about science and society*.

Barnes B, Edge D 1982 *Science in context*. The Open University Press
Edge D, Mulkay M J 1976 *Astronomy transformed*. Wiley-Interscience
Gibbons M, Gummett P 1984 *Science, technology and society today.* Manchester University Press
Gummett P 1980 *Scientists in Whitehall*. Manchester University Press
Merton R K 1973 *The sociology of science*. Chicago UP
Ravetz J R 1971 *Scientific knowledge and its social problems*. OUP
Rose H, Rose S 1970 *Science and society*. Penguin
Ziman J 1968 *Public Knowledge*. CUP
     1980 *Teaching and learning about science and society*. CUP

Science writing

At their best, professional writers about science can add a new dimension to their subjects that experts rarely achieve (at least nowadays). In practice many maintain a foot in both camps. One example is physicist Jeremy Bernstein whose literary skills have been rewarded by regular publication in the *New Yorker*. Horace Freeland Judson and Pamela McCorduck benefit from a wider perspective than any of the many scientists whose work they report. Norman Mailer and Tom Wolfe use the reportage approach, as does Tracy Kidder in a factually informative but less spectacular way. Arthur Koestler, Nigel Calder and Martin Gardner are all in their own way grand old men who enjoy a certain licence to impose their own views on their subjects, in each case adding a new element that goes beyond reporting into master journalism.

Bernstein J 1979 *Experiencing science*. Burnett Books/Andre Deutsch
              1982 *Science observed*. Basic Books, New York
Calder N 1978 *The key to the universe*. Penguin
Gardner M 1983 *Science: good, bad and bogus*. OUP
Judson H 1979 *The eighth day of creation*. Jonathon Cape
Kidder T 1982 *The soul of a new machine*. Allen Lane
Koestler A 1959 *The sleepwalkers*. Hutchinson
Koestler A 1971 *The case of the midwife toad*. Hutchinson
Mailer N 1970 *A fire on the moon*. Weidenfeld and Nicolson
McCorduck P 1979 *Machines who think*. W H Freeman
Wolfe T 1979 *The right stuff*. Cape

Chapter Six

Bibliography

The European Organization for Nuclear Research, CERN
Completed questionnaire from Roger Anthoine, Press and Visits Information, CERN
Goldsmith M and Shaw E 1977 *Europe's giant accelerator*. Taylor and Francis
CERN/LEP 1984. CERN, Geneva
Annual report 1983. CERN, Geneva
Schmied H 1975 *A study of economic utility resulting from CERN contracts*. CERN, Geneva

The North Atlantic Treaty Organization
Nato science committee year book 1982. NATO Scientific Affairs Division, Brussels
Rannestad, Andreas 1973 *Nato and science*. NATO Scientific Affairs Division, Brussels

The Organization for Economic Cooperation and Development
Ministers talk about science 1965. OECD, Paris
Problems of science policy 1968. OECD, Paris
Science and technology policy for the 1980s 1982. OECD, Paris

The European Southern Observatory
European Southern Observatory: an outline prepared on the occasion of the inauguration of the headquarters building at Garching on 5 May 1981. ESO, Garching bei Munchen
Woltjer L *ESO annual report 1983*. ESO, Garching bei Munchen

The European Molecular Biology Organization
European international collaboration in molecular biology during the 1980s 1978. EMBO, Heidelberg

The United Kingdom's participation in the European Molecular Biology Laboratory 1983. Medical Research Council

The Institut Laue Langevin
Completed questionnaire from Bernd Maier, Information Officer, Institut Laue Langevin
Brinkman William F (et al) 1980 *Report of the review panel on neutron scattering.* US Department of Energy, Washington
Herman R S 1981 Seventy-two hours in the life of an experiment. *New Scientist* 7 May: 362
Robinson Arthur L 1981 Will US skip neutron scattering derby? *Science* **211**: 259

The European Science Foundation
A study of manpower in astronomy in the countries represented in the European Science Foundation 1978. ESF, Strasbourg
Completed questionnaire from Natasha Weyer-Brown, Information Officer, European Science Foundation
Employment prospects and mobility of scientists in Europe 1980. ESF, Strasbourg
Flowers B 1979 *The European Science Foundation – an experiment in international collaboration in science and the humanities.* 10th J D Bernal lecture, Birkbeck College, London
Goormaghtigh, John 1982 Scientific Cooperation: The European Science Foundation. In Hurwitz, Leon (ed) *The harmonisation of public policy – regional responses to transnational policy.* Greenwood Press Westport, Connecticut
Nuclear physics in Europe: present state and outlook 1984. ESF, Strasbourg
Planetary science in Europe: present state and future outlook 1982. ESF, Strasbourg
Polymer research in Europe: universities and non-industrial laboratories: 1979 survey. ESF, Strasbourg

The European Communities
Biotechnology in the community 1983 Com (83) 672 final. Commission of the European Communities, Brussels
Danzin A 1979 *Science and the second renaissance of Europe.* Pergamon Press, Oxford
Eurofutures: the challenges of innovation 1984. Butterworth
Herman R S 1984 The West aligns its science. *New Scientist* 18 October, p 16
On laying the foundations for a European strategic programme of R&D in information technology: the pilot phase 1982 Com (82) 486 final. Commission of the European Communities, Brussels

Science and technology policy for the 1980s 1982. OECD, Paris

Economic summit
Herman R S 1984 The West aligns its science. *New Scientist* 18 October p 16
Report of the technology, growth and employment working group to the London Economic Summit 1984. Cabinet Office London

Council of Europe
Information report on the assembly 'Exercise in scientific cooperation presented by the Committee on Science and Technology' 1983. Council of Europe Document 5085

Chapter Seven

Bibliography

The World Health Organization
The work of the World Health Organization 1980–1 1982. WHO, Geneva

The International Council of Scientific Unions
The 19th General Assembly of ICSU 1982. ICSU Secretariat, Paris

The International Centre for Theoretical Physics
Behrman D 1979 *Science and technology in development – a UNESCO approach.* UNESCO, Paris

Some recent books

Irvine John, Martin Ben R 1984 *Foresight in science: picking the winners* Frances Pinter, London

Whitley, Richard 1984 *The intellectual and social organization of the sciences* Clarendon Press, Oxford

Ziman, John 1984 *An introduction to science studies* Cambridge University Press

Notes

Sources listed in the chapter bibliographies are referred to by author's name or title and year of publication only: for others a full bibliographic reference is given. The first number is the page number; the full reference follows.

Chapter 1
1   Stein, Gertrude 1984 *Wars I have seen* Brilliance Books, London p68
4   Gummett, 1980 p22f
5   Papon 1983 p80
10   Beyerchen 1977 pp123–132
13   Bush 1980 p22

Chapter 2
General
18   Salomon J J in Spiegel-Rösing, de Solla Price 1977 p52
18   ibid, p53, 54
Ireland
44   1981 *Science Budget 1981* p10
Italy
48   *Italy: a science profile* 1983 p10
Yugoslavia
74   Petak 1980 p10

Chapter 5
120 Barnes, Edge 1982 p183
120 Gibbons, Gummett 1984 p19
121 Irvine, John and Martin, Ben 1984 The writing on the wall *New Scientist*, 8 November 1984, p25 (first draft)
122 *Fundamental research and the policies of governments* pp11 and 18
123 Gummett 1980 p199
124 Schilperoort R A, R R van der Meer 1983 *The innovation-oriented programme on biotechnology in the Netherlands* Dutch Programme Committee on Biotechnology c/o CIVI, PO Box 18531, 2502 EM The Hague
125 ibid
125 ibid
126 ibid

Chapter 6
CERN
133 *CERN/LEP* 1984 p1

NATO

134	Rannestad, Andreas 1973 p15
134	ibid p159
134	ibid p143
134	*Nato Science Committee Yearbook* 1982 p7
134	Rannestad, Andreas 1973 p17
135	*Nato Science Committee Yearbook* 1982 p21
135	ibid p348
135	Nato Communiqué 1982

OECD

136	*Ministers talk about science* 1965 p17
136	ibid p161
137	ibid p158–60
137	ibid p163–4
138	*Problems of Science Policy* 1968 p143
138	ibid p143–4

ESO

139	*European Southern Observatory: an outline* 1981 p10

EMBO

140	Tooze, John 1981 A history of the European Molecular Biology Organization *EMBO Journal*, pilot issue, IRL Press Ltd, Oxford p1
140	*The United Kingdom's participation in the European Molecular Biology Laboratory* p6
141	ibid p7

ILL

141	Completed questionnaire from Bernd Maier

ESF

142	Flowers, Brian 1980 *International cooperation in science and humanities* Inaugural Einstein Memorial Lecture, Israel Academy of Science and Humanities p3
143	ibid p3
143	Flowers Brian 1979 p2
144	ESF 1983 *Annual Report* p14
144	ibid p16
146	*A study of manpower in astronomy* 1978 p16
146	*Planetary science in Europe* 1982 p7
147	ibid p117 (as quoted)
147	ibid p117
147	ibid p124
147	*Nuclear physics in Europe* 1984 p3
148	ibid p3
148	*Employment prospects and mobility of scientists in Europe* p10
149	ibid p11
149	ibid p23
149	ibid p24
149	ibid p29

EC

151	*Science and technology policy for the 1980s* 1982 p137
152	Danzin A 1979 p75
152	ibid p94
153	*Eurofutures: the challenges of innovation* 1984 p4
153	ibid p xi
154	*On laying the foundations for a European strategic programme of R&D in information technology: the pilot phase* 1982 p6

155   *Biotechnology in the community* 1983 ppE5, E6
156   *Stimulating European cooperation and scientific and technical
        interchange* 1984 p3
Summit
157–8   *Report of the Technology, Growth and Employment working group* 1984
        p6
Council of Europe
158   *Information report on the Assembly 'Exercise in scientific cooperation'*
        1983 p1
159   Council of Europe 1983 *Conference U-2000: preliminary findings*
        DECS/ESR (83) 55 p3
159   *Political declaration for the conference of European ministers
        responsible for research* (final communiqué of the meeting of research
        ministers held in Paris on 17 September 1984)
159   ibid
159   ibid
160   ibid
160   ibid

Chapter 7
172   *19th General Assembly of ICSU* 1982 p120
173   Behrman D 1979 (quoted in Aspen newsletter)

Name index

Adams, John   132
Aristotle   108
Armand, Louis   134
Aston, Francis William   10
Bernal, J D   12, 121
Beverton, Ray   168
Beyerchen, Alan   10
Bisogno, Paulo   168
Blume, Stuart   168
Bohr, Aage   11
Bohr, Niels   9, 11, 30, 118
Born, Max   9, 11
Bragg, W H   6
Bragg, W L   6
Bush, Vannevar   13–14
Cabrera, Blas   11, 58
Chadwick, James   9
Chevènement, Jean-Pierre   34, 36
Cockcroft, John   9
Crowther, J G   12
Curie, Marie   6
Curien, Hubert   36
Dahrendorf, Ralf   144
Dainton, Frederick   123
Danzin, Andre   152
de Broglie, Louis   10, 132
Dewar, James   6
Dias Agudo, F R   56, 168
Dornberger, Walter   10
Ehrenfest, Paul   9
Einstein, Albert   11, 112
Fabius, Laurent   36
Fermi, Enrico   9, 11
Feyerabend, Paul   119
Flowers, Brian   142
Fuchs, Klaus   17
Gibbons, Michael   120, 168
Gummett, Philip   4, 123
Haber, Fritz   6
Hahn, Otto   13
Heisenberg, Werner   9, 13
Hitler, Adolf   10
Irvine, John   120
Joliot-Curie, Frédéric   10, 13
Kendrew, John   140, 163
King, Alexander   136

Lakatos, Imré   118
Lenard, Philip   10
Levi, Marco Tullio   11
Leibig, Justus   2
Lysenko, Trofim   12
Maier-Leibnitz, Heinz   141
Martin, Ben   120
Meitner, Lise   11
Mill, John Stuart   3
Mitterrand, François   157, 159, 161
Néel, Louis   141
Newton, Isaac   118
Nunn May, Allan   17
Ochoa, Severo,   11, 58
Oldham, Geoffrey,   168
Oppenheimer, J Robert   17
Papon, Pierre   5, 168
Pasteur, Louis   5
Pauli, Wolfgang   9, 11
Planck, Max   9
Playfair, Lyon   4
Polanyi, Michael   12
Pontecorvo, Bruno   17
Popper, Karl,   117
Primo Yufera, E   168
Renan, Ernest   5
Rose, Hilary and Steven   121
Rothschild, Victor   123
Salam, Abdus   173
Salomon, Jean-Jacques   18
Schilperoort R A   124
Schneider, Christoph   vii, 168
Schrödinger, Erwin   9
Schwartz, Laurent   37, 168
Segrè, Emilio   17
Stark, Johannes   10
Szilard, Leo   140
Thomson, J J   9
Tooze, John   140
van der Meer, R R   124
von Braun, Werner   10
Walton, Ernest   9
Watson, John   140
Weizmann, Chaim   7, 11
Whewell, William   3
Ziman, John   168

Organization index

The country to which national organizations belong is indicated by a letter code shown below (the same as for motor vehicles).

Austria **A**
Belgium **B**
Denmark **DK**
Finland **SF**
France **F**
Germany **D**
Greece **GR**
Ireland **IRL**
Italy **I**

Netherlands **NL**
Norway **N**
Portugal **P**
Spain **E**
Sweden **S**
Switzerland **CH**
Turkey **TR**
United Kingdom **GB**
Yugoslavia **YU**

ABRC   *see* Advisory Board for the Research Councils
Academie de Paris   *see* Paris Academy
Academy of Finland **SF**   32
Academy of Sciences **A**   25
actions de recherche concertées   see Coordinated Research Programmes
Advisory Board for the Research Councils (ABRC) **GB**   72
Advisory Committee for Scientific and Technological Research **E**   59, 93
Advisory Council on Scientific and Industrial Research **GB**   7
AFRC   *see* Agricultural and Food Research Council
Agricultural and Food Research Council (AFRC) **GB** formerly Agricultural Research Council 71–2
ARC   *see* Agricultural and Food Research Council
Atomic Energy Commission **F**   34
Austrian Research Council **A**   23
Austrian Research Promotion Council **A**   23

Austrian Research Society **A**   23
BASF **D**   4
Bayer **D**   4
BRITE: EEC programme in research to meet the needs of industry   156, 163
British Council **GB**   48
British Westinghouse **GB**   4
Burroughs Wellcome **GB**   4
Cambridge Scientific Instrument Company **GB**   4
CEC   *see* Commission of the European Communities
Central Institute for Industrial Development (CIVI) **NL**   50
Central Organization for Applied Scientific Research (TNO) **NL**   8, 50, 51
Central School **F**   5
Centre for Energy, Environment and Technological Research **E**   60
Centre National de la Recherche Scientifique (CNRS)   *see* National Centre for Scientific Research
CNR   *see* National Council for Research
CNRS   *see* National Centre for Scientific Research

Collège de France **F** 13
Commission of the European
  Communities (CEC)   see also
  European Communities   143, 154,
  159, 162
Commission Supérieure des
  Inventions   see Higher Commission
  for Inventions
Consejo Superior de Investigaciones
  Cientīficas (CSIC)   see Higher
  Council for Scientific Research
Consiglio Nazionale delle Richerche
  (CNR)   see National Research
  Council
Coordinated Research Programmes
  B 27
COST   see European Cooperation in
  Scientific and Technical Research
Council of Europe   56, 98, 158–160
CREST   see Scientific and
  Technological Research Committee
Danish Research Administration
  DK 29
Department of Scientific and Industrial
  Research (DSIR) **GB** 7, 69
DESY   see German Electron
  Synchrotron
Deutsche Forschungsgemeinschaft
  see German Research Society
Deutsches Elektronen Synchroton
  (DESY)   see German Electron
  Synchrotron
DFG   see German Research Society
DG XII   see EC Directorate General for
  Science, Research and Development
Direction des Inventions Interessant la
  Defense Nationale   see Directorate
  for inventions concerning national
  defence
Directorate for inventions concerning
  national defence **F** 6
EC   see European Communities
EC Directorate General for Science,
  Research and Development
  (DGXII)   153–7, 162
École Centrale   see Central School
École des Mines   see School of Mines
École des Ponts et Chaussées   see
  School of Bridges and Roads
École Polytechnique   see Polytechnic
  School
EEC (=European Economic
  Community)   see European
  Communities

Emergency Association for German
  Science **D** 8
ESA   see European Space Agency
ESO   see European Southern
  Observatory
ESPRIT   see European Strategic
  Programme for R & D in Information
  Technology
Euratom   150, 151
Eureka   161–2
European Committee for Future
  Accelerators (ECFA)   132
European Committee for Research and
  Development (CERD)   148, 150,
  152, 153
European Communities (EC)   see also
  Commission of the European
  Communities   105, 143, 144, 148,
  149–157, 161
European Cooperation in Scientific and
  Technical Research (COST)   150,
  151, 159
European Geotraverse   145
European Joint Committee for
  Scientific Cooperation   158
European Molecular Biology Laboratory
  (EMBL)   see European Molecular
  Biology Organization
European Molecular Biology
  Organization (EMBO)   139, 140–1,
  159, 167
European Organization for Nuclear
  Research (CERN)   72, 132–3, 159,
  166–7
European Physical Society (EPS)   169
European Science Foundation   ix,
  142–9, 159–60, 169, 173
European Southern Observatory
  (ESO)   139, 159
European Space Agency (ESA)   147
European Strategic Programme for R &
  D in Information Technology
  (ESPRIT)   154–5
European Synchrotron   145, 166
European Training Programme for
  Brain and Behaviour Research
  (ETP)   144
FAST   see Forecasting and Assessment
  in Science and Technology
Federal Health Office **D** 4
Federal Ministry for Research and
  Technology **D** 38
Federal Ministry for Scientific Research
  D 38

Federal Ministry of Education and
Science **D** 38
Fonds National de la Recherche
Scientifique (FNRS) *see* National
Foundation for Scientific Research
Forecasting and Assessment in Science
and Technology (FAST) 153
Forschungskonzeption *see* Research
Programme
Foundation for Scientific and Industrial
Research (SINTEF) **N** 53
Foundation for Technical Services
(STW) **NL** 51
Fraunhofer Society for the
Advancement of Applied Research
D 38
General Electric Company **USA** 4
German Electron Synchroton (DESY)
132, 140
German Research Society (DFG) **D** 38
Government School of Mines **GB** 3
Higher Commission for Inventions
F 5
Higher Council for Scientific Research
(CSIC) **E** 8, 59, 91
Higher Education Council **TR** 67
Higher Education Guideline Bill **F** 35
Ilford **GB** 4
Imperial College of Science and
Technology **GB** 4
Institut Laue Langevin (ILL) 141–2,
166
Institut National de la Santé et de la
Recherche Médicale (INSERM) *see*
National Institute for Health and
Medical Research
Institute for Experimentation and
Research **A** 23
International Bioscience Networks
(IBN) 172
International Centre for Theoretical
Physics (ICTP) 172
International Council of Scientific
Unions formerly International
Research Council 7, 172
International Research Council *see
also* International Council of
Scientific Unions 7
Joint Research Centre (JRC) 150–1,
167
JRC *see* Joint Research Centre
Kaiser Wilhelm Society (Kaiser
Wilhelm Gesellschaft) **D** *see also*
Max Planck Society 4

Kaiserliches Gesundheitsamt *see*
Federal Health Office
Krupp **D** 4
Laboratory of the Government
Chemist **GB** 3
Ludwig Boltzmann Society **A** 23
Max Planck Institutes *see* Max
Planck Society
Max Planck Society (Max Planck
Gesellschaft) formerly Kaiser
Wilhelm Society 37, 91, 144
Medical Research Council (MRC)
GB 7, 70, 140
Ministry for Research and Technology
F 34
Ministry of Public Instruction **I** 48
Ministry of Research and Technology
GB 42
Ministry of Science and Research
A 23
mobilization programmes
(programmes mobilisateurs)**F** 36
National Academy of Sciences **USA** 7
National Board for Science and
Technology (NSBT) **IRL** 44
National Board for Scientific and
Technological Research (JNICT)
P 56
National Board for Technical
Development (STU) **S** 61, 93
National Board for Universities and
Colleges **S** 62
National Centre for Scientific Research
(CNRS) **F** 8, 34, 35, 37, 91, 168
National Council for Scientific and
Technological Research (CNICT)
P 57
National Foundation for Scientific
Research **B** 26
National Institute for Health and
Medical Research (INSERM) **F** 91
National Institute for Scientific
Research (INIC) **P** 57
National Institute for the Stimulation
of Research in Industry and
Agriculture **B** 27
National Physical Laboratory **GB** 4,
7, 91
National Research Council (CNR)
I 47, 93
National Science Foundation **CH** 65
NATO Science Committee *see also*
North Atlantic Treaty
Organization 133–5

Natural Environment Research Council (NERC) **GB**   71–2
Natural Science Research Council (NFR) **S**   62
Nederlands Organisatie voor Zuiverwetenschapelijk Onderzoek (ZWO)   *see* Netherlands Organization for Research in the Natural Sciences
Netherlands Organization for Research in the Natural Sciences **NL**   51
NHO   *see* Northern Hemisphere Observatory
Nobel's **GB**   4
Norges Teknisk-Naturvitenskapeliger Forskningsrad (NTNF)   *see* Norwegian Technical Scientific Research Council
North Atlantic Treaty Organization (NATO)   *see also* NATO Science Committee   102, 161, 169
Northern Hemisphere Observatory (NHO)   139
Norwegian Research Council for Science and the Humanities (NAVF) **N**   53
Norwegian Technical Scientific Research Council (NTNF) **N**   53
OECD   *see* Organization for Economic Cooperation and Development
Organization for Economic Cooperation and Development (OECD)   19, 23, 33, 44, 54, 56, 122–3, 135
Paris Academy **F**   7
Philips Research Laboratory **NL**   11, 52
Physikalisches Technisches Reichsanstalt   *see* State Physico-Technical Institute
Polytechnic School **F**   5
programmes mobilisateurs   *see* mobilization programmes
Research Programme (Forschunskonzeption) **A**   23
Risø National Laboratory **DK**   30, 91
Royal College of Chemistry **GB**   3
Royal College of Science **GB**   4
Royal Institution **GB**   3, 6
Royal Norwegian Society of Science and Letters **N**   53
Royal Society **GB**   3, 7

School of Bridges and Roads **F**   5
School of Mines **F**   5
Science and Engineering Research Council (SERC) **GB** *formerly* Science Research Council   70, 72
Science and Research Board **A**   23
Science and Research Conference **A**   25
Science Council (Wissenschaftsrat) **D**   vii, 168
Science Foundation **A**   23
Science Policy Council **SF**   33
Science Policy Office **B**   26
Science Research Council   *see* Science and Engineering Research Council
Scientific and Research council of Turkey (TÜBITAK) **TR**   68
Scientific and Technological Research Committee (CREST)   150, 153
SERC   *see* Science and Engineering Research Council
Society for the Freedom of Science **GB**   12
Solvay Congress **Int**   7
SRC   *see* Science and Engineering Research Council
Star wars   *see* Strategic Defense Initiative
State Physico-Technical Institute **D**   4
Strategic Defense Initiative (SDI) 'star wars'   161
Swiss University Conference **CH**   65
TNO (=Organisatie voor Toegepast Natuurwetenschappelijk Onderzoek)   *see* Central Organization for Applied Scientific Research
United Alkali **GB**   4
United Nations Educational and Cultural Organization (UNESCO)   172
University Grants Committee (UGC) **GB**   70
Weizmann Institute   11
Western Economic Summit: Technology, Growth and Employment working group   157–8
Wissenschaftsrat   *see* Science Council
World Federation of Scientific Workers   12
World Health Organization (WHO)   172

Subject index

academics   2, 39, 62, 86–90
acetone   6–7
age structure   28, 36, 75, 86–8, 148–9
agriculture   2, 4, 17, 26, 41, 99–101
Algeria   104
amateur scientists   108
ammonia   6
animal experimentation   98, 108
applied (tactical) research   ix, 2, 5, 6, 8, 11, 24, 123, 134, 135
Arab states   173
Aryan physics   10
astrology   109
astronomy   139, 146–7
atom bomb   13, 102, 132
atom secrets, leaking of   17
atomic energy *see* nuclear power
Austria (**A**)   23–5, 80, 89, 92, 104, 132, 169
Austria–Hungary   7, 11
aviation   5
basic research   ix, x, 19, 25, 26, 30, 39, 43, 47, 63, 71, 92, 94, 98, 124, 127, 134–5, 143
Belgium (**B**)   7, 26–8, 92, 131, 132, 139
biotechnology   124–6, 155–6
bureaucracy   84–5, 94
Canada   7
cars   5, 8
cause and effect   108
centres of excellence   159, 167
ceramics   8
chemical engineers   2
China   174
Christianity   1, 2
civil engineering   9
communication of research within scientific community   94
communism   11–2, 17

computers   13, 17, 42, 112, 115, 153–4
cordite   6
craft   108
creativity   ix, x, 95
culture and science   1, 107–14
Czechoslovakia   169
defence research *see* military research
Denmark (**DR**)   3, 28–31, 80, 91, 92, 104, 131, 132, 139, 161
economic change   x, 11, 14, 25, 106, 119
education   2, 78, 79–81, 107
Eire *see* Ireland
electrical equipment   5
electrometallurgy   5
emigation of scientists   10–13, 42, 80, 170–1, 173
employment   105–6
energy   104–5
engines   8
equipment for research   18, 19, 73, 94, 109
experiment   108
fascism   10–11, 45, 58
Finland (**SF**)   31–3, 80, 92, 132, 169
First World War   4, 5, 6–8
food   99–101
France (**F**)   A   5–6, 7, 12, 33–7, 80, 82, 84, 88, 89, 91, 92, 93, 102, 106, 131, 132, 139, 168
freedom of thought   108
genetics   10
geology   145
Germany (West) (**D**)   2–3, 7, 9, 10–11, 12, 17, 37–41, 80, 83, 85, 91, 92, 93, 104, 106, 131, 132, 139, 141–2, 168
government involvement in education and research before the end of the Second World War   2–10
graduate unemployment   24, 32, 39, 51–2, 63, 83

graduates, demand for in industry 83, 84–5
Greece (ancient) 1
Greece (modern) **GR** 41–3, 80, 82, 92, 131, 132, 135, 163
higher education, expansion of 11, 19, 79
higher education, qualifications for 24, 39
Hiroshima 17, 102
Hungary 169
industry 3, 4, 5, 8, 23, 30, 33, 52, 61, 113
industry, research in and by 3, 4, 10, 23, 33, 52, 58, 64, 101, 107, 119–20
innovation 19, 119–20
international collaboration 7, 15, 132–64, 165–7
Ireland (**IRL**) 17, 43–6, 80, 92, 132, 139
iron 8
Israel *see also* Palestine 140, 173
Italy (**I**) 3, 7, 9, 46–9, 79, 84, 85, 88, 89, 92, 93, 104, 106, 131, 132, 139, 168
Japan x, 4, 7, 152, 161, 171
land reclamation 9
logic 108, 116
magic 109
manpower 18, 34, 45, 136, 168
manpower, cutbacks in 27, 50, 72, 91
manpower planning 80, 97–8
Marxism 10
materials 8
materialism 152
mathematics 112–3
medicine 97–9
Middle Ages 1
military research 4, 5, 6, 7, 14, 17, 18, · 34, 69, 102–3
mobility 24, 94, 110, 148–9
multidisciplinary research 95
mysticism 116–7
Nagasaki 17, 102
national laboratories, links with universities and industry 93
nationalism 1, 10, 115
Netherlands (**NL**) 9, 11, 49–52, 80, 83, 86, 88, 89, 91, 92, 104, 106, 123, 124–7, 131, 132, 141, 168
networks, scientific 159, 163, 168
New Zealand 7
nitrates 6
Norway (**N**) 52–5, 89, 91, 92, 104, 131, 132, 161

nuclear physics 147–8
nuclear power 14, 17, 104, 150
numerus clausus 80
oil crisis 19, 104
optical equipment 4
Palestine 11
pattern 108, 116–7
peer review 12, 127
philosophy of science 117–9
political change x, 11–12
polymers 10
Portugal (**P**) 3, 7, 55–57, 80, 82, 85, 88, 89, 91, 92, 93, 102, 106, 131, 132
postdoctoral research 84–5
postgraduate training 26, 30, 36, 48, 57, 82–4, 85, 144
practical skills 94
pragmatism 11
Prussia 2
public interest in science and scientists 2, 95, 121, 127–9
quantum mechanics 9–19
radar 12, 17
radios 8
refrigerators 8
regional considerations 27, 29, 37, 60, 62, 64, 73–5
religion and science 1, 2, 108, 111, 115
research councils 8, 89, 127, 142
research institutes and laboratories 23, 25, 31, 32, 42, 44, 56, 65, 68, 70, 74, 91–4, 109
rockets 10, 13
Romania and Serbia 7
Rome (ancient) 1
Rothschild principle 123–4
rubber 10
scholarship 142
science budget 26, 63
science policy 18, 23, 26, 30, 34, 36, 42, 44, 47, 50, 54, 57, 63, 65, 68, 73, 122–7, 135–9, 152
scientific community *see* age structure, communication of research, emigration of scientists, international collaboration, manpower, mobility, public interest in science and scientists, structural problems of the scientific community
scientific enterprise (see also creativity, equipment, multi-disciplinary research, practical skills,

team work, technical support) 1, 12, 14
scientific ethos, European 107–14, 128, 175
Second World War 1, 12–13, 23, 102, 103
shipping 8
social change x, 8–9, 12, 25, 115
social contract for science 25, 106, 174–6
socialism 11–12, 121
sociology of science 119–122
sound ranging 6
Spain (E) 3, 11, 57–60, 88, 91, 92, 93, 105, 132, 139
Sputnik 17
steel 8
strategic science and research 25, 27, 46, 49, 55, 72, 89, 123, 124–6, 167
structural problems of the scientific community 18, 19, 40, 86, 148–9, 152, 168
students 25, 26, 29, 36, 39, 58, 88–9
submarines 6
Sweden (S) 3, 7, 9, 11, 13, 61–3, 80, 82, 83, 86, 89, 92, 93, 102, 105, 131, 132, 139, 169
Switzerland (CH) 11, 13, 80, 83, 91, 92, 123, 131, 132, 139, 169
synthetic fibres 10
teamwork 94, 111–2

technical support for research 19, 24, 35, 109
technology ix, 8, 9, 12, 14, 98, 120
telephones 8
trade unions 25, 35, 40
turbines 8
Turkey (TR) 66–8, 80, 92, 135
Union of Soviet Socialist Republics (USSR) 12, 13, 15, 17, 104, 169, 170
United Kingdom (GB) 6, 9, 12, 17, 68–73, 82, 83, 84, 86, 89, 92, 93, 95, 102, 103, 105, 106, 131, 132, 139, 141, 168
United States (USA) ix, 9, 11, 13, 14, 15, 17, 102, 103, 141, 152, 161, 169–7
universities x, 2, 3, 6, 9, 10, 11, 23, 24, 26, 29, 31, 34, 35, 42, 45, 50, 53, 55, 59, 62, 64, 67, 70, 72, 79–96, 109, 110, 148–9, 168
universities, state control of 88–9
university – industry links 25, 27, 29, 30, 40, 43, 45, 52, 61, 63, 82, 88
university, technical 3, 6, 29, 31, 42
vacuum cleaners 8
vocational training 41, 45, 80–1, 97–8, 107
weights and measures 4
young researchers, schemes to help see also age structure 24–5, 30, 71, 85–6
Yugoslavia (YU) 73–5, 80, 92, 105, 131, 132, 169